Arlington Bound

A Korean War Memoir

Corporal Robert H. Hickox
U. S. Army, Retired
"C" Company, 65th Combat Engineer
Battalion, 25th Infantry Division

Edited by John Faylo

HERITAGE BOOKS
2025

HERITAGE BOOKS

AN IMPRINT OF HERITAGE BOOKS, INC.

Books, CDs, and more—Worldwide

For our listing of thousands of titles see our website
at
www.HeritageBooks.com

Published 2025 by
HERITAGE BOOKS, INC.
Publishing Division
5810 Ruatan Street
Berwyn Heights, MD 20740

International Standard Book Number
Paperbound: 978-0-7884-4801-0

For Bob,

You once told me that a promise made is a debt unpaid. I made many promises to you and I have kept them all.

I promised to love you with all my heart. I promised to lay you to rest with your band of brothers in Arlington while bagpipes played *Amazing Grace*. I promised to share your story, your words, with the world and to find love again.

My debts are paid.

Forever in Camelot,
Mary

Table of Contents

List of Photographs

Robert H. Hickox
27 March 1930 – 6 April 2015

Preface

by Robert Hickox

Many books have been written regarding lives, fortunes, and misfortunes. A memoir is certainly not a new or unknown format for writing about life.

It is my belief each life is a story that should be told and preserved regardless of fortunes encountered because all lives contain wisdom to be gleaned for future generations.

Countless war stories have been written, often summarizing the exploits of many individuals along with the horrors of war. This too is a part of life, not an unusual design, but nevertheless a part of the whole…

Hopefully, this book will compile all these things as culled from my life.

I have always viewed life as a series of books, a book for each beginning and a book for each ending, and within these books, many chapters, each covering a certain period of life. When asked how I coped with some of the experiences in my life, I refer to my experiences as my "Little Books on the Shelf". Here I keep my memories, great and small, good and bad, and call upon them as the need arises. This is my way of handling things we try to forget but know we never can. In this way, I can take a certain book off the shelf when I wish, and when I am done reading, put it back. Some might feel this is simply an escape. I have found it most comforting.

In this memoir, I will try to cover many areas. I will briefly cover some of the hardships and joys of my early life. I will cover much of my adult life and the many happenings I have been privy to during these years.

Primarily I will cover my part *of* the Korean War. Notice I did not say my part *in* the Korean War. I do not want to write another "war story". God knows, there have been enough of them – too many wars, too many self-righteous heroes flaunting their heroic deeds. Do not mistake me. I have known many heroic men, and I wish in no way to taint their memory. I do not class myself among them. I hope to show only my participation in, and my observations of, that war.

I pulled my wartime service in Korea. Three Purple Hearts, a Bronze Star with Valor, a POW Medal for 30 months of captivity, and a bunch of other "stuff". I found myself in unique and questionable situations during that time and I feel I can contribute something to the history of the Korean War.

I hope you enjoy the books of my life.

Acknowledgments

I would like to thank everyone who provided material and emotional support for this project, especially the families of Korean War veterans mentioned in this memoir.

William H. Bowling appears courtesy of Deborah Jennings.

Timothy F. Casey appears courtesy of Nita Léger Casey.

John J. Doody appears courtesy of Jay and Mildred Doody.

Robert H. Hickox appears courtesy of Mary Hickox.

Duane K. Morgan appears courtesy of Becky Childers.

Aldin B. Saloway appears courtesy of Robert Hickox and Patrick Shaughnessy.

Michael A. Shaughnessy appears courtesy of Patrick Shaughnessy.

Alfred D. Thistle appears courtesy of Carol Thistle.

News item copy and photos originally published in the *Syracuse Herald Journal* appear courtesy of the *Syracuse Post Standard* and Editor/Managing Producer Steven Billmyer.

Material originally published in the KWVA 50th Reunion brochure and in *Greybeards Magazine* appears courtesy of the Korean War Veterans Association and President David H. Pickett.

Thanks to Dr. Shereasa T. Braxton, Middle School Reading Specialist, who line-edited this manuscript for publication.

Special thanks to Patrick Shaughnessy and his family for maintaining an impeccable Shaughnessy family record and for tirelessly hunting through the U.S. National Archives searching for paper records gathering dust in forgotten boxes.

Finally, I would like to thank Frederik Pohl for attending a 1984 science fiction convention and graciously allowing me to sit in a chair next to him while he signed his latest book and ask him stupid questions about the writing craft.

To all who have served, are serving, or will serve, thank you. Freedom isn't free. All gave some, some gave all.

Prologue

A LETTER FROM MARY HICKOX

Bob was the love of my life. For the thirty years we were married, I listened to his stories and adventures. When he told me he wanted to write it down and publish it, I encouraged him! He worked diligently until his age prevented him from typing. He switched to dictation.

Sadly, Bob passed away before completing his memoir. Years later, another love of mine agreed to finish the project and help me fulfill Bob's wish as I promised. I want to share his story with the world.

Thank you for reading.

0.2   17 APR 2021 – SYRACUSE, NY – MEETING ROBERT HICKOX – BY JOHN FAYLO

In the corner of the basement rested an old black lacquer trunk with brass edges and a latch, the trunk you imagine people used during the Civil War or carried aboard *Titanic*. The lock sealing the trunk seemed out of time, anachronistic, a modern finale used to secure an older story hidden within. I removed Mary's lock, as she had asked me to, and opened the trunk in search of the story Bob promised, a story told in little books, a story about Bob, Norma, and Mariko, a story worth telling.

The open trunk smelled old, musty, tired, as if it had guarded secrets far too long. I picked up a small book wrapped in tissue from several others placed neatly in the left separation of the upper tray. *Baby's Own Journal* containing a lock of Barbara Anne's hair clipped on 27 September 1956. Another book, *Baby Days*, listed gifts Robert Thomas received during his first Christmas: a plastic horse and a duck pull toy from Santa. A baptismal certificate for

Sandra Jean. Anniversary cards for Bob and Norma. Items in the family trunk were arranged neatly, stored with care in envelopes and smaller boxes, not tossed in randomly like the hope chest of a teenage girl eager to begin life.

Deeper in Norma's trunk, I found a photograph of Bob in Class A uniform. Corporal Robert H Hickox, U.S. Army Retired, "C" Company, 65th Combat Engineer Battalion, 25th Infantry Division. I found a box of modest envelopes each labeled with the award it had contained, awards now displayed in Mary's shadowbox upstairs. Bronze Star. Three Purple Hearts. Army of Occupation Japan – where he met Mariko – 1948 to 1950. Korean Service. Prisoner of War, 27 November 1950 to 24 April 1953. I found the pocket Bible Bob had with him the night he was captured.

I found an American flag folded in a triangle, small compared to the flag Mary displayed in the living room upstairs. The larger flag covered Bob's casket during his funeral at Arlington. After an honorary rifle rally, it had been folded with precision by Army Old Guard attending the casket and presented to Mary. Upstairs, a velvet bag containing three rifle cartridges fired during the rally rested near Mary's Arlington photo album.

I remember a photo of Mary Hickox using gold fingerpaint to place her handprint on Bob's casket while she said goodbye to her husband. Bob's daughter followed with a handprint applied in green fingerpaint. A bagpipe musician played "Amazing Grace"; the song Bob requested. Relatives said goodbye to Robert Hickox, a man they knew intimately, a man who shared their lives.

Quietly, slowly, I examined secrets hidden in Norma's trunk, learning about a man I never met, someone who chose to record his memoir in the form of little books. Each little book touched me and helped me imagine a world that existed before I was born.

Robert Hickox never considered himself a hero, yet his experience is larger than life, the product of a person raised during trying times who proved himself to be master of those times. Bob wanted to share his story with people willing to listen, with people like you.

And Bob tells his story well.

Circle

I spent thirty months as a prisoner of war in Pyuktong Prison Camp Five in North Korea. I was released on April 24, 1953, at Panmunjom on Day Five of Operation Little Switch. General Mark Clark led a United Nations force that met us at Panmunjom and escorted us to freedom.

At dawn, our North Korean guards in Pyuktong woke us up and herded us into trucks that would carry us to the prisoner exchange. We boarded the trucks quickly. We were dirty, stinking, and half-starved, but eager to return home. Nobody spoke.

When we reached the exchange point, a barren section of Korean wilderness, we got out of the trucks and traveled on foot. Our guards pointed out the direction to freedom and released us. We would never see them again. We crossed a small footbridge and met soldiers from the UN Force. We were free.

Our rescuers offered us new clothing. Without hesitation, we stripped off our prison uniforms, Mao-blue Chinese clothing given to us by our captors, and grabbed American clothing. We left our past in a pile near a bridge in the Korean wilderness. I left my food bowl, a little silver bowl I had eaten out of for three years while I watched fellow prisoners die from harsh treatment. I took my pocket Bible, a book I had when I was captured. Easy decisions.

At the UN camp, we were deloused, allowed to shower, and given our first square meal in three years. Then we were flown to Japan's Tokyo Army Hospital. I tried to call Mariko, my girlfriend in Japan, but they wouldn't let me. Nobody was allowed to communicate with the outside world until we had been debriefed in the continental United States. The Army arranged a short press conference and let photographers take pictures of us so our families would know we were safe.

I stayed in the Tokyo Hospital for about a week. One guy went AWOL from the hospital because he couldn't handle more confinement. I was okay with it.

The Army awarded me my third Purple Heart and a Bronze Star with Valor.

All one-hundred forty-nine POWs released were flown to Hawaii for a layover and then flown directly to San Francisco. We landed at night. Our group was divided into smaller groups and each person was flown to the Army Hospital closest to his hometown.

On April 30, 1953, I arrived at Valley Forge Army Hospital in Pennsylvania. More debriefing followed. An Army psychiatrist talked with me several times, apparently interested in my welfare. He sat in a chair in my room and attempted polite conversation. It didn't take long for me to figure out he was Army Intelligence, a CIC Major trying to squeeze me for details about our collaboration with the Chinese while we were in Pyuktong.

I stopped talking to him. I spent my time in Pyuktong being indoctrinated by Lin Shi-Zhong, a Chinese political officer from Malaysia who earned the nickname "Screaming Skull". Lin would sit in a chair across from me, just like the Army CIC Major, and carry on polite conversation. Thirty months with Screaming Skull was enough for one lifetime.

1.2   29 APR 1953 – SYRACUSE HERALD JOURNAL – HICKOX, FREED POW, GETS PURPLE HEART

MRS. DURWOOD C. HICKOX, 144 Stafford Av., expressed happiness today upon hearing that her son, Pfc. Robert H. Hickox has been awarded the Purple Heart.

Released last week by the Communists at Panmunjom, Hickox was one of six enlisted men and an officer who were decorated in Tokyo yesterday.

He was wounded in action on Sept. 2, 1950, when a bullet from a Russian burp gun went through his thigh, his mother said. "Luckily, it just zigzagged around and didn't hit anything important," she commented. Hickox was sent to Japan to recuperate in a hospital for six weeks, after which he was sent to the front. Only three weeks after that, Hickox was captured. Listed as missing in action on Nov. 27, 1950, it was a year before his family knew that he was still alive. First letter from captivity came Nov. 23, 1951, a day before Thanksgiving.

News of Hickox's award came hard on the heels of additional news from him yesterday. A telegram, sent before he telephoned his family last weekend, arrived yesterday morning. It read: "My loving family. Feeling good and looking forward to seeing you again. Impossible to express my joy at being released. Hope you received word of my return from prison camp. Will try to telephone you as soon as possible. Love to all the family. Bob."

1.3   CHATHAM, MASSACHUSETTS 1943
MY CHILDHOOD – LITTLE BOOK 1

It was about the middle of 1943 and my father was stationed at Chatham Massachusetts on Cape Cod. He arranged for a family move because he had attained a military rank high enough to allow him to live off-base with us. We packed up and moved to Cape Cod.

When we arrived, we were assigned housing in a lighthouse. For my stay in Cape Cod, we lived in the Chatham Lighthouse. Three other families were billeted at Chatham and the Coast Guard operated the lighthouse proper. It was fun. I had a whole beach to myself, and I could run across the road and gather a bucket of clams and shellfish fresh from the tidal pools. Not much swimming. Even during summer, the water was too cold. Despite this, I often went wading because several of the Navy WAVES stationed nearby would sunbathe on the beach – an enjoyable experience for a healthy thirteen-year-old boy.

Due to the continuous bickering of my parents, I moved into a little shed behind the lighthouse. It wasn't much, but I didn't have to endure their battling all hours of the night. I made myself a bunk and fixed it up in a "manly" but cozy way. Girlie pictures on one wall, a radio, a clock, and the necessary stash of snacks. I spent many happy hours in that shack.

To pass the time, I set traps to catch some of the big wharf rats living in the area. Some were as big as a housecat, so big I had to use traps used to catch muskrats. I loved skinning and tanning their hides, and I would proudly decorate my little shack by tacking their skins on the bare walls, much to the chagrin of my parents.

Another advantage of living in my little shack was the private view of other housing units. Two young couples lived in these units – and exactly half of these couples consisted of two young, beautiful wives who spent each night alone while their husbands were on duty at the naval base. These VERY young, VERY beautiful wives were unaware that from my vantage point, I could watch them getting ready for bed every night. They never pulled the shades and always lingered in front of open windows, perhaps to introduce a young man to the pleasures of life. Such was my introduction to the wonders of the female form. Although it was nothing more than observation, I like to think of it as my first sexual experience.

Strip shows continued every night. After a while, I became friendly with the women, an event that would lead to my downfall. One of the girls (ladies) became very friendly with me and invited me into her apartment during mornings when her husband wasn't home. I was happy to be with her. All we did was talk, play games, and eat the cookies she would bake. We became so friendly she told me I could visit anytime. I guess I took her "anytime" too literally and walked in one morning while she was still in bed. I walked into her bedroom to wake her up. She became startled and raised a ruckus. When her husband came home, she told him I had sneaked into her bedroom while she was asleep. He came looking for my sorry little butt. Fortunately, for one time in my life, my father interceded and probably saved my life. I talked my way out of that one by promising I wouldn't visit the woman again.

Oddly, the nightly strip shows continued. I didn't mention it. Why ruin a good thing?

1.4   SYRACUSE, NEW YORK, MAY 1953 – BOB HICKOX DAY – LITTLE BOOK 23 (intended)

NOTE: This section has been reconstructed from Robert Hickox email, working notes, and manuscript.

When I returned from Pennsylvania during the second week of May, I had a big homecoming welcome from the military, the city, and the county. People from the local news station picked me up at the hospital (Valley Forge, PA) and flew me home in a small private plane. I made them promise "no fuss". They said we would land on a secluded runway where my mother and father would be waiting.

As it turned out, when we landed and I stepped out of the plane, I saw a military band contingent from each branch of the service, a reviewing stand, and an official greeting. After the welcome, a motorcade delivered me to my house, Stafford Avenue, Eastwood, New York, a place I hadn't seen in five years.

Friday night. Big celebration. Norma, my old girlfriend, wasn't there. She didn't come to the airport either. She didn't know I wanted her to. Grandparents, distant relatives. More press and television people.

I had press people living in my house. Very disturbing.

Ate dinner, forgot what.

After dinner, I got rid of the press and got the nerve to call Norma. I asked her to grab a cab and come to my house. She did.

When Norma got there, I noticed a big change in her. She had grown up. Norma wasn't the high school girl I dated before I went to Korea. We stayed at the house and talked until 11:30 p.m. It was a nice night, so I walked her home. We had a long talk on her front porch. We discussed many things, too many to recall. I knew I loved her as much now as I did five years ago. We made plans to go out the next night.

People from the Saturday Evening Post offered me $10,000 for my story about being a POW for thirty months. I turned them down. I had had enough publicity, not all good, and I was tired of it.

During the weekend, Bob McKinney, an old buddy from Korea, came to visit me. He had a new car and we took off "to do" the town. Naturally, we got drunk, rammed another car, and totaled his car. When the cops came, I thought they were leaning on Mac a little heavily and without good reason. I was drunk. What did I know? I walked up to one of the cops and told him to leave my buddy alone. The cop turned around and shoved me, so I hauled off and hit him. I told the cop I had been shoved around in a POW camp for three years and I wasn't going to take it anymore.

Bob and I both ended up in the Syracuse City jail. I got us out by explaining that the Syracuse mayor was planning a big welcome home parade for me and a dinner in my honor at the Syracuse Hotel the following Wednesday. About 2 AM, I told the desk sergeant I wanted to make a phone call.

"Who do you want to call?"

"The Syracuse mayor."

"What do you want him for?"

"Well, he's throwing a big party for me next Wednesday. If his guest of honor is in jail, he's gonna be awful pissed."

The cop looked at me for a minute then said: "You two get the hell out of here. I don't want to see you again."

Ha! It pays to know people in high places.

The following Wednesday, there was another motorcade down Salina Street in Syracuse. Looked like the whole city turned out. I rode down Salina Street in a big gold Cadillac. Some smart-ass city official leaned over and told me the city used to give Cadillacs away to people like me – but now they offered to sell them to guests of honor instead. No car, but I received a watch from a local merchant.

After the parade, I attended a dinner for *me* at the Syracuse Hotel. A lot of speeches by politicians. The Syracuse mayor declared it "Bob Hickox Day" and had a big banner hung across the main street stating such. I had to give a short speech. I did not like all the attention. It's not exactly what someone who has been where I had been for almost three years wants.

After that dinner, there was another round of dinners and dedications around town that I had to attend. Even my old high school had a "Bob Hickox" night with more speeches and fanfare.

All I wanted to do was hide away somewhere, but everywhere I went I was hounded by politicians and news people. It was a harrowing experience – one I wouldn't wish on anybody.

Eventually, the fanfare ended, as all things do.

1.5   9 MAY 1953 – SYRACUSE HERALD JOURNAL – MEETING THE MAYOR – a warm greeting from Syracuse Mayor Corcoran.

Beverly Hickox, Mr. and Mrs. Hickox, Mayor Corcoran and Col. Robert P. Halloran

Robert Hickox Day May 1953

People from the Saturday Evening Post offered me $10,000 for my story about being a POW for thirty months. I turned them down.

– Robert Hickox

9 MAY 1953 – HOME-COOKED MEAL NO DREAM FOR BOB
– Concerning the Syracuse welcome received by Robert Hickox
upon returning home to his family.

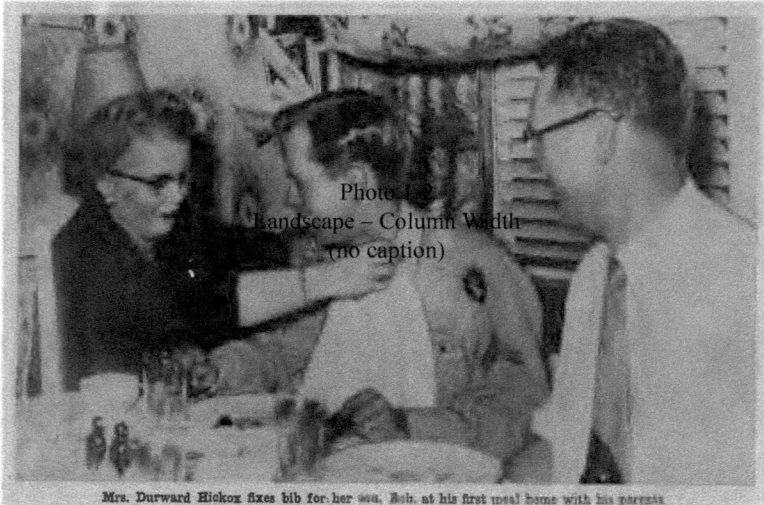

Mrs. Durward Hickox fixes bib for her son, Bob, at his first meal home with his parents.

Home after 27 months in a Communist prisoner of war camp,
Corp. Robert H. Hickox sank wearily into a chair last night, and
murmured, "I hope I don't wake up all of a sudden and find out it's
a dream."

The slender, 23-year-old soldier had just gone through a cheering
welcome as Syracuse went all out to honor its first returned prisoner
of war.

Corp. Hickox had arrived at Hancock Field at 5:25 P.M.
yesterday after leaving Valley Forge Military Hospital,
Phoenixville, Pa., on a 30-day furlough. Bands, color guards, honor
guards, city officials, and hundreds of cheering Syracusans were
there to greet him. It was almost too much for Corporal Hickox.
Last to come off the plane, he paused at the top of the runway,
looked out at the crowd in amazement, and grinned. After raising a
hand in acknowledgment, he descended to the runway and was
whisked into the arms of his family.

He shook his head later at his home. "I didn't expect anybody. It was a complete surprise. If there'd been a back door to that plane, I would have taken it."

10 May 1953 – A NEW WATCH FOR BOB – Ceremonial presentation of a gift donated by a local merchant.

WATCH REPLACED.—Corp. Robert Hickox receives a watch replacing one taken from him by his Communist captors from John D. Wilson, head of Wilson's Jewelers. Parents of the former prisoner of war, Mr. and Mrs. Durward Hickox of 144 Stafford ave., witnessed the presentation in the Eastwood store.

[The Chinese] dragged me around and started going through my pockets. They took my watch, graduation ring, and billfold. One took my New Testament Bible from my jacket pocket. He looked at it and motioned, wanting to know what it was. I made a praying motion. He put it back in my pocket. I have that Bible today.

– Robert Hickox

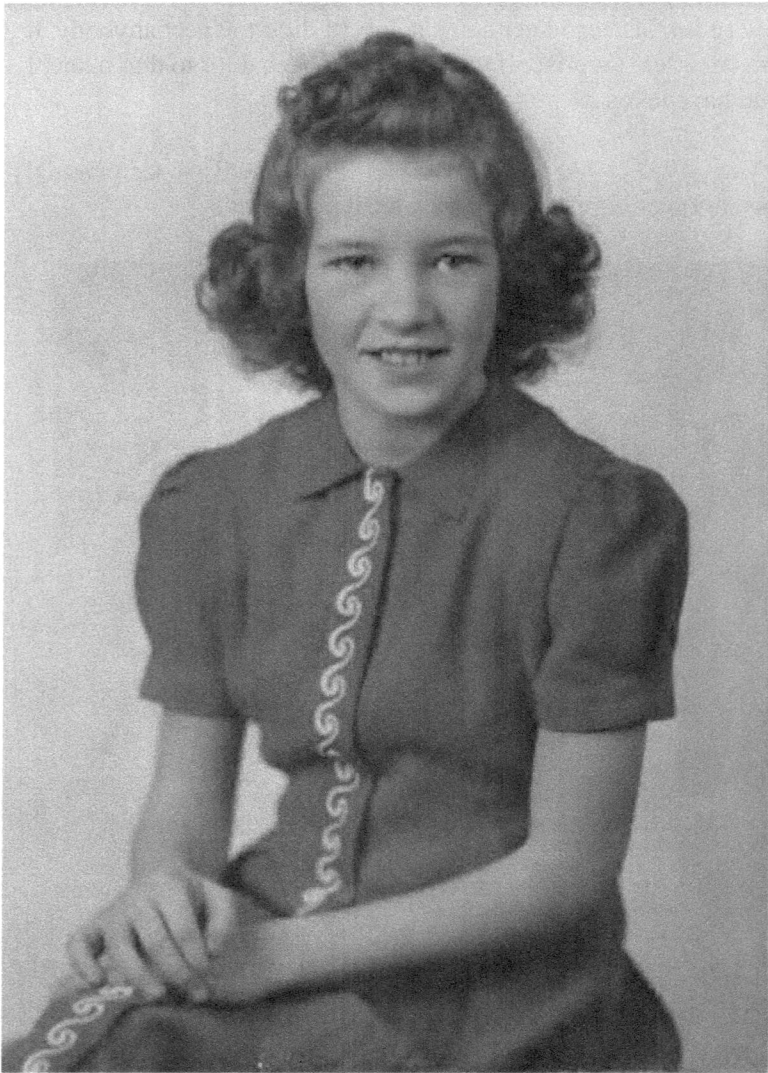

Norma "Kitten" VanPatten

Norma

2.1 EASTWOOD, NY 1946 – MY HIGH SCHOOL YEARS – LITTLE BOOK 1

During my junior year in high school, I met a beautiful young girl named Norma [VanPatten] and we became close friends. She went to my school and was two years younger than me. She was fifteen and I was seventeen. Before long I fell madly in love with her and on nights when I wasn't out looking for trouble with my friends, I was with her in the Eastwood Diner eating hamburgers, drinking shakes, and talking.

I traded time with my buddies for time with Norma. After work, I hurried down to the diner where she was waiting for me. Before long I walked Norma home every night while she held my hand. During that summer we strolled through the nearby park. By the following winter, everyone said it was "Bob and Norma forever".

When my gang got together, Norma was there with us, trying to keep me out of trouble. Norma knew I carried a hunting knife in a scabbard under my coat. When a street fight seemed likely, she made me give her the knife before the fight. I'm sure she kept me from killing someone, or more likely, getting killed. Everyone knew Norma was my girl and nobody messed with her. She made it clear to everyone that she was mine and nobody questioned it. We had good times together.

One night when Norma was home safe, Bob Ivison and I got drunk and tore up the town. Bob was quite a hell-raiser and a genius at hotwiring cars. He and I always had transportation. That night we wired a car in Eastwood and took off for the old Spinning Wheel, a local watering hole on the edge of town. Along the way, the police started chasing us. About a half mile from the Spinning Wheel, Bob made a sharp turn at an intersection and ran our stolen car into a gas station. The crash destroyed the car and didn't do the gas station much good. Bob and I took off on foot. We knew if we could reach the Spinning Wheel, our gang would cover for us. We reached the Wheel with police hot on our tail and ran inside. About fifteen minutes later, the officers came in looking for us. Everyone in the place swore we'd been there all night.

If you have friends in the right places, things go your way. Bob and I pulled a lot of stunts like that before we went into the Army and never got caught. Lucky, I guess.

2.2   EASTWOOD, NY, MAY 1953 – OUR WEDDING DAY – LITTLE BOOK 30

After the Syracuse Press Corps forgot about me, the hero, I spent time with Norma. Every night we went out. The old Anchor Room Bar threw a big party for me. Everything was on the house. Champagne, food, the works.

Several times I asked Norma to marry me. She said no each time.

I became dissolute. One night I arranged to fly back to Japan. I didn't see us working out. When Norma found out, she got really upset. A few nights later, at the house of some old school friends, Norma and I were sitting in the living room alone.

"What would you say if I said YES to that question you've been asking me all these years?" said Norma.

The next day, May 25th, I went to a jeweler and picked out an engagement ring. Then I met her after work and took her to the same jeweler so she could "pick out" the same engagement ring. It was one of the happiest days of my life.

We were going to wait until I got out of the Army before we got married, but we didn't know when that would be. I had planned a career in the Army. We changed our minds and decided to get married as soon as possible. We went downtown for blood tests the next day and decided to get married on June 2, a week later.

WEDDING BELLS. Corp. Robert Hickox, returned Korean war prisoner, and his bride, the former Miss Norma Van Patten, 1019 Tyson pl., leave Blessed Sacrament Church following their marriage this morning.

The blood tests didn't get back in time, so I had to get the City Clerk Edward Apps to open City Hall. He got a judge to waive the blood test requirement and issue the marriage license. More fun followed. Since we would be getting married in three days, I whipped off a telegram to the Commanding Officer of Valley Forge

Hospital requesting an extension of my thirty-day leave so I could get married. The answer came back: APPROVED. TAKE 30 DAYS MORE. CONGRATULATIONS.

We got a dispensation from the Bishop of Syracuse Catholic Diocese (I wasn't Catholic) to be married at the altar in Blessed Sacrament Church in Eastwood.

We were married on June 2nd, 1953, the same day as the Coronation of Elizabeth II of England. Dave Ianuzi was my best man. Norma's married sister Anita was the Matron of Honor. We caught a plane to Buffalo to begin our honeymoon. As we sat in a restaurant in Buffalo watching television news, we saw the Coronation of Elizabeth II followed by news of our wedding.

Two queens in one day.

2.3   VALLEY FORGE ARMY HOSPITAL – WARD 10 C-D, 16 JUL 1953 – NORMA'S LETTER TO BOB (EXCERPTED) – After the wedding, Robert Hickox returned to Valley Forge Army Hospital for continued care before discharge. Norma sent Bob one letter per day while he was gone.

Hi My Darling,

Well honey, here is your loving wife again. I can't say I worked hard this evening because I treated myself and went out for a while. I went up to Eastwood looking for a brown skirt. As usual, they had every color but brown. I stopped in the Anchor Room and had a couple beers. Terri was working tonight and Mary Ann was with her. They came back and joined me. I don't know if you know it or not, but Mary Ann chose not to live with her mother...

When I woke up this morning, I really felt lazy. I just love it when I have my monthly. I get so damn weak I wonder if I can raise my little finger.

I bought you a couple of things this noon. A tie rack, eight handkerchiefs, and two pairs of socks. I also made an attempt to clean those light brown shoes of yours.

I received that letter you were talking about [on the phone] *last night. I hate to have you so lonely and down in the dumps. I must admit, honey, it was a very serious letter and one that I read over several times. For one thing, don't ever be afraid of the future. Your wife is not weak and someone you have to drag behind you. I'm not afraid of the future as long as we are together. I'll be beside you all the way.*

You also talked in your letter as if I wanted you to change or be something different than you are. Remember honey, I fell for you just the way you are. I never want you to be different. There is one statement in your letter that made me mad and that is: [quoting Bob] *"I have to tell you, darling, that I am so afraid that once the novelty has worn off, you will regret marrying me, that perhaps I am not, or will not be, the person you thought I was." To begin with, honey, our marriage was not a novelty. It was something deep and truthful. The word novelty does not describe it now or at any other time. Honey, I will never regret marrying you as long as I live. Who should know you better than me?*

I know what you like and what you are thinking. I understand. You are my whole life, honey, and as long as we are together, you can bring nothing but happiness to me. I am more than willing to spend the rest of my life with you. If I wasn't, I wouldn't have said "I will." Honey, I want you to be the father of my children. You are a wonderful husband and you will make a better father.

...I will close for tonight, honey, as I am very tired. I will write tomorrow. Goodnight, honey.

All my love,
All my life,
Your loving wife,

"Kitten"

P.S. I love you and miss you my darling.
XXXXXX OOOOOO

2.4   EASTWOOD, NY, SUMMER 1947 – MY CAR THIEF DAYS – LITTLE BOOK 1

After graduation, I kept running with the gang, working at the railroad yard, and spending time with Norma. Foolishly, I dragged her along on some of our capers. Our gang – and Norma – never got caught and I believe that proved to be our downfall.

We were still stealing cars. A new friend opened up a chop shop and he paid us for all the "spare parts" we could find. We had quite a good thing going for us until one night we borrowed a car and stripped it clean just about the time the police found us. Three of us were gathered around the car finishing up when the garage door flew open. Cops rushed into the garage and arrested us at gunpoint.

They dragged us before the Justice of the Peace, Town of Manlius, a man who didn't appreciate being awakened in the middle of the night. He became judge, jury, and executioner. The justice asked me if I was guilty or innocent. Like a fool, I said: "Well, I was there and got caught so I guess I'm guilty." All three of us received one year in county lockup. After we heard our sentence, my first words were: "Ah shit, we ain't gonna be home for Christmas."

2.5   EASTWOOD, NY, AUTUMN 1947 – JOINING THE ARMY – LITTLE BOOK 1

Fortunately, one year was reduced to six months. One of the guys got his parents to hire a lawyer and he got us out on good behavior after four months. I was happy in jail though because I wasn't at home and didn't have to put up with my parents fighting. We were in a separate section reserved for juveniles so there wasn't any "funny stuff" going on even though we had some bad asses in there. I remember one guy who was awaiting trial for rape. He and I got into a fight and ended up in solitary for a couple of days.

Around November 1947, the three of us were back on the street and the old gang threw a party for us. They even invited a couple of beat cops to welcome us. After the party, reality set in. I had no job and was getting desperate for money. The railroad I worked for while in school offered to take me back, but I was too ashamed to go. Although I had saved about six hundred dollars before I got arrested, the money vanished while I was in prison. My parents said they spent it on legal fees, but I don't remember getting a single visit from our lawyer.

I was glad to see Norma again. When I was in prison, I wouldn't let her come see me. Norma's mother didn't want her to have anything to do with me and I can't say I blame her. Norma was waiting for me the night I was released, and we spent a lot of time together during the next month. I think she had a plan to rehabilitate me. I was disgusted with myself at that point. I had no direction in life and was slowly heading back into the same old routine. While avoiding home, I was drinking too much and becoming an alcoholic. One step away from jail, too. And I was just a kid.

One night in January 1948, while I was out with the guys and pretty drunk, someone came up with the bright idea of joining the Army. Well, that sounded good. Even in my drunken state, I saw the advantages of escaping the life I was making for myself. I knew I'd have no problem getting my parents to sign for me. They'd be glad to get rid of me. They always said I caused them too much embarrassment. My parole officer would release me if the Army would accept me.

Nothing to lose and a lot to gain.

Another reason I wanted to get away was because Norma and I broke up. During the past few weeks, we had some problems and broke up, 1948 style, and she started seeing someone else. I loved her very much. Perhaps more than a sixteen-year-old girl, 1948 style, could handle.

The next day, the five of us who made a drunken pact the night before went down to the Army Recruiting Center to sign up. We got the necessary papers and went home. My parents signed for me without even reading the forms. No problems with my parole officer either. He said it was fine and waved goodbye.

One of my buddies, Bob Ivison, was having a problem. His parents didn't want him to join so he asked me to talk to them. I went to Bob's house and gave his parents the old gung-ho speech about how great it would be for their son. Since Bob quit school in tenth grade, I told his parents how he could finish his education. He could learn a trade, make something of himself (the usual bullshit). Bob's parents changed their minds and signed his paper. I would regret my speech for the rest of my life.

Bob died in Korea.

Glory Boy

3.1 CAMP PICKETT, VIRGINIA, 1948 – ARMY BASIC TRAINING – LITTLE BOOK 2

We arrived in Camp Pickett after a long, tiring train ride. I spent years working at the railyard, but I had never ridden a train before. The most I had ever done was jump a freight car to get to work.

When I got to Pickett, my life changed suddenly. We were herded onto trucks that took us to a processing building that looked like a Nazi death chamber. Our sergeant swore at us and treated us as less than human. "Form two lines for physical examination." *Strip.* "Turn your head and cough". *Skin it back so the doctor can see it.* "Bend over." *Rubber glove. Flee to the showers to scrub up.*

After we showered and shaved (I didn't shave yet, but I faked it), we lined up and marched naked into a large room where we received uniforms from an evil man. No matter what size you told him, he would turn to another evil man and ask for "one extra-large". It would have been simpler if they told us everything came in one size. I received two sets of standard-issue clothing and signed for it all. They didn't hesitate to tell us if we lost anything, we had to pay for it. A statement of charges would be deducted from our whopping monthly pay of eighty-two dollars.

A sergeant ordered us to try on one complete uniform with old-style World War Two combat boots. My uniform fit fine – or would have if I had been six foot six and weighed two-fifty. I was five foot seven and weighed one hundred thirty pounds soaking wet. No amount of begging changed the minds of the evil men in Supply.

Barracks, bunks, footlockers, long marches under a hot Virginia sun. Thirteen weeks of pain. Inspections that involved bouncing quarters on a mattress. Cleaning floors with a toothbrush. Shit on a shingle for lunch. More inspections. Pretty easy compared to Korea.

The only real problem I had was with our designated drill sergeant who was lush. He would get drunk and come into our barracks at two in the morning, turn on all the lights, and order us to attention. Under ordinary circumstances, this would have been his prerogative, but six weeks into our training, he made a snide remark about us that was uncalled for. Under my breath, I called him a son-of-a-bitch. He heard me.

"What did you say Hickox?"

"I called you a son-of-bitch, sergeant."

He ordered me to do twenty pushups. I was athletic so twenty was easy for me. When I finished, I stood at attention. Meanwhile, my sergeant walked around the room harassing everyone. When he returned to me, he scowled.

"How many did you do, Hickox?"

"Twenty, sergeant."

"Dammit, Hickox. Do twenty more for telling the truth."

Too much. Punishing me for doing wrong made sense. Punishing me for obeying didn't. I blew my top and hit him so hard I sent him sprawling across the room. All hell broke loose. Some of the guys grabbed me. Confused by his inebriation, our sergeant stormed off to his quarters. Lights out.

Court Martial seemed likely.

The next morning, after calisthenics and breakfast, I reported to the Company Commander's Office as ordered. My sergeant was there. He denied everything. He was hot and heavy to press charges for insubordination and a dozen other misdemeanors. Before my CO passed judgment, several men from my barracks appeared and testified in my favor. My CO concluded my actions were justified. My sergeant was immediately transferred out of the company. I passed Basic Training and moved on to Camp Breckenridge, Kentucky, home of the famous 101st Airborne Division.

3.2   SYRACUSE, NEW YORK, 1948 – GOODBYE
LITTLE BOOK 2

After Basic Training, I went home to Syracuse on leave. It seemed like a strange place, as if home never existed. During the time I was away, I grew up. I was no longer the little boy who climbed aboard a train for Camp Pickett. I learned what I could do and no longer felt the desire to follow the ways of others my age who still lived at home. Even though I had just turned eighteen, I was no longer dominated by my parents or anyone else.

Several of the guys who enlisted with me were home on leave. A few were going to the 101st Airborne with me while others were shipping overseas. We were looking forward to military careers. Since we were enlistees (Regular Army), a career seemed like a good plan – after we celebrated.

We vowed not to leave Syracuse with any beer for non-military types to drink. We indulged heavily during our time home and amazed the girls with our great feats of derring-do and tales of adventure (or so we thought). We had a great time. Most of the guys teamed up with old girlfriends for one last fling. We told them disaster awaited us and it might be our last chance to see our women. The girls ate it up. I blame it on the uniform.

I got a chance to see Norma a few times while I was home, but she wasn't interested in renewing our previous relationship. She was hanging out with our old gang and playing the field when it came to dating. She was still in school, in tenth grade I believe, and here I was "a big man in uniform" asking for her affection. How could I expect her to react?

I spent my last night of leave at home with her, sitting on her front porch talking. We talked about many things. We talked about her schoolwork, her alcoholic father who had separated from her mother, her other relationships, and her hopes for the future. I heard a hint in her voice that there might be a future for us, but not now.

Feeling buoyed by this hope, I kissed her goodbye. After professing my undying love, I left.

I realized in my heart that night that I could never love another girl the way I loved her. What I didn't realize was the love I felt and the bond we shared would get me through my darkest hours while a prisoner of war in Korea.

3.3   CHINATOWN, SAN FRANCISCO, 1948 – BEER TALKING – LITTLE BOOK 4

After I washed out of Airborne, I requested a transfer to the Far East. I received orders for Far East Command along with a ticket aboard a train bound for the West Coast. The Twentieth Century Limited was the super-train of the forties. It had Pullman berths, plush seats, a bar, and an observation car. It was one of the few trains traveling coast to coast. I loved seeing America during the trip. And Uncle Sam paid for the whole thing.

I thought airborne training was going well. After two weeks of intense training that included night marches, bayonet practice, and jumping off twenty-foot towers, I prepared myself for my first jump. Exiting military aircraft while in flight. Not paratrooper. Nowhere did I see the word paratrooper. My first jump went well. The Company Commander called me into his office and rewarded me with a transfer to another unit. I was too short. My equipment weighed more than me and my instructors felt I didn't meet the high standards demanded by the 101st so they sent me to a repo depot in Camp Stoneman, San Francisco.

Cincinnati, Chicago, Deadwood, Reno. By the time the Twentieth Century Limited reached San Francisco, I teamed up with a guy named Goose, an Italian boy with a friendly smile. We found a cheap flophouse and headed up to Nob Hill to check out the mansions we were destined to live in someday. Then we went to Chinatown where all the action was, or so we had been told.

Chinatown was packed with import shops, curio dealers, and food carts. When it got dark, fireworks started going off everywhere. It was a sight to behold. Some of the prettiest girls I have ever seen played oriental instruments and the music became hypnotic. They had almond eyes and fancy hair arranged in beautiful long black tresses. Their Oriental clothing showed all the colors of the rainbow. The experience made me long to sail for the Far East, a place I had always dreamed about. I could hardly wait to sail under the beautiful Golden Gate and head for what I believed to be Paradise.

As the night wore on, we consumed most of the beer available while seeing the lights of the city. Goose concentrated on all the pretty but unavailable girls on the street. My thoughts were on the wonders I imagined I would find in the Far East.

The next morning, we crawled out from under our gear, which had somehow become strewn all over the room, and took a taxi to Camp Stoneman. When I arrived, I checked the roster board and saw a familiar name. Bob Ivison. My old friend who helped me drive a stolen car through a gas station. I hunted Bob down and we had a great reunion. He arrived in Stoneman a week before me and had a good idea of the camp layout and schedule.

One night we caught a bus to Frisco and tried to drink it dry. Somehow, we ended up in Oakland, the twin city across the bridge. We were stone drunk in an unknown bar when some guy offered to buy us drinks. A soldier never turns down a free drink, so we said: "Why not?" Suddenly this old fart started putting the moves on us. We looked around and realized the whole bar was nothing but queers. Our first thought was to run. Then our new friend pulled out his wallet to buy another round and we noticed this guy was loaded. Twenties and fifties bulging out. Bob and I looked at each other and decided to play along to see if we could acquire his wealth.

When we finished our drinks, our friend suggested we get a hotel room at a place he knew. No good mother's son would agree to such an arrangement, but here we were three thousand miles from home, drinking in a strange place with a queer who was asking to get rolled. Our drunken booze-washed brains saw an opportunity to pick up some big bucks.

We caught a taxi to a flop hotel. Don't know where. Bobby and I figured when we got ready to go to bed, one of us would crawl in with this guy and the other would hit him over the head with a large brass ashtray we found in the room. That done, we would lift his wallet, take his money, and hit the road. We flipped a coin to see who would get into bed with this creep and who would nail him with the ashtray. Lo and behold, yours truly lost. My job was to slide into bed with this jerk and wait for Bobby to pop him.

Off to bed for everyone. I lay there next to this stinking pig waiting for Bobby to make his move. I heard Bob start to snore and I thought: *No, you bastard, don't you dare go to sleep.* To my surprise, my bed partner started snoring too. I sat up in bed and called out to Bob. After a couple of snorts, he woke up. I told him the guy was sleeping and we didn't need to hit him.

We got up and put on our uniforms. Bobby found the guy's pants and removed his billfold. Bingo! Payday. Three hundred bucks. While our pal snored, we snuck out. Bob and I divided up the money, had breakfast, and caught a shuttle to camp for reveille.

A week later, Bob shipped out for Japan. I sat around Camp Stoneman waiting for orders. When I had given up hope, I saw my name on the board. Far East, Japan. I shipped out next week. My time at Stoneman was at an end and I was on my way to all the great adventures I had imagined.

Typhoon

A few days after leaving the States, we sailed into Hawaii aboard a decrepit old Liberty Ship named *General D.E. Altman*, a leftover transport from World War Two troop carrying days. Except for the disgusting conditions aboard the vessel, our voyage was uneventful. Lower ranking personnel, including me, were bunked below deck – way below – in tiers four high. Everyone became seasick the first day out and remained that way for the entire trip so you can imagine conditions below deck.

Fortunately, I didn't have to endure this evil for long. About the time I was ready to join the multitude barfing in the hold, salvation found me. I was appointed as an MP (Military Policeman) to guard the dependent quarters on the upper deck. Ahhh! Fresh air and sunshine. My duties consisted of guarding a single stateroom door – guarding precious wives and daughters who were on their way to Japan and other ports to meet up with military spouses and fathers serving in the Occupation Forces. Now this was terrific duty! Talk about the fox in the chicken coop.

I was on duty for four hours and off eight. I had an MP armband and carried a .45 caliber sidearm that made my little five-foot-seven-inch frame seem about seven feet tall. I was obligated to run errands for my trusts but that wasn't entirely bad. They were quite generous and often invited me in for a few moments of rest that included coffee and conversation. Not exactly allowed by my superiors, but it seemed good to be among civilized people after witnessing the drama below deck.

The mess hall, or as they say in the Navy, the galley, was open to MPs twenty-four hours a day. Since MPs and Navy personnel were the only ones who could keep food down, it was quite pleasurable to drop by day or night for a meal. The food was good, but I found the fresh air and warm breeze on deck more to my liking. I spent hours watching dolphins swim alongside our vessel. When the galley crew threw garbage off the fantail, sea creatures surfaced in droves to eat. It was quite an experience for me to absorb.

**

Hawaii was beautiful, everything I expected it to be. Lush, tropical, and warm. It was a sight to behold the islands rising out of the Pacific. The contrast of dark volcanic peaks against the green of thick tropical forests and beaches nearly white was everything you could want in Paradise.

After our ship docked, they turned us loose on the unsuspecting natives of these beautiful islands. Two days with gorgeous hula girls begging to adorn us with flowered leis. As each man left the ship, he got a kiss and a lei while a Polynesian band welcomed us with Hawaiian music.

Drinks, music, stories. Surfers riding huge waves. Beautiful girls. Drinks, music, stories.

During our last night in Hawaii, we were guests of honor at a hotel luau arranged by the Army. Roast pig, vegetables, seafood, and poi. Poi is a native dish that resembles wallpaper paste. You eat it with your fingers from a small bowl. Not much taste, but filling. We were served local brews by *Wahinis*, unmarried Hawaiian women, until we couldn't walk. We crawled to our rooms, satisfied, knowing tomorrow we would continue our journey to the Land of the Rising Sun.

**

Early the next morning, the NCO in charge of our detachment woke us before dawn and ordered us to grab our gear and report to the dock for embarkation. With weary eyes and aching heads, we gathered our belongings, showered, shaved, and dressed. We stumbled out of the hotel to the military buses bound for *General D.E. Altman*. Hopefully, she had been cleaned up a little.

At the dock, we lined up for roll call. When they determined everyone survived the previous night of revelry, we were ordered to board the ship and remain in quarters. Most of us disobeyed. We stayed on deck and waved goodbye to the *Wahinis* while the Polynesian band played "Aloha Oh". Soon our ship was underway, *en route* to our next destination.

Normally it would have taken four or five days to reach Japan, but we had no such luck. We were two days out of Honolulu when a violent storm hit us. Once again, I was thankful for my duties as an MP located on the upper deck. As our ship tossed and turned in the wild sea, conditions below deck became worse than they were previously. The typhoon raged for twenty-four hours. We were nervous and extremely glad when it was over.

I remember our ship running along the edge of the typhoon. I hung onto the gangway for dear life and watched the sea rise over the bow of our vessel. Thirty or forty feet above me. Standing on the deck of an aging Liberty Ship and watching a wave rise that high over her bow is a frightening experience I wouldn't care to repeat. The typhoon cost us a day of travel. We avoided the worst of the storm and rode out the rest as best we could while trying to pacify women and children in the dependent cabins. After the storm passed and moved northwest into the Pacific, we had smooth sailing – until we received an urgent message from a Navy vessel two-hundred-fifty nautical miles north of our position.

The vessel had been disabled by the typhoon and was requesting medical assistance. A crewman aboard that ship came down with a critical case of appendicitis and needed to be evacuated immediately due to a lack of medical facilities. So, we headed back into the typhoon.

Without hesitation, our glorious captain followed the code of the sea and changed course to help the disabled vessel. After a day and a half fighting the typhoon, we came alongside the stricken vessel. The crew put a line between both ships and hooked a stretcher to it. I'm sure there's a name for the procedure, but being a dumb Army rookie, I wasn't blessed with that knowledge. They hoisted the sick man between the two rolling ships and brought him aboard. During the transfer, both ships were rolling in the sea while the wind howled through their superstructures. Everyone below deck was puking constantly. Thank God for my MP post.

***

We turned the sick man over to medical personnel in Subic Bay, Philippines Naval Station. The Philippines was an unscheduled stop for us, but what the heck, why not use a typhoon as an excuse to see another country?

Now that *General D.E. Altman* was out of bad weather, we were in no hurry. We'd get to Japan sooner or later. I never figured out why they sent us to the Philippines instead of Japan (which was closer), but who am I to question military decisions? We offloaded military dependents after we docked. Maybe that was the reason.

I was getting anxious to see the glorious Orient. No passes were allowed in the Philippines and we weren't allowed off the ship, so my observation of that country was limited. I spent my time leaning over the rail and hollering at the natives as they walked by. The landscape was mountainous and very tropical, more so than Hawaii. The people appeared very poor. They had been devastated by World War Two and had not yet recovered.

The Philippines belonged to the United States until 1946 when we granted them independence. Prior to that, the Philippines was a U.S. protectorate similar to Puerto Rico, Alaska, and Hawaii. The islands fell to the Japanese at the beginning of World War Two and were retaken by our troops under the leadership of General Douglas MacArthur. The Philippines was new to this independence thing and the country was going through pangs of distress as they developed self-rule. The Philippine people had close ties with the U.S. and their young men fought side by side with ours during the war. Strong feelings of friendship and camaraderie developed between our people, and it showed in the way they treated us.

The Philippines was a very friendly place. I would have loved to have had more time to become acquainted with the people and customs, but alas, we put to sea again, bound for Japan.

4.2   JAPAN, JULY 1948 – CAMP KANAOKA
LITTLE BOOK 5

It was a bright, sunny morning when our ship sailed into Yokohama Harbor. As I stood on the deck of *General D.E. Altman*, I realized my long sea voyage was nearly over. Two weeks that lasted forever. We covered eight thousand miles since setting out from Golden Gate in San Francisco. It was an educational and exciting trip. Little did I know what lay ahead.

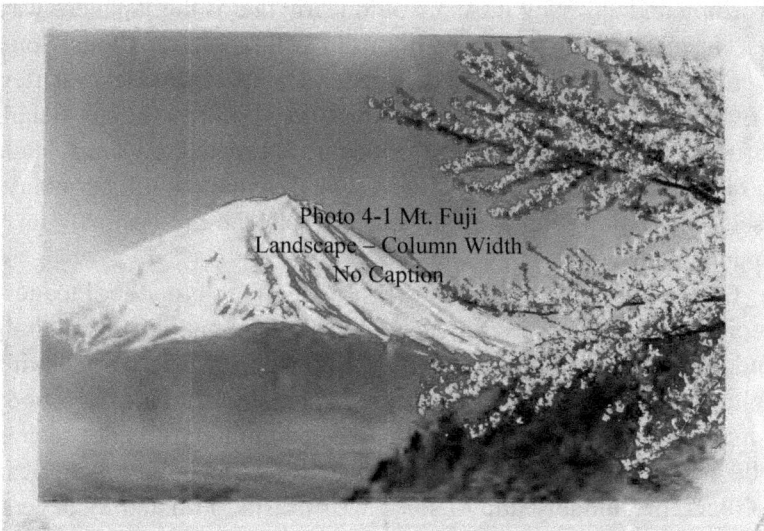

Photo 4-1 Mt. Fuji
Landscape – Column Width
No Caption

Japan is spellbinding and beautiful. Earlier, when we approached Honshu, the main island of Japan, I couldn't see anything from my position on deck because of dense fog covering the land. Then, suddenly, I saw the most spectacular sight I have ever beheld. Off the bow of *General D.E. Altman* a mighty snow-covered peak rose into the sky and disappeared in the clouds. Mount Fuji seemed to float overhead, suspended above our vessel. I was stunned by this beautiful, unnatural phenomenon, so unlike paintings I had seen before. Fuji is awesome, magnificent, magical. I was looking at it with my own eyes. Fuji, the sacred mountain of the Japanese, floated above me as I stared.

General D.E. Altman pulled into a huge dock and crewmen tied her off. After gangplanks were lowered, we gathered on deck with our gear. Roll call. An order for all troops to disembark the ship. We were assigned to military trucks alphabetically by last name, a lengthy operation. While I waited, I watched Japanese dock workers, hundreds of small sun-browned people speaking an unfamiliar tongue, running everywhere performing their duties. It was a strange sight for this uninitiated G.I. to see so many people working and enjoying it. As I would learn, that is the Japanese way.

The military trucks carried troops to different destinations. Some were assigned to the divisions, some to Eighth Army Headquarters FECOM (Far East Command) in Tokyo, and some to details throughout Japan. Unassigned troops were billeted to Camp Zama, a replacement depot where they would remain until permanent assignments were handed out. Zama was to be my destiny. Hurry up and wait.

Camp Zama was thirty miles south of Tokyo, the Japanese capital, and proved to be an austere place. The barracks were drab, and the camp was surrounded by a fence topped with barbed wire. When I saw it, I thought they sent me to prison. Not far off. Nobody could leave the camp because the local community was not secure. The Japanese populace showed no love for occupying American soldiers, presumably due to some "rowdyism" initiated by several American G.I.s in a nearby town.

I stayed in Zama for approximately two weeks. We spent our time performing limited duty, raiding the Base Exchange for snacks, and watching movies about the horrors of venereal disease. I attended several orientation classes explaining how to get along with Japanese people, which from the Army point-of-view meant how not to associate with them.

Eventually, I received my orders. I expected to be assigned to an infantry unit as a grunt, so I was delighted to see I was assigned to an engineering battalion. I knew little about engineering, but it had to be better than infantry. And you get to blow shit up.

I packed the next day and hopped aboard an Army bus headed two hundred miles south to the town of Kanaoka. Kanaoka is a small unremarkable village containing a few shacks and a small railroad station. A short distance outside Kanaoka was the camp of the 65th Engineer Combat Battalion, 25th Infantry Division. Kanaoka became my new home for the remainder of my stay in Japan.

Photo 4-2
Landscape – Column Width
No Caption

4.3   KANAOKA, JAPAN, SUMMER 1948 – MARIKO – LITTLE BOOK 5

Shortly after I arrived in Kanaoka, I met a pretty, dark-eyed little Japanese girl named Mariko. We spent a lot of time together and eventually bought a house in the city of Wakayama, about sixty miles southeast of Osaka. I put the house in Mariko's name because

American military personnel were not allowed to buy Japanese property. Kanaoka is only twelve miles from Osaka, making travel to our house easy. I spent most of my off-duty time at the house with Mariko and we got along fantastically. Mariko loved me and I was more than fond of her.

I brought Mariko into camp for Friday night dances, even though I didn't dance, and we went shopping in Osaka quite often. In Osaka is a huge department store called Takashimaya, a foreign-national-only store where Japanese were forbidden to shop. I bought her clothing and items unavailable to her in the few existing Japanese stores and we occasionally bought mail-order items from the Montgomery Ward catalog. We took trips around the island and saw many wonderful things. We had great times and shared a very warm, loving relationship. I often wonder how different things would have been if I had married Mariko and brought her back to the States.

Mariko and I were together for most of my stay in Japan. When I got off work, I headed for the train station and grabbed a train to Wakayama and Mariko. Under military law at the time, this was illegal and could have earned me six months in the stockade if I got caught. It was worth the risk. Besides, Japanese people on trains always hide an adventurous G.I. from the military police.

As much as I felt for Mariko, my thoughts always came back to Norma. I loved Norma and longed for her. Many times, I questioned my decision to leave her and join the Army. Then reality set in. We were too young. She was still in school and I needed a fresh start. Now I had my new home and Mariko. Life seemed good, very good.

4.4   SARASOTA HERALD-TRIBUNE, 1 JULY 1990 – A letter from Colonel John J. Doody, U.S. Army retired.

July 5 will be the 40th anniversary of the first ground combat action in the Korean War. Just as that conflict is known as the "Forgotten War", so have the events of its earliest days been forgotten.

Our armed forces at that time were victims of the huge force reductions and budget cuts of the late 1940s. The units of our division reflected this. They were at half strength and the majority of our weapons and equipment (most of which did not operate properly) were left over from combat actions in World War II.

Our battalion, which was commanded by Lt. Col. Charles B. Smith, had undergone an aggressive training program during the first six months of 1950. It was probably as prepared as any other unit in Japan at that time. However, with their personnel and equipment shortfalls, the men were not "combat-ready". Part of this battalion was the first to be committed to action. It was called "Task Force Smith".

Task Force Smith was composed of 406 infantrymen of the 1st Battalion, 21st Infantry Regiment, and a field battery of 105mm howitzers, all from the 24th Infantry Division. Total strength was 540 soldiers. Its mission was to block the invading North Korean Force, which turned out to be a well-trained, well-equipped, and combat-ready division about 10,000 strong.

Although tremendously outnumbered, our force did cause the enemy to slow down and to deploy its units. A very heavy price was paid for this effort in killed, wounded, and missing-in-action.

Today we are again looking at severe reductions in our ground force effectiveness to include personnel, equipment, and training cutbacks. We better keep up our guard and not disregard history. Never again should we have to repeat the events that occurred on the fifth of July, 1950.

4.5   27 NOV 1950, KUNU-RI KOREA – THE CHINESE OVERRUN – LITTLE BOOK 12

I got back to my unit in time for Thanksgiving. I spent two months in Japan recovering from a leg wound I suffered during a firefight along the Pusan Perimeter. The supply guys scraped up turkey for everyone in the company. November 23, 1950, was the last square meal I would eat for another three years. Turkey served on Army plates at a cold table in a part of North Korea I can barely remember. But I shared it with my guys.

We were with Task Force Dolvin on the run to the Yalu River. After we got zapped on Nov 27th, what was left was taken over by Gen Murch and became Task Force Murch. We were overrun by 30,000 Chinese People's Army troops. There was a ROK Division on our right that gave way and let the Chinese flank us. The 24th Regt was supposed to come between us and the ROKs, but they screwed up and moved too far forward, several miles ahead of the line. It's a wonder they weren't cut off and wiped out. They managed to get out, but it left our flank naked. The Second Division on our right took a licking too. Total fiasco.

I was on Hill 222 manning a .30 caliber machine gun. Chinese parachute flares lit up the sky above me and I could hear their bugles and whistles in the distance. They came over the hills like ants. I used up three boxes of ammunition shooting at them. I sent my assistant gunner, "Baby Face" Buli, to get another box.

Al Thistle, a company NCO, came to my position. He slapped me on the shoulder and told me to destroy my weapon and retreat. Our unit was out of ammo. Every man for himself. Al disappeared. I used a grenade to destroy my weapon. When I fell back toward our rear, I picked up an M-1 rifle someone dropped and loaded it. At that moment, a Chinese grenade, a World War Two potato masher, landed near me. The explosion cracked the rifle stock and knocked me to the ground, paralyzed from the waist down.

I crawled toward a bush and tried to hide. More Chinese flares appeared overhead. The whistles kept blowing. When the battle was over, I was taken prisoner and sent to Pyuktong Prison Camp Five where I spent thirty months in captivity. [Dates: 27 November 1950 to 24 April 1953 – ed.]

Tiger Survivor

Early in the summer of 1948, I was sent to Osaka for a six-month course in Army administration and the Japanese language. I was doing well in Japanese, thanks to Mariko and our friends, but much of what I knew was slang or worse. It seems we always pick up the seedy side of a language first.

I packed my belongings and went to Osaka. I was familiar with the city, so it was nothing new. My quarters were directly across the canal from the Division Stockade, good ole Lightning University, a place where those in need of an education are granted sufficient time to learn the error of their ways. Was the Army brass threatening me with an implied message?

I settled into my new routine and learned all the paperwork, rules, and procedures the Army defined as mission-critical administrative functions. Each day I had a class in conversational Japanese. I enjoyed my new duties. For several weeks, I practiced speaking Japanese among the populace, mostly in local tea houses.

Even though Mariko came to Osaka on weekends, I missed her very much. Things were different and I longed for the times we had in Wakayama. Mariko told me she had to go to her family's house in the country for a few days and would contact me when she returned. Mariko's family were farmers, as were most Japanese, raising rice and vegetables to trade. Money was scarce and produce stores were nonexistent. When Mariko left, I became discontented.

On the following weekend, I received my pass and went out on the town. I drank too much and took a train to Wakayama to stay at our house. Even with Mariko gone, I had several Japanese friends I could get together with and have fun. One of my friends was an American *nisei* named Don Koyama. Don was an American of Japanese descent who returned to Japan in 1939 to visit his family. While in Japan, he was conscripted into the Japanese Army as an intelligence officer because of his English language skills and background in American culture. He served the Japanese during World War Two and when the American Army occupied Japan, he switched sides and worked for American Army Intelligence. One of many people I crossed paths with during my tour of duty.

In Wakayama, time passed quickly. Too much *sake* and *beeru*. Before I knew it, Tuesday came. I had been AWOL for two days. Considering this, I decided I wouldn't get into much more trouble if I stayed a few extra days. As the weekend approached, I thought it might be a good idea to return to Osaka and check in. Without further ado, I caught the train back to Osaka.

When I reported, I was immediately confined to the barracks. I figured that on Monday I would be kicked out of school and sent back to Kanaoka for punishment. When Monday arrived, I was ordered to put on a Class A uniform and report to the school CO. He escorted me to a jeep, and we drove a few blocks to the Goshu building, known as Division HQ. Military police escorted me upstairs to a paneled waiting room where I sat for a long time. I twiddled my thumbs endlessly. Eventually, a Major entered the room and told me the General would see me.

At that point, I expected the stockade or a firing squad, not a general. I would have preferred a firing squad. I followed the Major into the office of General William B. Kean, Division Commander, U.S. Army, 25th Infantry. The Japanese school I attended was the pet project of General Kean. He took pride in his school and the men he selected to participate.

General Kean sat behind his desk. When he looked up, I saluted.

"Sit down, son."

I was shocked.

"Did you have a good time while you were AWOL from my school?"

"Yes, sir."

"Good. I'm glad to hear it."

General Kean proceeded to tell me how the school was his special project and how much it meant to him. I heard angels singing *Nearer My God to Thee* every time he mentioned his beloved school.

"Are you willing to return to my school and continue your studies and refrain from going AWOL again?"

"Yes, sir!"

"Alright, you are dismissed. Behave yourself. Have a good day."

Osaka culture 1948 – Museums, Kabuki, and Takashimaya Department Store.
Courtesy Mary Evans Picture Library

5.2   KANAOKA, JAPAN, 1948 – BLACK MARKET PRINCE – LITTLE BOOK 5

I completed school early in the Fall with no further incidents. I moved back to Kanaoka and resumed my duties as Company Clerk. I was charged with maintaining and updating service records for the battalion. Promotions, demotions, transfers. And PX ration cards.

All personnel joining the battalion received a ration card for cigarettes and goodies. All personnel leaving the battalion were required to surrender their ration cards to *me* for record keeping and destruction. Another case of the fox guarding the chicken coop. I used those cards to supplement my meager PFC pay with black market trading. A carton of cigarettes costs one dollar American and sells on the black market for four thousand yen, a neat profit of nine dollars American per carton. If someone had ten or twenty ration cards, he could buy his Japanese girlfriend quite a few nice things. The black market was rampant, and everyone participated.

Enough said.

5.3   17 MAY 1948 – JAPAN – KANAOKA BULLETIN – FREE WEEKLY MILITARY NEWSPAPER – Regarding events of interest to members of the 65th Engineer C Battalion stationed at Kanaoka Japan. Bob had copies of this periodical in his collection and likely enjoyed the publication. This issue predates Bob's stay in Kanaoka but demonstrates typical newspaper content.

The Southern Contingent

(photo unavailable)

The Southern Contingent – A new arrival to the 65th Engineer Combat Battalion is Lt Hoge of "Vuhginia" [Virginia] (smile when you say that) flanked by Captain Sibley and Captain Moore of Alabama and "Jawja" [Georgia] (smile when you say that one, too). Lt Hoge will become the A Company Commander when Captain Killian returns to Denver, out where the "deer and the antelope play". Welcome to the 65th Lt Hoge.

After his recent fire at his quarters in Hamadera Park, SSGT Fisher of A Company dropped in to see us. He said that he was grateful to everyone for their kindness and consideration towards him in this unfortunate period. SSGT Braun and Tec-5 Smith of the Kanaoka Fire Department also shared in Sgt Fisher's praise for their excellent skill in battling the flames. The Fishers are now living in the gas building in Osaka.

***

PILL PUSHER'S COLUMN
You have heard men all through the Army, especially the men of Kanaoka, say over and over that "You never had it so good!"

Well, the Medical Detachment has the same deal. Tec-4 Livesay, the terror of the [Kanaoka] post baseball team, just a little less than a month ago, extended his enlistment to 5. Maybe he wanted to stay away from the steel mills in Philadelphia.

Tec-5 Corey, Captain Caruthers dental assistant, who hails from St Louis, has decided he can pull his term with ease. Result: "He made it 4".

***

KANAOKA BULLETIN is printed for free distribution to the troops of the 65th Engineer Combat Battalion APO 25, commanded by Lt Col H. A. Holstrom and the 25th Quartermaster Company APO 25, commanded by Lt Col A. A. Hall. Authorization is by the 65th Engineer Combat Battalion. Supervision is by the 65th Engineer Combat Battalion TI&E Office. Newspaper Officer, 1st Lt G. E. Newton; Editor, Tec-5 G. W. Monett; Photos, Tec-5 T. E. Williams; "A" Company, Pfc Douglas & Tech-Sgt P. Tom; QM Company Pfc Cardonell; Medics, Tec-4 Ayers. Local news may be printed without first obtaining clearance through the Public Information Officer.

5.4   PYUKTONG PRISON CAMP FIVE, KOREA, 28 NOV
       TO 14 DEC 1950 – DEATH MARCH TO PYUKTONG –
       LITTLE BOOK 13 (intended)

NOTE: This passage is reconstructed from email between Robert
Hickox and fellow veterans who remained in contact using internet
message boards. According to Bob's working notes, he intended to
discuss this material in Little Book 13.

After the annihilation of the 65th Engineer Combat Battalion
during a battle near Kunu-ri on 26-27 November 1950, surviving
American soldiers were detained in a shed located at the bottom of
a hill. After the death march began, POWs and their captors traveled
at night and hid in deserted villages by day to avoid detection by
UN aircraft. Most soldiers wore a standard issue three-season
uniform that proved worthless against the bitter cold encountered in
the icy Korean highland. Bob wore winter clothing, issued to him
as a stopgap because the Army had no uniforms his size. -ed.

5.5   8 JAN 2000 – ROBERT HICKOX EMAIL TO [PMA---] –
       (excerpt) – Trading war stories regarding combat and
       conditions endured by POWs after capture in both Viet
       Nam and Korea.

PMA---: We were so wiped out after Dak Seang [special forces
camp] things are a blur. Broke my back at Dak Pek [special forces
camp], fell out of the air at 3,500 feet AGL [above ground level].
Then in April, [I] was hit in the back with a grenade. ...the kneeling
blond in the photo is Jerry ----, caught and cut to pieces. If they got
you in Laos, no POW. Cut your belly open and stuck a flamethrower
inside ya. My last two rounds in the pistol were for me.

ROBERT HICKOX: We were compounded in deserted Korean
villages, i.e. mud and straw huts. [They packed us twenty-five men
to a ten-foot square hut. So tight, if one guy wanted to roll over, we
all had to roll.] No heat. Fire under the floor. At forty below, no less.

[They dug trenches under the floor of each hut and jammed burning sticks into the trenches to warm the hut. You could feel the coals beneath you. The fire was so hot, it woke up hog lice living in the floor. Lice started biting my leg. They did so much damage to me, you can see the pockmarks to this day.]

It was the winter of 1950-51. I was just north of the Yalu River, near the town of Antung, close to a Chinese airfield. Yes. Regardless of what you have heard, our guys flew across the border to bomb that airfield.

Picked up my second Purple Heart on Sept 2, 1950. Tangled with a "Burp" gun and came out on the short end. Those damn M-1 rifles. Too heavy for close fighting. Would much prefer lighter and more firepower. [Like an M3 Grease Gun – ed.] Got hit in the right thigh, straight through, spent two months in Japan in a Kobe hospital, and volunteered to return to Korea. Bad move! Taken POW 11/27/50. So much for being home for Christmas.

I understand the Jerry ----- you mentioned was captured and killed, correct? Bad news! The North Koreans were similar [to the Chinese] in the early days of the war. They were taking no prisoners. We found forty-six of our men with hands tied behind their backs with wire and shot in the back of the head. And a lot of similar cases. When we pushed north, [the Koreans] executed over a hundred Americans near Seoul. We decided early on to keep something for ourselves [a bullet or grenade -ed.] to avoid capture. I didn't have much of a choice when I was captured. [I was paralyzed below the waist.] I was lucky they were Chinese and not North Koreans. The South Koreans weren't much better. Hell, they killed their own people along with a few Americans.

5.6   13 MAY 2002 – EMAIL TO BILL BOWLING (65TH ENGR CMBT BN – BAR GUNNER) – Regarding a book published by Lawrence E. Donovan describing the death march to Pyuktong.

I received your note and the excerpt from the book by [Lawrence] Donovan. ...He and I were in together, but they kept him longer. ...I never got along with him too well. He was kind of a publicity hound, got his name in a lot of books and articles.

The shed he mentions is where they put us prior to the death march. [DONOVAN: We were marched down the valley to a kind of shed, where others of my company were being held prisoner.] Sergeant Harper was one of those carried on a bamboo mat stretcher. He was with us only a few days. The Chinese made us leave him and other severely wounded behind.

The Chinese turned us over to the North Koreans for most of the march (with a few Chinese observers). The North Koreans let us know they were in charge by dispensing "justice".

The priest [Donovan] refers to was Father Kapaun (He spelled it wrong). [DONOVAN: A thing I shall never forget is the death of Father Capon, a Catholic priest who somehow had been put in with the POWs. ...I'll never know what the father did to enrage the Chinese, but one night they took him away and beat him to death.] Actually, [Kapaun] was a chaplain in the First Cavalry. He died from a leg wound because the chinks wouldn't let one of our American doctors treat him. A [medical officer] named Captain Anderson wanted to amputate the leg after gangrene set in, but the Chinese wouldn't let him. Kapaun died from infection. I agree [with Donovan], if ever a priest should be considered for sainthood, it should be Kapaun.

[According to records,] Donovan and I were in the same medical detail in Kanaoka for a while.

By the way, my estimate of the total dead at Camp #5 would be around 2600. I knew when we buried them across the river, they would never be recovered. I doubt if any of them will ever be.

5.7   21 DEC 2002 – EMAIL EXCHANGE BETWEEN JIM BELCHER AND ROBERT HICKOX – Regarding the anonymity of author Lawrence E. Donovan.

BELCHER: Al forwarded me a letter he received from this Donovan guy that none of us can remember. Sounds like he's made a career out of being a POW, which is okay.

HICKOX: Al sent me a copy of that letter too. Hell, I was a POW with him, and I don't remember him. Al does though.

Al forwarded other letters from Donovan to me, and I agree with you. He does seem to have made a career out of being a POW. I know several others who have done the same thing. The President of the KWVA, Harley Coon, is another one who always manages to find a camera to get his picture in something.

As far as I know, Donovan was in the same camp as me, at least for a while. I would have to check on that to be sure. The plain truth is that later, in late '51 and '52, there were some guys who made too much trouble and were hurting all of us, so the chinks moved them to another camp. Don't know if he was one of those or not.

Guess they were the ones who got the medals when they got back. Ha!

5.8   10 JAN 2002 – EMAIL TO BILL BOWLING (65TH ENGR CMBT BN – BAR GUNNER) – Regarding events that occurred during the death march.

We lost a lot [of our guys] on the death march. If you were sick, you died. If you fell out of ranks, you were shot or bayonetted. [I was temporarily paralyzed below the waist.] If it wasn't for a couple of guys who half-carried me for two weeks, I would never have made it. I don't know who they were, but they were terrific.

A lot of our guys got dysentery during the march from bad food. Half a bowl of millet or a barley ball per day. It tore our guts up. [Separate email: Most of the guys taken prisoner didn't even have winter clothes. I was fortunate that I had a wool sweater, but some of them got caught in their sleeping bags and didn't even have pants or shoes.]

About the second week into the march, when I could walk again, the North Koreans ordered us to fall into formation. I had reached a point where I didn't want to go any farther. The North Korean Major in charge of the death march [allegedly nicknamed Tiger. See "Greybeard" magazine, March-April 2003, page 4, Tiger Survivors Story. -ed.], came strutting by. When he passed me, I said something to him. He started hollering at me and slapped me across the face. Out of reflex, I hit him as hard as I could. He went flat on his back. He grabbed for his pistol, one of those big things with a wooden handle they can make a rifle out of (don't know what they're called). He got it halfway out of the holster, then changed his mind and jammed it back in. He got up and wiped himself off. He looked at me then stormed off. I don't know why he didn't shoot me on the spot. I figured I would get pulled out of rank later and shot, but it never happened. Maybe he figured I didn't have long to live.

They marched us every night from sundown to sunup [for about two weeks]. Probably covered twenty-five to thirty miles per night. [The chinks were terrified of our planes. During daylight, we huddled in abandoned huts and sheds. During the three weeks from 28 Nov through 14 Dec 1950], we covered a lot of Korea, picking up prisoners. Considering the cold, it's a miracle anyone survived. I felt the butt of one of their damn rifles more than once.

[SEPARATE EMAIL: I would put Kenny's figures on the death march closer to 3500, considering the number we lost along the way. By the time the chinks got us to Pyuktong, they probably picked up close to 5000, which is what we had in camp at the beginning. We probably lost 700 or 800 on the march. When you add all the guys that were wounded, all the guys that didn't have clothes and froze to death, those that died from disease, those unfortunate ones the gooks (both NK and Chink) executed for no reason other than to set an example, and those who couldn't walk, [you get 800 dead].

5.9   18 APR 2001 – ROBERT HICKOX EMAIL TO JIM BELCHER – Regarding a Siberian Tiger attack on Bob's death march group.

Personally, I remember a lot more guards than that. I remember them walking along both sides of our column and every time somebody would stumble or fall, they would get a rifle butt in the head. Or worse. The only happy time on the march was when the gooks all started hollering one night and come to find out a Siberian

Tiger had grabbed one of the guards and took off with him. At least that's what the guards told us. [See Biography #7 -ed.]

5.10   030 JAN 2002 – EMAIL TO BILL BOWLING (65TH ENGR CMBT BN – BAR GUNNER) – Regarding a weapon Bob carried during the death march.

The amusing part of this sad tale is that I still had that M-2 bayonet in my boot [after capture] and it was there for about three weeks. [The whole death march.] I forgot about it completely. Since the chinks never gave us a chance to take our boots off (if we had any to start with), I never noticed. When we got to the POW camp, after the long march (about 3 weeks), I reached down into my boot and there was the bayonet. Ha! Well, I figured right off that since I wasn't going to stab anybody I should ditch it. If the North Koreans found it on me, I probably would have bought myself a bullet in the head. I laugh every time I think about it. They stripped me of everything else, watch, ring, billfold, but never checked my pant legs or boots.

5.11   HONSHU JAPAN, FALL 1948 – TOURING JAPAN WITH MARIKO – LITTLE BOOK 5

During my absence from Kanaoka for training in Osaka, my company acquired a new CO, a West Point grad. He was stricter and more military than Captain Schmidt had been, and he curtailed my duties and activities. My leave and free time remained the same though, and I still spent time in Wakayama with Mariko.

It was getting later in the year and the air was cooling off from the extreme heat of the southern Japanese summer. Sightseeing became enjoyable. Mariko and I visited shrines and temples in Osaka, Kobe, and Kyoto. We went to museums and Kabuki theaters. We traveled through the countryside and saw many wondrous things. I learned about Geisha and Samurai. I studied Bushido and the great histories of Japan. I delved into the ancient religions of Shinto and Buddhism.

Mariko helped me put to rest many of the fallacies people in the United States invented during World War Two regarding the people in Japan. We visited the cities of Hiroshima and Nagasaki, two cities the United States devastated with atomic bombs to end the war. The inhabitants were rebuilding, but vast destruction could still be seen. In two blinding flashes, a quarter of a million people died and ushered in an era of man's inhumanity to man.

Photo 6-1 – Pyuktong 5
Landscape – Column Width
(viewed from the gutter edge)
CAPTION: (below)

Pyuktong 5 POW camp operated by China and North Korea.

Dead Man's Bowl

6.1 PYUKTONG PRISON CAMP FIVE – CHINESE PROPAGANDA PUBLICATION – (excerpt) – Explaining why North Korean Prison Camps are the most humane in the world.

SHALL BROTHERS BE... Published by the Chinese People's Committee for World Peace, 1952. Page 11.

Not At All What The Colonel Said Would Happen.

I consider myself to be an average POW and am sure my story is similar to that of thousands of other men who find themselves prisoners of the Korean People's Army and the Chinese Volunteers.

I landed in Korea on the first day of April and joined the Third Division. On arriving at this point, my group received a lecture from a Colonel concerning battle conditions and what to expect should we be captured. He told of many atrocities committed by the Chinese and Koreans, such as having your hands tied behind you and being shot in the head, or else possibly being tortured to death. He added that it would be better to fight to the death rather than surrender. I listened to these tales of horror and decided then and there that I should fight to the bitter end if I ever faced capture.

...My unit was forced to fall back to prepared positions where we were expected to hold out against all attacks. The Chinese Volunteers rushed forward and took us prisoner, and I expected to meet my fate at any moment. Much to my surprise, after giving up our weapons, we were treated very kindly. One of the Chinese soldiers took some of his own food and shared it with us. I didn't eat much for I was still suspicious and couldn't understand these

actions. This wasn't at all what the Colonel said would happen. Instead of death, we received food; instead of torture, cigarettes. My doubts were fast fading away but I still refused to place my complete confidence in them.

No Barbed Wire

We marched to a place a short distance away where there was a volunteer who spoke English. He told us we would not be harmed and that we would start our trip to the prison camp immediately. Because of the long duration of our trip, I didn't believe there was a prison camp. After many days of travel, my doubts came crashing down once more for we arrived at the camp and were given food and rest.

My ideas about a prison camp had to be revised also. No barbed wire enclosed us and only a few guards were to be seen. Day by day, conditions improved. The quality of food became much better and besides, we got more of it. Rations of sugar and tobacco were issued every three days. New clothes and toilet articles were given to us. In a short time, we began to look like new men.

...the library is stocked with English language books and newspapers from England and the United States and also China. ...Instead of being treated as prisoners, we are being treated as equals. It is nothing to see the [Chinese] volunteers and the G.I.s playing ball games together and discussing various topics.

If anyone back home thinks we are ill-treated, I wish they could see how happily we are all working and playing together. An air of friendship prevails between us, American, British and Chinese alike, our main interest is the same, peace, not only here in Korea, but for all the peoples of the world.

Norman Wilmer, 55002931.

6.2   PYUKTONG PRISON CAMP FIVE – DEAD MAN'S
        BOWL – This section is reconstructed from Robert Hickox
        email and an interview with Mary Hickox.

EXTANT HICKOX EMAIL:
        The chinks gave us a little metal bowl to eat out of. It
        held about a half a cup, which was more than we usually
        got to eat. I really wish I'd kept that little bowl. I didn't. I
        threw it away as soon as I came across "Freedom Bridge".
        I'd like to have it for a souvenir now.

INTERVIEW WITH MARY HICKOX – Regarding the use of food
        bowls belonging to POWs who died during the night.

Q: Tell me about Bob's bowl.

MARY: They gave him this little [silver] bowl to eat out of. Half a
        cup of boiled cucumber soup a day. He hated cucumbers
        after that. Sometimes he would get rice. It might have a bug
        or a piece of hair in it. A lot of guys would refuse to eat it.
        One guy refused to eat his rice because it didn't have milk
        and sugar on it like his momma used to make. They all died.
            Bob ate everything. Bugs. Millet. Fisheyes. When they
        gave them meat it might be a fish head. Bob would suck out
        the eyes because they were protein. Most guys wouldn't
        touch the eyes. He would find pigweed in the yard and eat
        it. I don't know what pigweed is, but he would boil it up
        and eat it.

Q: How would he boil food his food?

MARY: The huts had trenches under them. The only heat they had
        came from burning sticks the Koreans used to shove into
        the trenches. Bob would put the pigweed in his bowl with
        some water and place the bowl in the trench so it would
        boil. It was the only way you could eat the millet. He

called it chicken feed. He said it would break your teeth if you ate it raw.

Q: Did anybody steal food or eat the other guy's fish head?

MARY: When someone died in the middle of the night, the guy sleeping next to him might roll the body over, so it looked like he was sleeping. Then they took the dead guy's bowl and put it on the floor near his feet like normal. When the Koreans came in to hand out food, they would fill the bowl and move on. It was one extra meal. Later when they discovered the guy was dead, the Koreans would take his bowl.
        Bob said he never did that, but he saw other guys do it.

Q: What happened to Bob's bowl?

MARY: He threw it away. When they got off the truck [after Little Switch], they stripped off all their clothes and threw them in a pile. They didn't want anything the Chinese gave them. Bob threw away his bowl and everything else he had. He wanted to forget. He told me he wished he kept his bowl. He knew the story behind every dent and scratch in it.

23 SEP 2004 – ROBERT HICKOX EMAIL TO COMMAND SERGEANT MAJOR TIMOTHY F. CASEY U.S. ARMY (RET) POW COORDINATOR – Regarding POW murders in Pyuktong Camp Five.

HICKOX: I'll offer an observation [regarding your comment]. Those that play "hard ass" are the ones who probably would not like their prison records scrutinized closely. Things happened in the first year I'm sure they would not like brought to anyone's attention. Yet they will be the ones who make the most noise and are the most critical of others. I know of several, should the truth be known, who should have been strung up for murder. And they were the ones given all the medals when they returned. I don't suppose any of the guys [you mentioned] ever talk about stealing food from the sick, hiding bodies of dead comrades so they can get that extra ration, or stealing clothes off the sick? I would think not. Yet I have seen it.

CASEY: Nobody ever mentioned to me some of the negative things that happened in the early stages of captivity, at least not at reunions. They have mentioned them in phone conversations. Hunger drives people to do bad things. Two people mentioned the murder of fellow POWs. While on burial detail, one said he noticed [corpses] that had black-and-blue marks on their throats. He suspected they were killed by other POWs. Stealing food from the sick, bullies overpowering weaker guys to get their rations, and so on. [I've] heard of getting dead man's ration – that seemed acceptable to them. As is stripping clothes from the dead, not the sick.

6.3   TEAHOUSE   WISDOM,   JAPAN   1949   –   THE HONEYPOT – LITTLE BOOK 5

Not long after I arrived in Kanaoka, I discovered the fine nectar of Japanese *beeru* (beer), *sake* (rice wine), and the notorious rotgut called *suntory* (whiskey). These three evils were to cause me all kinds of problems during my time in Japan. Whenever I had a pass, I headed for the nearest tearoom to indulge in one (or all) of my passions. Alcohol and wisdom do not mix.

I lost track of time – hours and even days – and my name kept popping up on AWOL reports. My CO and First Sergeant were lenient with me, more so than they should have been. I suffered only token punishment. They reminded me I had changed in rank so often [for going AWOL and later being promoted to the rank I lost] that I should have been a general. I didn't get the hint and continued to bounce around between Corporal and Private.

I got together with my buddies quite often, with or without our girlfriends, and had some riotous times. One guy worked in the medical detachment and had access to medical alcohol. Now this was potent stuff, around one hundred twenty proof, and would burn the roof of your mouth off if you attempted to drink it straight. Mix it with a little fruit juice, however, and it goes down easily. We would grab a bottle of medical alcohol and crawl into one of the *hooches* in Kanaoka and get drunker than hootie-owls (as Bob Ivison used to say).

One night, we got pretty "buzzed". We went over to HQ and, using my key, went into the office and borrowed a couple of uniforms. I took Lt Cameron's uniform. My buddy took Lt Shaughnessy's [the Battalion Adjutant]. We proceeded to go down into the town of Kanaoka and pull "bed check" on all the guys shacking up. We would just walk in and nail them in bed. Talk about "shittin' and gittin'". We had a ball and none of them ever caught on. [Especially Jim Belcher. See Bio-2.1. -ed.] They just saw "brass" and hopped to attention. When we finished our bed check we went back to camp and put the uniforms back. Nobody knew.

***

As bizarre as it seems, the Japanese use human excrement to fertilize their crops. Most Japanese houses have a honey pot in the backyard. A honey pot is a deep hole in the ground where they keep their excrement until it ripens. Then they scoop it out and fertilize their crops.

One evening our group was sitting in a local teahouse drinking Asahi beer with our boots off and uniforms askew. Suddenly a jeep pulled up out front and the mamasan hollered "MP! MP!" We fled. I headed for the back of the house and jumped out of an open window. I ran across the backyard toward camp – without my boots. Suddenly, I felt the ground give way. Before I realized what was happening, I was waist-deep in shit.

I crawled out of the honeypot, a wet, stinking mess with no boots. I headed for camp. When I got there, I avoided everyone and ran for the showers. I dove in fully clothed. After the first shower, I removed my clothes and took another. I bundled my filthy clothing and tossed it. I got a clean uniform from my room and pretended nothing happened.

I thought I had gone through the ordeal unseen, but several people in the teahouse witnessed what happened and reminded me for months. I don't know what happened to my filthy uniform. With luck, it disintegrated in its own stench. I never found my boots either. Probably ended up on the feet of a Japanese black marketeer. Everyone escaped the wrath of the provost marshal, although nobody did it as fragrantly as me.

***

I have never seen anyone mention in any [POW experience] book how we made our booze.

The floor of the compound [Pyuktong Camp Five] was made of dirt and easy to dig a hole in. We got ahold of some of those big earthen jugs the Koreans used and would sink one into the floor and put a cover on it. We would fill it nearly full of water from the river and, over a period of time, we would each contribute a handful of whatever we could spare of rice, millet, or corn, and throw it into the jug. Then we would cover the jug with dirt and let it ferment for a few weeks. When it smelled "ripe", we would uncover it, scrape out the fermented stuff on top, strain the rest through a piece of cloth, and create white lightning.

I think one of the Southern boys came up with the idea. Throughout '51 and '52, we had a steady supply of hooch. The Chinese could never figure out where we were getting it. It never occurred to them to dig up the floor. They seldom pulled a complete strip-out inspection.

It wasn't Jack Daniels, but it wasn't bad.

6.4   KANAOKA JAPAN, WINTER 1948 – MEMORIES OF MY OLD FLAME – LITTLE BOOK 4/5

NOTE: The following passage was constructed by merging two portions of Robert Hickox's original manuscript.

The winter months of 1948-49 passed slowly. I kept myself busy with work at HQ. I spent weekends in the beer hall at camp or in Wakayama with Mariko. On more than one occasion, I found myself thinking of Norma. We had written but hadn't stayed in close contact. She was young, just finishing school and I wanted to give her as much space as possible. Secretly, I hoped we had a future.

I wasn't sure what direction I wanted to go. I was happy with Mariko and my life in Japan. I considered renewing my enlistment indefinitely. On the other hand, I was still in love with Norma.

I didn't write my parents either. I tried to let go of that miserable part of my life. My CO called me on the carpet for not writing to my mother. I told him I didn't want to write her, and he shouldn't ask why.

I knew little of what was happening back in Syracuse. Outside of Norma, I didn't care. I left all that when my Liberty Ship passed the Golden Gate. I was confused, not due to a lack of options, but because I had too many.

I remembered time I spent with Norma, time that seemed so long ago. I remember visiting her after I washed out of airborne school.

When I got back to Eastwood after my airborne training disaster, the first thing I did was get on the phone and call Norma. She told me she wasn't busy and would be glad to meet me at our old haunt, the Eastwood Diner. I offered to pick her up. I didn't have a car, but I had money now and I took a taxi everywhere. She declined and said she would meet me at the diner.

After getting settled at home, I walked – hell ran – to the diner. There she was, sitting in our usual booth. The jukebox was playing "Far Away Places", our favorite song. I damn near broke down crying. I walked up to her and kissed her, then sat down. We ordered coffee and talked. Several cups later, we were still talking.

As the sun was setting, I suggested we scoot across the street to the Anchor Room, an old hangout for our childhood gang, and get some dinner. We walked across the street holding hands for the first time in a long time.

While the owner, Callahan, roundly welcomed me with free beer, Norma went to a phone in the back and called her mother. When she returned, I grabbed my beer and we moved to a booth in the back. We ordered dinner and drinks. Back then people served minors. Besides, she was with a soldier.

During the following days, we went to movies, restaurants, and hit the amusement rides at Suburban Park near Manlius. We roller-skated under the stars. I spent every moment I could with her, keeping in mind she was attending school every day – except those days she skipped to be with me. Her mother worked every day, so I wrote Norma's excuses for school absences.

We spent many evenings, cold as it was, walking through the park holding hands, throwing snowballs, and laughing. I hoped our time would never end.

Norma, Eastwood, and my old life were far away from Japan where I was now. Far away from the beer hall where I spent cold winter nights drinking with my buddies. Far away from Wakayama where Mariko and I shared a home.

6.5   9 AUG 1948 – JAPAN – KANAOKA BULLETIN – FREE WEEKLY NEWSPAPER – Regarding events of interest to members of the 65th Engineer C Battalion stationed at Kanaoka Japan.

The week for the Engineers is started off by welcoming back Sgt Carnes to the Company. Sgt Carnes has been to the States for a furlough which he spent at his home in Oklahoma. He has been away from the Battalion since April. We suppose that it is good to be back here away from the high prices in the States. The Battalion is in a very distant way related to the local broadcasting station in Osaka – Mrs. Girard – Division R&U Clerk – Steno is the wife of Lt Girard of station WVTQ – any requests?

Thomas W. Iles
(photo unavailable)

MAN OF THE WEEK

Shown on the cover this week is a picture of Recruit Thomas W. Iles who is a member of the 65th Engineer Combat Battalion. He entered the army on the 8th of May 1942 and received his basic training at Jefferson Barracks, MO. After receiving his basic, he went on duty at an Army Sponsored Show which was held at Indianapolis, Indiana. He then was sent to the Air Corps at Syracuse NY as a cook.

On 17 April 1943, he landed in England and at that time he was transferred to the infantry. In May of 1944 [typo 1945 -ed.], he was landed in France and was assigned to the 102nd Infantry Division in Holland. He fought on through from there to the border of Germany where he won the Silver Star and the Bronze Star. He won the Silver Star by knocking out a German tank that was stopping an attack he was in. He won the Bronze Star by stopping a German counterattack that would have seriously hurt his outfit.

[After the war ended], his next assignment was with the 25th Infantry Division Military Police. After this, he was with the Headquarters Company as a Supply Sgt where he extended his enlistment two more years. At this time, he was transferred to the 65th Engineer Combat Battalion which is located at the beautiful Kanaoka Barracks.

He plans to make the Army his career and he has a pretty good start with six years.

FOR INFORMATION
All Japan Swim Meet
See Cpl. Eugene Brown, Special Service

Eighth Army Special Service is sponsoring an All-Japan Swimming Meet which will be held at the Meiji Pool in Tokyo August 26 through 28.

Participation in this meet will be on an individual basis but with a maximum of three entries from each corps, division, and base in each event. The events will include 50, 100, 200, 400, and 1800-meter races, 100-meter backstroke, 200-meter breaststroke, 300-meter medley relay, 400-meter relay, and fancy diving. The 300-meter relay will be composed of three men and the 400-meter relay of four men.

In last year's All Japan and Inter-Command meet, Pfc Siera of First Cavalry broke the 200-meter freestyle record, the 400-meter record, and swam with the 400-meter relay team which set a record. In addition to Pfc. Siera, Lt. Glynn, 25th Division, Cpl. Quigley, 25th Division, Pfc. Kornfield, and Pfc. Herbert Martin, Eighth Army, were chosen to represent the Far East Command in the All-Army Olympic tryout held in Hawaii.

***

KANAOKA BULLETIN is printed for free distribution to the troops of the 65th Engineer Combat Battalion APO 25, commanded by Lt Col H. A. Holstrom and the 25th Quartermaster Company APO 25, commanded by Lt Col A. A. Hall. Authorization is by the 65th Engineer Combat Battalion. Supervision is by the 65th Engineer Combat Battalion TI&E Office. Newspaper Officer, 1st Lt G. E. Newton; Editor, Tec-5 G. W. Monett; Photos, Tec-5 T. E. Williams; "A" Company, Pfc Douglas & Tech-Sgt P. Tom; QM Company Pfc Cardonell; Medics, Tec-4 Ayers. Local news may be printed without first obtaining clearance through the Public Information Officer.

6.6   5 FEB 2000 – ROBERT HICKOX EMAIL TO [LEO---] –
Regarding Don Koyama.

Don Koyama was a *nisei*, an American citizen. [He] was
conscripted into the Japanese Army Intelligence Service. After the
Americans [occupied Japan], he dropped out of sight for a while
then resurfaced as a volunteer for American Intelligence. He served
the U.S. faithfully for a couple of years. [When] he had enough, he
dropped out again and resurfaced in Wakayama.

At the time I met him, he was the biggest underworld black
market name in that area. We became close friends. I would invite
him to my house and vice versa. I was a small fish, but he could
peddle anything I could maneuver [like American cigarettes. -ed.].
He was a Ju-jitsu black belt. Whenever we would meet, his
introduction would be to throw me around the room. He was a real
character. He told me anytime I wanted anything in Wakayama, just
mention his name.

I did this several times and was surprised at the fear and respect
people had for him. I could walk into a restaurant or teahouse, order
anything I wanted, and tell them: "Koyama pay." Nobody
questioned it. I always informed Don of the charges. I never had to
pay him back.

I learned the extent of Koyama's influence one night when I was
walking down the street [in Wakayama] with Mariko and got
attacked by a huge Ainu. He beat me badly. Some people took me
to my hooch and Mariko took care of me. The next day, Don
dropped by to see how I was doing. He mentioned the Japanese man
who attacked me and told me not to worry. He won't harm anybody
anymore. It had a chilling effect. I made sure I stayed on Don's good
side thereafter.

Koyama kept the MPs away from Wakayama. When I left for
Korea, he was still in business. Last I heard, several years ago, he
returned to the U.S. and was living happily somewhere in the
Northwest.

6.7   PYUKTONG PRISON CAMP FIVE – CHINESE
         PROPAGANDA PUBLICATION – (excerpt) – Regarding
         the excellent standard of medical care provided for POW
         patients.

         SHALL BROTHERS BE... Published by the Chinese
         People's Committee for World Peace, 1952, Page 58

Life In The Camp Hospital

*The men who were so sick that they were expected to die were
given the best of medical care available, and also a special diet of
four to six meals a day. The doctors and nurses are looking in on us
every few minutes day and night, and medicine is given at all hours
around the clock. We are all now on the road to recovery and some
of us are getting fat. I myself am very fat and healthy now.*

Richard W. Godlewski, RA 12341853. L. Co, 38th Regt, 2nd Div.

6.8   PYUKTONG PRISON CAMP FIVE – 26 APR 2002
EMAIL TO BILL BOWLING – Regarding the quality of medical
care in the prison camp.

Speaking of teeth, did I tell you how the Chinese cured a
toothache I had? I got an abscessed molar (big one) and the chinks,
out of the generosity of their hearts, had three big Mongolians hold
me down while a fourth one pulled, not one, but TWO of my teeth
with a pair of pliers. One molar on each side. Why the hell they
pulled the good one I'll never know. Some kind of voodoo, poopoo,
horseshit. I can't believe the idiots didn't break my jaw. But that
was medicine in the POW camps.

Robert Hickox (left) and Robert Ivison (right).

ICE RIVER

7.1   KYOTO JAPAN, SUMMER 1949 – TOURING JAPAN WITH BOB IVISON – LITTLE BOOK 5

Sometime in the late summer of 1949 I was summoned to the Company C Orderly Room and informed I had a visitor. I had no idea who it might be. I didn't know anyone outside the camp who might show up here.

I walked into the company office and noticed a tall skinny guy waiting for me.

"Hey Bob," said my friend and fellow troublemaker Bob Ivison.

I had last seen Bob Ivison at Camp Stoneman California before we shipped out. I lost track of him and had no idea he was stationed in Japan. As it turned out, he was assigned to Company E, 35th Infantry Regiment, 25th Infantry Division, stationed at Otsu, Japan, only forty miles from me. I have no idea how Bob located me. More than likely, his mother told him. Or Norma. He was a more dedicated letter writer than I was.

It was great to see Bob again. With the good auspices of First Sergeant Frankfurter (or so we called him.) [MSGT Leroy Francard. -ed.], I received a three-day pass on the spot. Bob and I took off to do some sightseeing.

We spent time in Osaka. I showed him Osaka Castle, the ancient home of the Shogun. For the heck of it, I showed him my old quarters where I stayed when I attended General Kean's Japanese language school – right across from "Lightning University", the Division stockade. We patronized a few finer establishments for beer and then went to Wakayama to meet Mariko and see my house.

From there we traveled to Kyoto where I showed Bob many of the Shinto and Buddhist shrines I discovered during my previous trip with Mariko. Fortunately, the Great Buddha of Kamakura was nowhere in sight. Otherwise, Bob and I might have climbed it.

The following spring, when I received amphibious training prior to Korean deployment, I was in Kamakura checking out teahouses with friends. Kamakura is an old religious site, more conservative than most temples. The Great Buddha statue is sixty feet high and highly revered by the local citizenry. When I saw Buddha, I accepted his challenge. Having visited several tearooms and feeling no pain, I decided to climb the Great Buddha. After considerable effort, I managed to reach Buddha's lap where I sat and caught my breath. My climb up evoked wrath among devoted worshippers and the climb down nearly got me killed. I managed to escape with my life, mostly due to the nonviolent nature of Buddhist monks.

Bob and I spent the remaining two days on a cultural tour. We visited museums during the day and enjoyed hospitality in some of the finer establishments at night. I was eager to push boundaries like Bob and I did in the old days, but Bob had become a conscientious soldier unwilling to buck the system.

We had a terrific time. Bob filled me in on events back in Syracuse. When it was time to say goodbye, I tried to talk him into going AWOL and spending a few more days touring Japan. Sadly, but firmly, Bob told me he needed to return to camp. We promised to keep in touch.

Is there no end to Army brainwashing?

7.2   KANAOKA JAPAN, FALL 1949 – AWOL TWICE WITH PAY – LITTLE BOOK 5

During a period of restlessness, I pulled one of the biggest screwups of my life. I left camp on an after-work pass I wrote for myself [because I was the] company clerk and went to Wakayama. This time I decided to stay awhile.

Since Wakayama was already an off-limits city due to civil and political (Communist) unrest, it was an ideal place to be if you were avoiding military police because no MPs were allowed in the city without a warrant. That's one of the reasons I bought a house there.

Wakayama might have been a dangerous place for me, an American soldier, if not for my good friend Don Koyama, a former Japanese Army Intelligence Officer who ran the black market and ruled the city with an iron fist. Whatever Koyama-san wanted, Koyama-san got. Whoever was a friend of Koyama-san had nothing to fear. Mention of his name was enough to get me anything I might want, from free beer to transport out of Japan if I desired. Koyama-san was powerful and feared in Wakayama and he was my friend.

After I had been AWOL for two weeks and enjoying the good life, I ran out of money. I could have floated on Koyama's name for a bit, but it was the first of the month and my pay was waiting back at camp. I figured, what the heck, I'll go in and collect my pay along with a few cartons of cigarettes and return to Wakayama.

I hopped a train back to Kanaoka, brazenly walked through the main gate unchallenged, and stood in the pay line. When they called my name, I saluted and went through the routine to collect my whopping ninety-seven dollars. Nobody froze my pay for being AWOL. Apparently, the company clerk [me] was not doing his job. I added on a few cartons of cigarettes I could sell for several thousand yen and headed out of camp.

My boss, Second Lieutenant Hayward Cameron, ran into me near the gate. He looked surprised. He could have placed me under arrest right there, but he was too nice a guy. Instead, he asked me where I had been, what I had been doing, and if I planned on remaining in camp. I assured him I would report as usual on Monday morning. He let me go. Bad decision on his part.

I grabbed a train back to Wakayama and stayed another week. I sold the cigarettes for enough money to last a long time. By the end of the week, my conscience was bothering me. Or perhaps it was images of Lightning University, the stockade across the street from my quarters, haunting me. If I stayed AWOL for one more week, they could nail me for desertion. I didn't want that. Desertion is serious. I decided to return to camp and accept my punishment.

I got a train back to Kanaoka and turned myself in. I was instantly confined to quarters and "placed in chains". Sergeant Frankfurter (so we called him) [MSGT Leroy Francard. -ed.] notified me I would be facing a Summary Court Martial.

Since the whole thing took place on a Friday, I was stuck in quarters for the weekend. This seemed unreasonable to me, so that night I crawled out a window and headed into town. Nobody would miss me before Monday, and I planned to be back by then.

I headed for the nearest tearoom and settled into a couple of bottles of Asahi *beeru*. After one bottle, a jeep pulled up out front and the *mamasan* hollered "MP! MP!" Even though I was wearing my boots, I didn't get away. The goon squad arrested me on the spot and dragged me back to camp where I was incarcerated in a one-cell jail in the provost's office. Sergeant Frankfurter notified me my Summary Court Martial had been upgraded to a Special Court Martial. I was charged with AWOL, resisting arrest, and crimes against the Army. If convicted, I faced six months in the stockade, a reduction in rank to zero, and loss of all pay and PX allowance.

This did not make me a happy camper, but I had nobody to blame but myself. Second Lieutenant Cameron told me he never heard of anyone who had gone AWOL, returned to camp and got paid, and then went AWOL again.

My Special Court Martial convened on Tuesday morning. They took me from the Orderly Room in handcuffs. Sergeant Frankfurter was dancing with glee. Guards escorted me to the HQ Building where a panel of officers sat, presided over by a Lt Colonel. My shackles were removed. I approached the court and saluted.

"Pfc Robert Hickox reporting to the Court as ordered."

The Lt Colonel looked at me for a moment then fingered through a file stuffed with papers. He frowned.

"What did you say your rank was, soldier?"

"Pfc, sir."

"I have a copy of a company order signed by First Sergeant Frankfurter on behalf of the company commander. This order reduced you to the rank of Recruit on your first day of AWOL. Were you aware of this order?"

"No, sir. Since I was AWOL, I couldn't possibly know about it."

The Lt Colonel studied papers in front of him.

"Son, if you were not present when this company order was issued, and you were not made aware of it later, there is nothing this court can do. It must be ruled you were summarily punished by company order and reduced to the rank of Recruit in your absence. This court is dismissed."

I thanked the court, saluted, and walked out the door.

7.3   PYUKTONG PRISON CAMP FIVE, KOREA – CHINESE PROPAGANDA PUBLICATION – (excerpt) – Describing typical daily life in a prison camp along the Yalu River.

SHALL BROTHERS BE... Published by the Chinese People's Committee for World Peace, 1952, Page 9

Lenient Treatment Policy

Leisure hours were passed away playing games, swimming or sunbathing. The river is on our doorstep and many pleasant afternoons were spent in the sun, dozing, chatting, or idly watching the swallows skimming over the river's ruffled surface. This helped us forget we were POWs for a few fleeting hours. To relax in this manner was very helpful, it gave our minds, usually full of contradictory and conflicting thoughts, a much-desired rest.

And then we were told about the Lenient Treatment Policy – now we were interested! All the "whys" and "wherefores" came to light and we finally realized that this policy was adopted for our benefit and the benefit of all POWs of the differing nationalities.

PAGE 27:   *"How We Spent Christmas."*

Three days before Christmas, we were busy preparing for the holiday. Evergreen boughs were cut and brought to our various companies and arches were built over the entrances of the company areas and each squad room. Colored paper was issued to every squad to decorate the arches and Christmas trees that were set up outside rooms.

...Christmas Eve's supper was really something special. Extra-large rations of pork, fish, and gravy with plenty of good white bread filled everyone to the bursting point. Then, after this

enjoyable meal, we went to the theatre to see a show put on by talent
selected from among the men of the camp.

7.4   PYUKTONG PRISON CAMP FIVE, KOREA (WINTER
          – 1950-51) – LITTLE BOOK 17 (intended)

          30 MAY 2002 – ROBERT HICKOX EMAIL TO BILL
          BOWLING – Regarding the POW experience.

I don't know if you remember Kenny Johnson. He was from
downstate NY [Johnstown] and was taken POW when I was. He
died in the camp. He was a close friend of Jim Belcher and me.
    …Kenny starved to death and died in my arms. He couldn't eat,
even when there was something to eat. A lot of men died that way.
They developed dysentery and then lost their appetite and died. I
tried to force feed [Kenny] but he couldn't take it. It's one thing to
see someone executed or beaten. As a prisoner, you come to expect
that. But seeing men starve and die when medicine would have
helped is beyond me. That was the hardest thing for me to handle.

7.5   18 OCT 2003 – ROBERT HICKOX EMAIL TO ROB
          YOUNG – Regarding POW casualties at Camp Five.

There were around 5000 in Camp #5 during the winter and
spring of 1951. Over 1600 died during the first winter in our camp.
Almost a thousand more died during the ensuing two years. I helped
bury most of them. [By carrying their corpses across the frozen river
to mass graves on the far side. -ed.]
    Johnny Johnson was the person who kept the names of those who
died. [He recorded names] on scraps of paper and brought them
back in a toothpaste tube (don't know where he got that). He was in
another camp. I think the one at Mampo, northeast of us a little. He
got a Silver Star a couple of years ago for his effort. Some things
take a long time and recognition comes slowly from the Army.

Some 4000 died while POW, almost a 40% death rate, higher than any war other than the Civil War. [Separate email: I know we were burying twenty-five to thirty guys per day during the winter of 1950-51. War is a shitty game.]

By the way, my estimate of the total dead at Camp #5 would be around 2600. I knew when we buried them across the river, they would never be recovered. I doubt if any of them will ever be.

NOTE: Bob spent the rest of his life searching maps of North Korea to locate POW graves so bodies could be recovered. Due to time and erosion, he was unable to reproduce his trips across the ice.

7.6   18 OCT 1948 – JAPAN – KANAOKA BULLETIN – FREE WEEKLY NEWSPAPER – Regarding events of interest to members of the 65th Engineer C Battalion stationed at Kanaoka Japan.

Some of the things that happened in the Company during the past week were the football game that was held at Gifu and the stage show "Kiss and Tell".

We lost the game at Gifu by a score of 46-8 but a good fight was put up by the men of Kanaoka.

Last Wednesday, the stage show "Kiss and Tell" was shown here at Kanaoka Barracks. It was a show that was enjoyed by all that attended, and we know that a lot of effort was put into it to make it the good show that it was. Our new Sergeant Major, MSGT Miller was most hospitable to the cast. He entertained them royally at the NCO club. The old Sergeant Major, MSGT Berwick of Brooklyn (Yerks), New York says "Give me a few days after I get back and I'll have my Brooklyn accent again."

We are all going to miss "Pop" Gregory when he leaves for the States, but don't worry as he is going to be back. "Ole Pop" really helped us out a lot getting ready for the Annual General Inspection. The picket fence in front of A Company particularly is a big improvement. Speaking of the AGI – we're all glad it's over for another year.

Page 3 .   ****WEEKLY NEWS****   18 October 1966

FLASH

BATTALION STRENGTH INCREASED BY ONE
OCTOBER 13 TH

ERIN GOBRAUGH

27TH WARD CHICAGO

Photo 7.2
Portrait + Centered
CAPTION (below)

28TH STATION HOSPITAL

HAMADEN PARK

        In this corner we have Patricia Ann Shaughnessy,
weighing five and one half pounds, and contender for
the loudest crying in Southern Honshu. She is dressed in
three cornered pants and is teething on a clay pipe.
Her parents are betting on her to win the Irish Crown
for "MISS KANAOKA" of 1966.
        Congratulations Lt and Mrs. Shaughnessy.

In this corner we have Patricia Ann Shaughnessy, weighing five and one-half pounds, a contender for the loudest crying in Southern Honshu. She is dressed in three-cornered pants and is teething on a clay pipe. Her parents are betting on her to win the Irish Crown for "Miss Kanaoka" of 1966. Congratulations Lt and Mrs. Shaughnessy.

Only known photo of the stage show "Warrior's Husband" which played at the
Kanaoka Theater at 1930 hrs 14-21 October 1948.

***

A clear-headed, clean-mouthed soldier who respects women and
fears God is of far more value to his country than the other kind.

COME TO CHAPEL SUNDAY – BRING A BUDDY.

***

KANAOKA BULLETIN is printed for free distribution to the
troops of the 65th Engineer Combat Battalion APO 25, commanded
by Lt Col H. A. Holstrom and the 25th Quartermaster Company
APO 25, commanded by Lt Col A. A. Hall. Authorization is by the
65th Engineer Combat Battalion. Supervision is by the 65th
Engineer Combat Battalion TI&E Office. Newspaper Officer, 1st Lt
G. E. Newton; Editor, Tec-5 G. W. Monett; Photos, Tec-5 T. E.
Williams; "A" Company, Pfc Douglas & Tech-Sgt P. Tom; QM
Company Pfc Cardonell; Medics, Tec-4 Ayers. Local news may be
printed without first obtaining clearance through the Public
Information Officer.

7.7   KANAOKA   JAPAN,   MAY   1950   –   OFFICER CANDIDATE SCHOOL – LITTLE BOOK 5

In May 1950, I received word the Army was offering testing for Officer Candidate School. With my record, I didn't feel I was a good OCS prospect. I figured, what the heck, I'll take the test for fun. I thought I was as smart or smarter than most of the officers I encountered during my career.

On a bright, sunny morning I reported to the testing room with a whopper of a hangover from the night before. The test measured IQ with some questions about military decorum. A passing grade was 110. I thought officers were smarter than that. I finished the test and staggered out of the room, never expecting to hear from the Army.

A few weeks later, an Army representative notified me I scored 142 on the test and was being considered for OCS. If accepted, I would receive orders to return to CONUS (Continental United States) to begin Engineer Officer Training. A short time after that, I received notification of acceptance.

Returning to CONUS created a dilemma for me. I didn't want to leave Japan and Mariko but returning to the States would allow me to see Norma. Graduating from OCS would give me the rank of Second Lieutenant and a better rate of pay. I could spend more money on Mariko.

I made a stipulation that if I accepted a commission, I would be allowed to return to Japan and my old unit, the 65th. Requests are seldom sanctioned in the military, but someone acquiesced and guaranteed me a slot with my outfit upon my return. I must have had a guardian angel, probably Lieutenant Cameron. Now all I had to do was wait while my paperwork wound its way through a maze of red tape and chain of command.

***

In June 1950, my unit began training intensely for combat deployment. Rumors circulated that the company would be leaving shortly for extended maneuvers. I had no idea where they were going, but I wanted to go with them. As an HQ clerk, I was not obligated to remain with the unit unless I chose to. Our company received orders to move to Yokohama for amphibious maneuvers.

This was the first time I had to play soldier since basic training. I didn't have the foggiest idea what amphibious training involved other than water. I was issued appropriate clothing (one size fits all) and basic equipment. Someone assigned me to a platoon and a squad, again something I had not dealt with since basic training. Our unit set up tents, unboxed provisions, and accepted a spartan lifestyle. Our mess trucks were never far behind so meals were plentiful. As a newbie, I wasn't asked to do real infantry work. Life went on around me while I watched and offered help.

We had a young Second Lieutenant [nicknamed "junior". -ed.] who was a real idiot. He was nineteen years old and wet behind the ears. Platoon Leader. You can lead a horse to water, but you can't make him drink. He screwed up everything he touched. We muddled on despite him. This kid attached himself to me for some reason, probably because he knew I was familiar with paperwork and Army organization. He was forever on my butt asking me questions or making stupid suggestions. I didn't like him, but shortly I would discover other people I disliked more.

In Yokohama, we spent our time on weapons training and learning landing craft features. I practiced going over the side of an LST on a rope ladder and ending up in an LCP, a small unstable craft used for landing troops on an enemy-held shoreline. Boats bounce up and down in the water making it easy to get hurt. We had several men injured during training. I witnessed a soldier in another platoon get caught between the LST and his LCP and get crushed.

Nobody was playing games here.

We spent three weeks in Yokohama practicing amphibious maneuvers and hostile landing zone skills. We stayed aboard an LST [USS Union] and practiced drills at sea.

On June 27, 1950, a calm Sunday morning, we were summoned on deck and solemnly informed North Korea had invaded South Korea. We were ordered to report to our respective units, collect our gear, and return to our home garrisons. Nobody knew what lay in wait for us.

Waegwan Bridge over the Naktong River. Hill 303 is visible lower right.

Hill 303

8.1 WASHINGTON DC, MAY 1953 – HONEYMOON – LITTLE BOOK 33 (intended) – This section has been reconstructed from Robert Hickox's working notes and an interview with Mary Hickox.

INTERVIEW WITH MARY HICKOX:

Q: Where did Bob and Norma go on their honeymoon?

MARY: They didn't have one. They stayed with Norma's mother because they didn't have any money. Bob was on leave from the Army at Valley Forge Hospital. He had to stay where they could contact him.

Q: In Bob's working notes, right after the wedding, he wrote: "Went to Washington to see Bob Jones. Gave Norma a tour." Did he ever talk about that trip?

MARY: Never heard anything about it.

NOTE: Robert Hickox's email identifies Bob Jones as a fellow POW he remained in contact with but provides little detail regarding the relationship.

ROBERT HICKOX WORKING NOTES:

We stayed with Norma's mother for three months until I was discharged from the Army on August 1, 1953. After I returned to Eastwood from Valley Forge Hospital (my final visit), things grew difficult in the household. According to Norma's mother, we stayed out too late, never helped around the house, and didn't have jobs.

I was offered a job at the Army Recruiting Office in Syracuse. I considered taking it, but Norma and I decided to go to Pensacola Florida and stay with friends. I bought tickets on a Greyhound Bus and we headed out.

8.2   PYUKTONG PRISON CAMP FIVE, KOREA, WINTER 1952 – MY ESCAPE TO MANCHURIA – LITTLE BOOK 20 (intended)

NOTE: This escape account is summarized in an email excerpt dated 2 February 2002 to Bill Bowling, 65th Engineer Combat Battalion.

I've got a pile of stories I can tell you that you'll never believe. I got away with some things I should have been shot a dozen times for. Just that lucky rabbit's foot, I guess. Ha!

Do you remember the story of the ring I brought to DC [during the 25th Infantry Division 50-Year Reunion held 26 to 28 July 2001 – ed.] and showed everybody? It was given to me by a Chinese girl, supposedly a nurse, who had been conscripted into Mao's army after they took over. A couple of us were planning to escape and she was sneaking us food to take with us. She gave me the ring to barter with if I had the opportunity. It's 22k gold. She thought we might be able to trade it for something.

Well, we took off in the winter of '52 and walked across the river to Manchuria. I swear, the mountains only got bigger and more rugged. We damn near froze to death. We found a farmhouse and thought maybe they would help us. No such luck. Even though we weren't in Korea, everybody on that side of the river was a member of the militia. They caught us and turned us over to the chinks [Regular Army] who brought us back to camp.

We were gone only a couple of days, but they put us in lockup for a week anyway. We had to write confessions about how bad we had been. The gal disappeared and I never saw her again. They said she was transferred out for reeducation. Apparently, they discovered she helped us. She was sympathetic to Chiang Kai-shek and the Kuomintang. I often wonder what really happened to her. Anyway, the chinks never found the ring and I snuck it home with me.

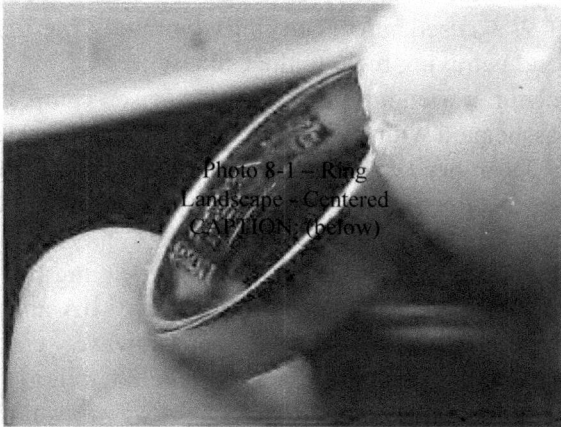

Photo 8-1 – Ring
Landscape – Centered
(CAPTION; below)

Kuomintang POW gift.

[A literal translation of the inscription reads: *north-capital city-gold-flea market-divine house (food)*. A modern rendering might be: Beijing Jewelry Store (high-end) 22k gold. -ed.]

8.3 SYRACUSE, NEW YORK, SUMMER 1953 – FBI HARASSMENT – LITTLE BOOK 35 (intended)

NOTE: This section is reconstructed from Robert Hickox's working notes and interviews with Mary Hickox.

After I returned to the United States, the FBI interrogated me several times in the Syracuse Federal Building. Rarely was it a pleasant experience. I got the impression they were looking for something to pin on somebody, maybe me, maybe someone bigger. I never found out what the FBI was searching for, but I suspected a handful of people.

Claude Batchelor was an American soldier assigned to the 8th Cavalry Regiment in Korea. He was taken prisoner on October 31, 1950, and spent the war in a POW camp. Batchelor [allegedly] collaborated with his Chinese captors by writing propaganda letters denouncing capitalism and demanding UN Forces evacuate Korea. Fellow POWs accused him of carrying Communist literature around the camp and betraying them to the Chinese.

Paul Schnur, a friend of mine from the prison camp, had family members associated with the American Communist Party.

During December 1951, dozens of POWs, myself included, sent out Christmas Greetings to our families in America via Radio Peking. Our Chinese captors forced us to include statements praising the North Korean peace effort and denying the torture of American POWs. Many of us were listed as MIA and figured a Christmas greeting would let our families know we were still alive. Unfortunately, those greetings made us look like traitors.

I spent thirty-three months in Pyuktong Prison Camp #5 watching 2600 American soldiers die over two winters, so handling FBI bullying was no problem for me. Not so with Norma.

When the FBI knew Norma was alone, they would call her on the phone and claim they had taken me prisoner and planned to kill me unless she brought the "evidence" of my Communist activity to such and such a person. Norma grew up in rural Eastwood and had no idea how to handle death threats made by a mysterious voice on the phone. The pressure got to her. She started drinking heavily.

I told Norma to call me if she got a threatening phone call. Call me wherever I was, no matter who I was with, and ask to speak directly to me. If she heard my voice, she would know I was alright.

The mysterious phone calls continued. So did Norma's drinking.

8.4   10 NOV 2001 – ROBERT HICKOX EMAIL TO AL
        THISTLE – Regarding FBI harassment.

Believe me, Al, if I seem a little defensive on that issue [collaborating with the enemy] it's because the CIC, CIA, FBI, and Army Intelligence (there's an oxymoron) worked me over pretty well when I was released. I wasn't alone in this, but it went on for a while. Mostly subpoenas to different committees and summoned as a witness to various court martials. Spent most of two years under their thumb and got tired of the insinuations [of me collaborating with the Chinese]. There were times when I cursed the fact I could use a typewriter. The army took advantage of me because of it (no gripes there) and even the enemy took advantage of it. [They made me type documents for the Chinese officers in Pyuktong.] I should learn to keep my mouth shut. Ha! I think I was the only one in the POW camp who could type. Apparently, anyway. And I was damn anxious to get those POW lists into the hands of the UN Armistice Commission [in time for the 1953 POW exchange]. You can bet I made sure my name was on there.

8.5   29 DEC 2001 – ROBERT HICKOX EMAIL TO BECKY
        CHILDERS (excerpt) – Bob clarifies his transition between
        Company clerk and HQ clerk.

Becky,

Well, I see someone has been telling tales out of school. YES! I was the "little prick from headquarters".

...to set the record straight, when we were in Japan, I was Company clerk for a while and then transferred to HQ to work in the Personnel Records Section. That put me in charge of records belonging to everybody in the battalion. I guess they all thought, because I worked with the "bigshot", and didn't have to do any inspections, reveille, guard duty, or KP, that I was some kind of spy and that I knew off the top of my head all the bad things in their records. Heck, I only had about 1200 records to maintain. I couldn't memorize them all.

Ha! Anyway, I never knew they felt that way. I knew they were careful what they said around me. Heck, I was too busy trying to keep my butt out of the stockade to worry about their records. Anyway, we got along okay, and when I volunteered to go to Korea with the company and quit the HQ job, everything was okay. Not many of them knew I threw away a commission just to go to Korea with the company. If I had kept my HQ job, I would have been guaranteed Warrant Officer and my OCS orders would have followed. But I wanted to play soldier. Ha! Bad move!

It was funny when the guys brought that [nickname] up in DC. We all had a big laugh over it.

Bob

8.6   KANAOKA JAPAN, 27 JUNE 1950 – EMBARKING FOR KOREA – LITTLE BOOK 6

We broke camp, collected our gear, and loaded onto our trucks in short order. Back at Kanaoka, you could feel an air of urgency and dread. We knew this was serious business.

Officials at Kanaoka told us President Truman had ordered General MacArthur, Supreme Commander Far East Command, in effect Governor of Japan, to immediately commit a contingent of Army and Air Force to South Korea to stem the tide of North Korean incursion. Due to a shortage of Combat Engineers in the Far East, our company had been selected for assignment TDY with elements of the 24th Infantry Division to Korean action. The 24th Infantry was currently garrisoned south of Kanaoka, closer to the Korean peninsula, and was more available. The balance of the 25th Infantry Division, Tropic Lightning, and our battalion would follow.

END ROBERT HICKOX MANUSCRIPT
BEGIN RECONSTRUCTION ROBERT HICKOX
WORKING NOTES AND EMAIL

LEFT TO RIGHT: Alfred Thistle, General John Wilson, "Baby Face" Buli, Stan Wegrzyn, Daryl Hormann.

8.7   31 JAN 2002 – EMAIL TO BILL BOWLING (65TH ENGR CMBT BN – BAR GUNNER) – LITTLE BOOK 7 (intended) – Regarding Master Sergeant Frankfurter.

Finally, just before amphibious maneuvers, they stuck me in a room with Francard [Sgt Frankfurter, or so we called him -ed]. This was not a good thing. I told you about the AWOL, breaking arrest, etc. for the Special Court. [I was done for] but, thanks to Francard, I beat it. Francard busted me while I was gone [so they couldn't touch me]. Ha! That did not make him any happier. I told Francard I never wanted to catch him on a hill I was on or I'd shoot his ass. So, I guess a few of us weren't too fond of Francard. Surprised me he lived long enough to get a field commission.

8.8   25 JUN 2003 – ROBERT HICKOX EMAIL TO ROB YOUNG – PUSAN LANDING – LITTLE BOOK 8 (intended)

We landed in Pusan on July 5th with parts of the 24th Infantry Division. Our company was the only one in the battalion to go TDY because they needed demolition people to stop the gooks. After Taejon, I don't think we did such a good job. We got our asses kicked. We got hit pretty hard, but nothing like the 24th. [See 4.4 Colonel John Doody letter. -ed.]

A hell of a way to get broke in in our little "police action". They told us we would only be there a couple of weeks, just directing traffic. Yeah, that's what they said, honest.

We had some wounded but didn't lose our first man until around the 13th of July '50, and that was by accident (spelled stupidity). A squad returned from a mission and was getting off the truck (deuce-and-a-half) and a Sergeant reached up to take a man's weapon, grabbed it by the barrel, and bang, that was it for him. A stupid accident. The Sergeant should have known better. Sometimes we don't think until it's too late. [Brenna, Odell C, 29 Jul 1950 -ed.]

We joined the rest of the battalion after Taejon and were dispersed, company and platoon, to individual units that needed us [attached], primarily the 27th Regt., 35th Regt., and the Marines (after they got there).

For a while during July, it looked like we were going to lose the [Pusan] Perimeter.

…Our biggest weakness during the first month was the lack of reliable equipment. Too often guns wouldn't fire, grenades wouldn't explode, and our little [2.26 inch – 57mm] bazookas would bounce right off those damn T-34s. All we had was leftover WW2 equipment and most of it was no good…

8.9   8 SEP 2003 – EMAIL EXCHANGE BETWEEN ROB YOUNG AND ROBERT HICKOX – Regarding obsolete weapon systems used by UN Forces in Korea.

ROB---:   There are many gloomy things to say about the lack of preparedness of the units we took to Korea. Our weapons were relics from World War II. Many had been condemned by our division ordnance inspectors as unfit for combat. This was a true evaluation. They were not. As an illustration of this, …I taught a class on flamethrowers the month before we went to Korea. We had to cannibalize all eight in the Regiment to get two working models for our class. All eight had 503 PIR stenciled on them. The 503rd was a parachute regiment that parachuted onto Corregidor five years earlier.

HICKOX: It was an absolute travesty to put men in that position with the weapons and material we had to work with. I have often read about our "lack of training" and "what lousy soldiers" we were, to which I reply: "Bullshit!"

            …Our problems were, as you mentioned, weapons left over from WW2. Grenades that wouldn't blow or would blow too soon. A worthless [2.26" – 57 mm] bazooka that couldn't stop mosquitos to say nothing of T-34s. As a combat engineer outfit, we used a lot of explosives, primarily dynamite and C-4. Most of our dynamite was left over from WW2 and completely unstable. We refused to carry the stuff in our truck. It separates after a few years and you've got pure nitroglycerin, very dangerous crap. The C-4 worked fine, but most of the blasting caps were past their prime and wouldn't set off the charge.

Early in the war (July, August), we didn't have any clothing or equipment other than what we had used in Japan for training and most of that was shot. We were fighting in OD Class A for the first month of the war. For the [close range engagements] we were doing, I hated that M-1 with a passion. It might be fine for picking off a gook at 300 yards but was too heavy for the close-up work we were doing. I would have given my left nut for a good, light automatic weapon like the gooks had. I tried the [M3] "grease gun", but that damn thing burned up barrels faster than I can smoke cigarettes. Had an M-2 carbine for a while but lost that. I ended up with a .45 sidearm when I was put on the MGs [.30 cal and .50 BMG -ed.] I used to envy the gooks with their Burp Guns [even though they jam].

But we all fought, held our perimeter, and after Inchon, whipped their asses.

8.10   25TH INFANTRY DIVISION HISTORY – AUG 1950 – BOOK IX – (public domain) – Regarding the activities of Task Force Kean.

NOTE: The following excerpt summarizes command and support items connected with Task Force Kean as recorded in the Division Activities Report for August 1950. On August 7, Task Force Kean began an offensive against the Korean People's Army in the area around Masan. The task force advanced toward Chinju amid heavy fighting. Due to enemy pressure along portions of the Pusan Perimeter, support for Task Force Kean shifted to other units. By August 14, Task Force Kean occupied positions it held before the offensive.

COMMAND – Withdrawal of Task Force Kean from Chinju occurred so rapidly some scheduled demolition projects were not completed. The heavy rock base under Korean roads required extra preparation time for emplacement of a sufficient cratering charge.

S3 OPERATIONS SECTION – During the advance of Task Force Kean, close support of attacking infantry units was a priority engineering mission. After the planned withdrawal, demolition of targets in the former task force zone became a priority. Demolition sites were selected by reconnaissance, plotted on a map, and assigned an index number. These numbers were used to distribute workload to each company.

S4 LOGISTICS & SUPPLY – In preparation for the Task Force Kean offensive, two units of Bailey bridge, each containing 130 feet of double bridge, arrived on 7 August. The M4-A2 floating bridge with transportation arrived later. After the offensive, the Bailey bridge was returned to Eighth Army while the M4-A2 bridge platoon was deployed in reserve at Chinhae.

NOTE: Appendix IV contains a detailed record of the 25th Infantry Division Activities Report for August 1950.

HOSTILE DEATHS – 65TH ENGR BN – KOREA – FIRST CASUALTY THROUGH TASK FORCE KEAN

42 Total Casualties   7/18 – 8/22, 1950

(See Appendix IV)

8.11   15 JUL 2003 – ROBERT HICKOX EMAIL TO ROB
        YOUNG – Regarding UN equipment used in Korea.

When we first got to Korea, all we had were the M-24 Chaffee
tanks, lightweight (18 tons) and they were no match for a T-34. We
only had the M9A1 2.26" [57 mm] bazooka that wouldn't penetrate
C-rations. No good against a T-34. I have seen shells bounce off.
Then we got the M20 3.5" [88 mm] bazooka which could stop a T-
34. I have used that and found it very effective (and fun. Ha!)

We also got the M26 Pershing tank about the end of September
or the first of October '50. That was a heavy tank (41 tons) and had
a PE shell that could penetrate a T-34. That and a bazooka leveled
the playing field. Later in '52, the Marines (of course) got the M46
Patton, about the same weight as the Pershing but with heavier
armament. That's what saved their asses at the Chosin reservoir.

...If we had the equipment that came later in the war, we would
have made out a hell of a lot better. We, that were first over, didn't
have shit as far as equipment. Just leftover WWII crap that we had
been using in training and most of it didn't work/fire/explode, or
whatever the hell it was supposed to do.

8.12   14 APR 2001 – ROBERT HICKOX EMAIL TO JIM
        BELCHER – Regarding Bob's customized M-1 rifle.

I'll tell ya, Jim, Bob [McKinney] has a hell of a memory. I asked
him if he could remember what I had written on the forend of my
M-1 in Korea. He says "Hell, yes. It was KITTEN in big yellow
letters." Surprised the hell out of me that anyone would remember.
That was my nickname for my girlfriend and later wife [Norma
"Kitten" VanPatten]. I always said I wanted it to be the last thing
the gooks saw.

8.13   21 OCT 2001 – EMAIL EXCHANGE BETWEEN BILL
        BOWLING, JIM BELCHER, AND BOB HICKOX –
        LITTLE BOOK 8 (intended) – Regarding a 23 August 1950
        firefight on Hill #303 along the Pusan Perimeter.

BILL BOWLING: On 8/23/50 the North Koreans overran our
        forward machinegun position manned by Scott and
        Capretto [aka "Coffee bean -ed.]. [We] sent Jim [Belcher]
        and Harold Terry up to help [them]. That's when Jim and
        Terry got it. Some of us pulled them out while others gave
        cover fire. Akers and I got Terry out. He was already dead.
        You [Bob] might know this.

JIM BELCHER: …Bob, I know my problem comes from layin' in
        the hospital for almost two years. During that time, I cussed
        the whole damn world cause #1, I wasn't with you guys,
        and #2, I was sure you'd all been killed and nobody gave a
        shit. I guess I created my own problem, but I was still young
        and dumb.
            I'll never forget that little chink walking right up to that
        .30, lowering his burp gun and blowing me away. Then the
        [other] chink kid with a G.I. handkerchief knotted on his
        head laid that pig sticker in my back for the final touch. I
        understand the burp gun, but for the life of me, I'll never
        understand that last one from that kid. EMAIL DATE: 15
        May 2001. [Jim Belcher was shot seven times and
        bayonetted twice. -ed.]

BOB HICKOX: I remember that August 23, 1950, very well.
        [Chief] Saloway, the Indian fellow, and I were in a foxhole
        about halfway up that ridge when Akers came by and said
        they (Terry and others on top) had been overrun. We
        grabbed our weapons and took off up the hill.

When we got to the top and found Jim [alive] and Terry's body, I just about lost it. Terry had been a close buddy [of mine] in Kanaoka. I remember Akers asking Jim if he was alright. Jim was sitting there [dazed] complaining because the North Korean officer took his watch and kept asking him for cigarettes.

I remember seeing Terry. At that point, I lost it. I swore I would never take a live gook after that. I remember a ring Terry always wore. I saw it there and I wanted it to remember him, but I knew it wouldn't be right to take it. About then, Akers sent me and a couple of others around the hill to look for more of our guys or any gooks who might have stayed behind.

When we got back, they had taken Jim down. We went to our foxhole. I don't know when the others were taken down. I didn't know Scott and Capretto were there. I think Akers knew I wasn't in good shape, so he sent me on patrol.

I didn't realize you were up there. Maybe I just forgot. It was a long time ago. I wasn't aware of too much after seeing Terry. I just went around hollering and shooting and chasing gooks.

Don't know if you remember, but one night the gooks put a mortar or rocket into a tree right behind where Chief [Saloway] and I had our foxhole. Blew the tree all to pieces. It was dark and nobody could see anything so Saloway and I hunkered down.

"Anybody get hit?" someone hollered.

"I think they got Hickox and Saloway."

Chief and I crouched in our hole for a few minutes listening to our obits.

"I hate to rain on your parade," I said, "but we're alive!"

Just one of the lighter moments.

8.14   HOSTILE DEATHS – 65TH ENGR BN – KOREA

CPL Bobby J Arnette
SWA   8/23/1950   ENGR   E4   Lee, VA

CPL James T. Belcher
SWA   8/23/1950   Medical Det   E4   Muhlenberg, KY

PFC William R Capretto
SWA   8/23/1950   ENGR   E3   Los Angeles, CA
AKA - "Coffee Bean"

PFC Robert F Scott
KIA   8/23/1950   ENGR   E3   Kenton, NY

SGT Harold Terry
KIA   8/23/1950   ENGR   E5   Jasper, MO

Six Additional Casualties   8/24 – 8/26/1950

SWA – Seriously Wounded in Action
KIA – Killed in Action   (See Appendix)

Masan

1 SEP 1953 – ROBERT HICKOX WORKING NOTES –
MONEY HONEY – LITTLE BOOK 36 (intended)

We left Syracuse on September 1st, 1953, for Pensacola Florida
by Greyhound bus. Norma had never been out of New York State
before and it was quite a thrill for her. It took us about four days to
get to Pensacola. Norma had some discomfort. Her feet and ankles
swelled up from sitting on the bus. The ride was exhausting.

When we got to Pensacola, we took a cab to the Marion family
house (our friends). They had a small place and two kids. Quite
crowded. We stayed with them occasionally but spent many nights
in a hotel. The situation drove us nuts and I couldn't stand the
husband. Obnoxious bastard. He made excuses for us exceeding our
welcome. Norma and I stayed out too late. We were never around
for dinner. We didn't appreciate the hospitality. Norma and I
decided to hit the road.

I landed a job in the new Monsanto Plant they were building in
Pensacola, as [an ethnic servant (racist) – ed.], but it would be about
three months before the plant began operating. We couldn't wait
that long, so I got a job with a Pensacola newspaper.

While sitting in a bar one morning, we noticed an ad in a local
newspaper for a couple to accompany a woman to San Francisco in
her car and share expenses. Road trip. Norma called the woman. We
met Vera and made travel arrangements. She was traveling to Frisco
to catch a boat to Japan to be with her husband.

We left in Vera's car the following weekend and headed for
Frisco. Wonderful trip. New Orleans, Mobile, Austin, Phoenix, and
other cities throughout the southwest on the road to Los Angeles.
Vera knew someone in Catalina Island so we spent time on the
beach. When we got tired of the sun, we headed to San Francisco.

We said goodbye to Vera and wished her well in Japan. We had a wonderful time traveling with her. She was in no hurry and liked to stop and explore new places. It was one of the biggest thrills of Norma's life. Norma, a girl who had never been out of Eastwood.

Norma and I got a hotel room. After we settled in, I gave Paul Schnur a call. He lived with his parents on Nob Hill. Paul was an old buddy of mine and a POW in my camp. He agreed to a visit. I knew San Francisco well, having departed for Japan through the Golden Gate years before. We took a cab to the Schnur mansion.

After Paul Schnur was released from POW in Korea and returned to the States, he got fingered by the FBI and Army Intelligence because of his father's association with Vincent Halloran, the American Communist Candidate for President. Paul's father was deeply involved with the Socialist Party and American Labor Unions. Probably not the wisest choice of associates for me under the circumstances, but Paul was a friend and he wanted us to stay with him in the family mansion.

So, we did.

High class. Waiters, maids, the whole deal. I met several Congressmen and a couple of Senators – or ex-Senators – I don't recall names now. Too many champagne bottles rolling across the floor. After the glitz wore off, things started to get uncomfortable. Every dinner at the Schnur mansion or in public became a Communist political meeting or a Socialist Labor Rally.

We stayed with Paul for about two weeks and got a rich man's tour of Frisco, but the experience was wearing on us. I didn't care for the Communists and Norma was uncomfortable with nonstop upper-class treatment. Not our style. I told Paul we would be more comfortable staying in a hotel for a few days.

The dinners continued. Paul loved having us there even though I told him we had to leave town. The whole thing might have gone on forever except for Norma and I running out of pocket money.

I took my Leica 37mm camera I bought in Japan for $160.00 and sold it for $600.00. That gave us enough travel money to get back home. I didn't want to go back to a town where I had no job, but Norma and I decided it was best to return to familiar territory.

We said goodbye to Paul Schnur (for real this time) and got on a train (coach) for Syracuse. Long journey back home. Coach is hell – but not as bad as a bus.

We left San Francisco in early December 1953 and headed east. Our train followed a northern route through the Rocky Mountains, Great Salt Lake, and the plains states. We stopped in Chicago for a week to visit with Aunt Doris and Uncle James Charbonnier. We went to the Chicago Zoo. We had dinner at the historic Palmer House Hilton. A good time.

Norma started feeling nervous again. She felt everything was too "uppity". The Charbonniers lived in an upscale neighborhood on the shore of Lake Michigan. Very nice house. Norma lasted a week.

We got back on a train to Syracuse. Arrived in the middle of December. It was cold, and we didn't have heavy clothes. Also, we had $40.00 left to our name and no place to stay. I had no intention of staying with Norma's mother even though she wanted to.

We took a cab to the Syracuse Hilton Hotel and hid in the room because we couldn't afford to pay the hotel bill. Things were getting desperate. Against my will, Norma called her mother, who, oddly enough, was happy to hear from us. She told Norma I had a pile of checks from the government waiting for me at her house. When we got to Norma's mother's house, I opened my checks. Seven hundred bucks from Uncle Sam for no reason I could remember.

Not bad. Now we could pay the hotel bill.

9.2   SYRACUSE NY – TWENTY-FOUR HOURS LATER – FBI HARASSMENT – LITTLE BOOK 48 (intended)

A car pulled up to the curb. Two FBI agents got out, faced me, and assumed intimidating poses. At least they would have seemed intimidating if I hadn't seen the inside of a Korean prison camp.

One agent explained at how Norma and I had been followed around the United States. He listed every city we visited, who we spoke with, and what restaurants and movie theaters we frequented.

I waited for him to finish talking. When he did, I said: "Well goddamn, I hope you enjoyed your trip!"

9.3   25TH INFANTRY DIVISION HISTORY – SEP 1950 –
        BOOK IX – (Public Domain) – Regarding combat along
        the Pusan Perimeter.

        NOTE: This passage summarizes Command and Support
        items connected with the Breakout from Pusan Perimeter as
        recorded in the Division Activities Report for September
        1950. The UN counteroffensive along the Pusan perimeter
        coincided with the 15 September UN invasion at Inchon.

COMMAND – As the Division swept up the west coast of Korea
toward Kunsan, engineer platoons were attached to three armored
spearheads to clear mines and breach obstacles. A D-4 bulldozer
transported on a 6-ton cargo truck proved to be of great value
because the combination could keep pace with the column advance.
Three armored sweeps covered the area from: 1) Chindong-ni to
Sacheon to Chinju; 2) Chinju to Hadong to Kunsan; 3) Chinju to
Hamyang to Kunsan. Rearguard engineer companies strengthened
bridges and improved bypasses.

S2 INTELLIGENCE – Due to a fast-moving situation, maps were
requested faster than they could be supplied. The problem was
solved with support from the US Air Force who flew maps to the
forward areas.

MAINTENANCE – During the first part of September, a shortage
of tires of all sizes became critical. Tires for 4-ton and 6-ton trucks
became available after making a special trip to the Pusan Ordnance
Depot. By the end of the month, this shortage ended and most
vehicles received new tires.

NOTE: Appendix IV contains a detailed record of the 25th Infantry
Division Activities Report for September 1950.

9.4   29 DEC 2001 – ROBERT HICKOX EMAIL TO BECKY
CHILDERS (excerpt) – Following up on posted military history
describing a combat action along the Pusan Perimeter involving
Bob's unit.

Becky,

*I found the web page: "50 Years Ago Today – 4 September 1950"
to be interesting. I back paged to the first and second of September
to see what they said.*

*Generally speaking, if they refer to the 27th Regiment in any of
these actions, C Company was usually attached. Their CO, Mike
Michaelis, loved us. Ha! Every time he needed help or had a dirty
job to do, he called on C Company 65th. He once said: "I would
rather have C Company 65th Engineer with me than any infantry
company." (Thanks a lot Mike) He later became a General and died
a few years ago of cancer. Great soldier, and a good leader.*

*The reason I wanted to read about the first part of September
1950 is because that's the action where I picked up my first Purple
Heart. From what it says, we must have been somewhere near
Masan, South Korea. I walked right into a "burp gun"* [Russian
PPSh-41 – ed]. *Oh well, I needed the vacation anyway.*

9.5   27 JAN 2002 EMAIL FROM BILL BOWLING TO BOB
       HICKOX – LITTLE BOOK 8 (intended) – Regarding
       circumstances surrounding a firefight that occurred along
       the Pusan Perimeter near Masan on 2 September 1950 and
       resulted in Bob's first Purple Heart. As seen from Bill
       Bowling's perspective.

Your messages are always appreciated. You did not offend me. I
wish the war had been put on hold. We would not have lost you for
thirty-three months.

Yes, I remember when you got hit the first time. I couldn't tell
you where we were. Just somewhere way south in Korea. I

remember they told us to attack a hill and take it. I remember marching single file on each side of the road for a long way. I also remember we found a G.I. lying in the middle of the road with his hands tied behind his back and shot in in the back of the head. The grave regiment came down the road in a 2 ½ ton truck filled with dead G.I.s. One body fell out of the truck, so we hollered for them to stop. We halted until they got the guy back on the truck.

We got to the foot of the hill we were supposed to attack. You said you went up the right side of the hill. I am mixed up. I thought I went up the right side and you and Saloway went up the left. Not that it makes a difference.

I know I was more afraid of our own people than the enemy. Everyone took off up that hill screaming. Some were behind shooting. I have never seen so much G.I. equipment left behind [from the previous assault]. I don't know what outfit tried to take the hill before us, but it looked like they chucked their equipment and took off. On the way up, I picked up full belts of BAR [Browning Automatic Rifle] ammo. I also saw a BAR and other equipment on the way up.

I have to tell you this story. It wasn't funny at the time. When we got near the top, we were told to get over the crest as soon as possible so we didn't skyline. I came over the crest like a bat out of hell looking for a foxhole. I spotted one and headed for it. When I got about twenty feet away, I saw a North Korean sitting in it. I moved my BAR around to shoot him. When I looked again, I saw somebody had already shot his head off. I cleared that foxhole twenty feet in the air.

[vague insider references]

TOPIC CHANGE: The discussion jumps to the Battle of P'ohang-dong along the Pusan Perimeter.

HICKOX: Some of us were swimming in our shorts [planting demo on the Yongdok bridge]. I got caught in an undertow. Scared the hell out of me. I got out and stopped swimming. Remember our ship in the cove? It would fire about 6 or 8 rounds then move back into the channel. That's where they had us load the bridge to blow. After we left, MacArthur waded ashore with his 1st Cav. Big headlines. Ha, ha. I agree with you it was all politics.

I know we loaded 3500 pounds of TNT on that [Yongdok] bridge. I can't remember if we blew it. I know they moved us there with the [27th Regiment] Wolfhounds. C Company got assigned to the Wolfhounds most of the time. The Wolfhounds were considered the best. Maybe we shouldn't have been so good. We might not have been there on the 26th [annihilation of 65th Engr Combat Bn]. I know we were with the group spearheading for the Yalu [River]. We were sent with the Wolfhounds to Yongdok. The South Koreans [ROK] were fighting in that area and didn't think they could hold the line. The Wolfhounds were known for holding, so they sent us wherever they thought there was going to be a breakthrough. Just our luck to go with them.

9.6   28 JAN 2002 EMAIL TO BILL BOWLING (65TH ENGR CMBT BN – BAR GUNNER) – LITTLE BOOK 8 (intended) – Regarding circumstances surrounding a firefight that occurred along the Pusan Perimeter near Masan on 2 September 1950 and resulted in Bob's second Purple Heart. As seen from Bob Hickox's perspective.

From maps I've been looking at, I got hit the first time around Masan. I thought it was closer to Taegu, but that doesn't jive with what I've read. Doesn't matter.

I remember that day clearly. I remember we got off the trucks and walked a long way. It was hot. I was so goddamn tired I didn't think I could walk much farther. When we got to the base of that hill, we stopped so they could pick up some dead G.I.s. The last thing I felt like doing was going uphill. Ha! I remember somebody saying we had to take that hill before nightfall (or something like that). I was thinking: *Why the hell don't they truck us up there so we won't be so damn tired.* Of course, I knew why.

I don't remember who was on my right side. Probably you were. I knew [Chief] Saloway was on my left. I thought I had the right flank, but it makes more sense to have [you with] a BAR [Browning Automatic Rifle] there.

We started up the hill, all hollering and making noise. I was about two-thirds the way up the hill when a bush [camouflaged enemy soldier] stood up in front of me, maybe fifteen to twenty feet in front of me, and cut loose with a burp gun [Russian PPSH-41]. I saw bullets drawing a line on the ground and I tried to get that damn M-1 around to fire but didn't make it. I swear, Bill, if I had an M-2 or a grease gun, I could have nailed him easily, but that damn M-1 was just too much for close quarters. Anyway, I could see he was going to cut me in two if I stood still, so I jumped in the air toward the bushes. (SEPARATE EMAIL: I didn't think I could outrun those bullets. I was always a lousy runner. I took gymnastics in school because I couldn't run around the track. Ha! I think that's what saved me. I did a double back somersault with two forward twists – or something like that. Ha! That sucker would have killed me for sure if it hadn't been for Saloway. I've been told Saloway chilled him [with his BAR].) As I left the ground, he nailed me in the leg.

Man, I will never forget that feeling. It felt like somebody whacked me full force with a 2 x 4. He started to make another pass at me and I thought I was a goner. Before the bullets reached me, the firing stopped. They told me [Chief] Saloway got him.

I crawled down the hill on my elbows. All I could think of was those bloodthirsty guys behind me. I expected to get my head blown off by the first chink who saw me. Fortunately, somebody friendly dragged my sorry ass off that hill.

TOPIC CHANGE: The discussion jumps to the Battle of P'ohang-dong along the Pusan Perimeter.

HICKOX: Now that you mention the undertow there at Yongdok, I think we were all swimming in there the same day. I remember a group of us. Thought for sure I was a goner. If someone else hadn't been there, I would have been "sleeping with the fishes". So that's where MacArthur made his big "like Luzon" landing with the Cav? I forgot about that.

I forgot about the Yongdok bridge. I remember the ship out there and I remember us charging the bridge to blow it. I don't remember if that was the bridge Sergeant Daryl Hormann and I stayed behind to blow or not. Somewhere there was a big bridge we charged. After the rest of the platoon pulled back, Hormann and I were sitting next to a little shack looking at all the detonator wire leading to the plungers. We were ordered to stay and watch for activity near the bridge then blow it. Can't remember whether we did or not. I just remember the two of us sitting there feeling lonely.

I'll always be grateful to Hormann. One day we were out picking up some of our own "Bouncing Bettys" and this stupid ass (me) stepped on one. I knew right away I was in trouble. I called Hormann. He was Sergeant in charge. He disarmed the darn thing so I could move. Talk about not breathing. Ha! I was a hell of a lot more cautious after that.

NOTE: A Bouncing Betty is a bounding mine. When triggered, the mine is launched into the air at a height of three feet. The explosion produces a lethal spray of fragments.

9.7   14 APR 2003 – ROBERT HICKOX EMAIL TO ROB YOUNG – Regarding the simultaneous wounding of several individuals discussed.

I think the reason we all got wounded about the same time (Sept 2-6) was because that was the last major offensive by the North Koreans and they threw everything they had into it. Sorta their last hurrah. I think I was up around Taegu somewhere when I was hit [closer to Masan -ed.]. We were trying to defend the [Pusan] Perimeter to keep from getting our butts shoved into the ocean. A lot of us got hit during that period. But we held 'em, didn't we?

No, we didn't get across the Naktong. We (my company) charged a bridge over the Naktong to blow if the gooks started to cross. We blew the bridge when they started their offensive. [Later,] when our troops started to advance, they didn't have a bridge to cross. After we blew the bridge, we were assigned [as infantry] to the 27th Regiment and stuck on the hill where I was hit.

9.8   HOSTILE DEATHS – 65TH ENGR BN – KOREA

Seven Casualties   9/1/1950
(See Appendix)

PFC Robert H Hickox
SWA   9/2/1950   ENGR E3   Onondaga, NY
AKA: "Little Prick From HQ"

PFC Aldin B Saloway
KIA   9/2/1950   ENGR E3   Lake, MT
AKA: "Chief"

SGT Daryl E Hormann
SWA   9/2/1950   ENGR E5   Roberts, SD

Eight Additional Casualties   9/2/1950
(See Appendix)

SFC William E Akers
SWA   9/4/1950   ENG   E7   Warwick, VA

PFC Garabed E Kenoian
SWA   9/4/1950   ENGR E3   Providence, RI
AKA: "My Little Arab Buddy"

PVT Oscar M Morales
KIA   9/4/1950   ENGR E2   Webb, TX

CPL James G Seidl
SWA   9/4/1950   ENGR E4   Taylor, WI

PFC Leonard D Stamper
SWA   9/4 1950   ENGR E3   McLennan, TX
AKA: "Stumpy" or "Spider"

Eight Additional Casualties   9/3 - 9/6/1950
(See Appendix)

Five Casualties   9/7 - 9/10/1950
Six Casualties   9/12/1950
Seven Casualties   9/13/1950
Twenty-Three Casualties   9/14/1950

OPERATION CHROMITE – AMPHIBIOUS INVASION

BATTLE OF INCHON   9/15 – 9/19/1950
Five Casualties   9/15 – 9/18

PUSAN PERIMETER OFFENSIVE

VERSUS KPA   9/15 – 9/22/1950
Six Casualties   9/20/1950
Three Casualties   9/21/1950

KEY: SWA – Seriously Wounded in Action
KIA – Killed in Action

9.9   21 APR 2001 – ROBERT HICKOX EMAIL TO JIM
         BELCHER – Regarding a lapse in Bob's memory of the
         campaign.

    Duane [Morgan] kept telling me about the company being on
Old Baldy for 28 days and how they were getting hit about every
day. It didn't ring a bell with me, so I asked him where this took
place. Seems the hill Chief was killed on, the one I was hit on,
became known as "Engineer Ridge". After that, they went on to Old
Baldy. Well, I missed that party because I was lying in a hospital in
Kobe getting my hole plugged up. No wonder I didn't remember
the company on Old Baldy.

9.10   18 NOV 2002 – ROBERT HICKOX EMAIL TO COMMAND SERGEANT MAJOR TIMOTHY F. CASEY U.S. ARMY (RET) POW COORDINATOR – Regarding alleged collaboration with the enemy.

Shortly after I arrived at Pyuktong in January 1950, I was interrogated by an English-speaking Chinese who told me he had attended Texas A&M and Syracuse University. Since I was from Syracuse and was familiar with the university and its professors, I told him I had attended school there for two years before joining the Army. Since I conversed with him on this subject, it went into my camp record. I guess that's why a lot of English-speaking Chinese liked to talk with me.

Attending Syracuse University wasn't true, but I never corrected myself. I believed from all I read [in the camp library] and heard [people revealing their schooling level through conversation] that I was one of the better-educated men in camp. It bought me no favors but earned me a small degree of respect. The Chinese had a great deal of respect for people with an education because so few Chinese had one. [Political Commissar] Lin let me get away with a lot because [he believed my SU story].

In the camp, I decided to keep my mind busy. If it meant reading Karl Marx, so be it. It was a way to pass the time and not worry about "Momma's home cooking". A majority of the men sat around camp doing nothing except talking about food and what they were going to do when they got home. I didn't want to do that. I saw too many men die crying for momma. I immersed myself in the things available to me. [I didn't consider reading to be Un-American.]

The Beehive

10.1   25 JAN 2002 EMAIL TO BILL BOWLING (65TH ENGR
        CMBT BN – BAR GUNNER) – LITTLE BOOK 8
        (intended) – Regarding evacuation after the 2 Sep 1950
        firefight near Masan.

I remember telling the medic I didn't want any morphine. I told
him to save it for himself. He'd need it before the night was over.
Real heroic. Considering I laid in the back of a jeep for a wild ride
through roadblocks, I was just as happy with an M-2 and a couple
of banana clips.

About 10:00 PM, I realized I could use a couple of shots. I was
on a train headed for Pusan. No medical personnel in sight. I was in
a rail car with a bunch of screaming gooks, all wounded. I passed
out. The next thing I remember was a room filled with cots with
clean sheets and nurses (not on the cots with me) pumping juice into
me. I remember asking a nurse how close the North Koreans were.
She said they were about twelve miles outside the city. I don't think
they were that close, but I could hear artillery.

The next day they sent me to a hospital in Kobe, Japan. I don't
remember the trip.

10.2   14 JAN 2002 EMAIL TO BILL BOWLING (65TH ENGR
        CMBT BN – BAR GUNNER) – LITTLE BOOK 8
        (intended) – Regarding hospitalization in Japan.

        NOTE: This passage was reconstructed from Email sent to
        Bill Bowling and Robert Young.

After I got [to Kobe], the staff told me when I got up and around,
they would like me to stay at the hospital and work in their
administrative section because of my clerical background. I waited
quite a while before telling them I wasn't interested. I wanted to go
back and finish [conquering] with my company (remember "Home
by Christmas"?)

About a month later, I told them I would like to go back to my
company when I was able. I was in a wheelchair at the time. The
doctor said I would probably be there for a couple of months, which
would take me to late December or January.

Sometime around the first part of November 1950, I got crutches
and was ready to roll. I asked for – and miraculously received – a
pass from the hospital. I headed downtown. Bad news! As usual, I
went AWOL and lit up the city of Kobe. Stayed drunk for about five
days. Even managed to get into a fight with a Marine and *wupped*
him with my crutches.

10.3   THE BEEHIVE GENTLEMAN'S CLUB – (where I
        wupped a Marine with my crutches)

While I was recuperating from my wounds in Kobe, I met what,
to this day, I believe to be the most beautiful girl in the world. I took
a pass with a buddy and went to a local tearoom (beer joint). The
address was #1 Chome, Moto'machi, Kobe, Japan. I will never
forget that place. The name of that joint was "The Beehive" [where
you could find your honey -ed.]

The first afternoon, I went in (on crutches) for a beer, and there
at one booth was this gorgeous raven-haired girl. She looked so

different from the rest, I asked about her. It seems she was Eurasian. Her father was a British naval officer and her mother was Japanese. Her name was Frances Howard (common Japanese name). [Women named Frances are everywhere in Japan. -ed.]

She was sitting with a couple of other girls. We went over and asked if we could join them. Sure, why not. It was apparent they didn't speak much English. For a while, [my unnamed buddy and I] were making comments as G.I.s are want to do. Since I spoke quite a bit of Japanese, having gone to school for it in Osaka, I knew what they were saying – but they didn't know what we were saying.

Suddenly, after I made a crude remark, this beautiful doll looks at me and starts chewing me out in the most perfect "King's English" you've ever heard. She spoke perfect English, had been educated in England, and owned the Beehive along with her father. Boy, did I feel like a fool.

She got a kick out of it. We got along fabulously for a couple of weeks before I shipped back to Korea. We spent several days and nights together. Now in all honesty [Email to: Robert Young], she was one gal I would have gladly brought back to the States, although she was better off than I was.

Some of the "houses" were U.S. Army-operated, but not all. The [Army] girls were generally pretty clean. They would get themselves checked out often because, as they told me, that was their livelihood, and they couldn't afford to get a disease.

[disappointing topic shift]

NOTE: Robert Hickox working notes indicate he got into a fight with a United States Marine in the Beehive Gentlemen's Club. No existing Hickox documents describe this fight.

10.4   14 JAN 2002 – EMAIL TO BILL BOWLING (continued)

After a few more days, I decided to get back to the hospital. I lost one crutch and the other wasn't in good shape. And I was starting to sober up. When I got back to the hospital, I was not welcomed with open arms. The doctor who told me I would be there for a couple of months suddenly discovered I had made a remarkable recovery. He felt I should leave immediately. Funny. Doctors have no sympathy for heroes.

It was "Goodbye, Bobby" and on the boat to Korea. I got back with my company around Thanksgiving, [two days before the Chinese overrun]. I was still on one crutch. Every time I tried to jump off the truck, I fell on my face.

Looks like I outfoxed myself, as you would say.

10.5   HOSTILE DEATHS – 65TH ENGR BN – KOREA
(See Appendix)

One Casualty	9/25/1950
Six Casualties	9/26/1950
Two Casualties	9/29 – 9/30

10.6   SYRACUSE   NY,   DECEMBER   1953   –   FBI HARASSMENT – LITTLE BOOK 51 (intended)

After we returned to Eastwood from our trip across the States, Norma and I found an apartment on the south side of Syracuse. Kirk Avenue, fourth-floor attic. Wow! Taj Mahal! (Not really.) At least it was better than living with Norma's mother.

We had a basic two-room setup. Living room, kitchen, bathroom (barely). Our Murphy bed pulled out of the living room closet. Cozy little firetrap. We called it home.

The FBI bugged our apartment several times. In a place that small, bugs are easy to find. [And you can speak directly into the bug without letting the FBI know you are aware the device is present. Ha! -ed.]

Norma decorated the Christmas tree in our apartment. Our first tree together. We spent Christmas with my parents. My father picked us up and took us to their house on Stafford Avenue. Norma decorated the Christmas tree there too. My uncle, Ray McGann, offered to get me a job at Easy Washing Machine Corporation on the north side of Syracuse. Ray was a plant foreman. He got me a job as a material and product inspector. I worked there for about five months before I got laid off. I wasn't crazy about the job anyway and I hated waiting for the bus at 5:30 every winter morning.

During spring, Paul Schnur came to visit us. He slept on the floor of our apartment. He brought friends with him, so our apartment was packed. No Communist meetings. No champagne. We showed Paul and his friends around Syracuse. Good time.

I knew Paul was on his way to New York when an FBI man leaned out the window of his car while I was walking and asked me why Paul Schnur needed to visit Syracuse. He followed his question with threats and bullshit. I kept walking.

10.7   28 AUG 1948 – TROPIC LIGHTNING 25TH INFANTRY DIVISION WEEKLY MAGAZINE – Bob had a copy of this publication in his collection. As a member of the 25th Infantry Division, Bob likely enjoyed the contents of this weekly magazine during his free time.

BASEBALL

The 25th Division Baseball team won a three (3) game series from GHQ by taking the second and third games after losing the first. The games were played at Camp Gifu Saturday, Sunday, and Monday. Summary of the games are as follows:

Saturday   Four errors allowing five (5) unearned runs cost the Division team the ball game. McCauley with three (3) hits for four (4) trips to the plate led the batting attack for the 25th Division.

	R	H	E
GHQ......................	5	8	0
25th Division................	3	8	4

<u>Sunday</u>   GHQ was leading the Division 4-3 with two (2) out in the 9th inning when Russell hit a 400-foot home run to end the game. Russell and Bowen with three (3) hits each led the batting attack for the 25th Division.

	R	H	E
25th Division…………	5	9	3
GHQ……………….....	4	6	2

<u>Monday</u> In the final game of the series, the Division team pounded out twelve (12) hits for a 9-5 win. McAuley and Bowen with three (3) hits each paced the Division team. One of the McAuley hits was a 425-foot home run with one man on base.

	R	H	E
25th Division…………	9	12	3
GHQ……………….....	5	7	4

HIGHLIGHTS IN THE WEEK'S EVENING RADIO PROGRAMS
AUG 30 – SEP 5

<u>Monday</u> 30 Aug

1900 – EVENING SERENADE
1930 – ON STAGE AMERICA
2000 – THEATER GUILD
2100 – WVTQ WORLD NEWS
2115 – MAGIC CARPET
2130 – AMOS AND ANDY
2200 – ONE NITE STAND

<u>Tuesday</u> 31 Aug

1900 – TO THE REAR MARCH
1930 – FIBBER AND MOLLY
2000 – BOB HOPE
2030 – RED SKELTON
2100 – WVTQ WORLD NEWS
2115 – MAGIC CARPET
2130 – MYSTERY PLAYHOUSE
2200 – ONE NIGHT STAND

<u>Wednesday</u> 1 Sep

1900 – MAIL CALL
1930 – MAYOR OF TOWN
2000 – HARVEST OF STARS
2030 – BING CROSBY
2100 – WVTQ WORLD NEWS
2115 – MAGIC CARPET
2130 – THE WHISTLER
2200 – ONE NITE STAND

<u>Thursday</u> 2 Sept

1900 – VILLAGE STORE
1930 – FRANK MORGAN
2000 – FANNIE BRICE
2030 – DICK HAYMES
2100 – WVTQ WORLD NEWS
2115 – MAGIC CARPET
2130 – FAMILY THEATER
2200 – ONE NIGHT STAND

<u>Friday</u> 3 Sep

1900 – COMMAND PERFORMANCE
1930 – DENNIS DAY
2000 – MUSIC HALL
2030 – BURNS AND ALLEN
2100 – WVTQ WORLD NEWS
2115 – MAGIC CARPET
2130 – INNER SANCTUM
2200 – ONE NITE STAND

<u>Sunday</u> 5 Sep

1900 – JACK BENNY
1930 – PERCY FAITH
2000 – CHARLIE MCCARTHY
2030 – MERRY-GO-ROUND
2100 – WVTQ WORLD NEWS
2115 – MAGIC CARPET
2130 – SCREEN GUILD
2200 – AMERICAN ALBUM

<u>Saturday</u> 4 Sep

1900 – LONE RANGER
1930 – MUSIC FROM AMERICA
2000 – OZZIE AND HARRIET
2030 – HIT PARADE
2100 – WVTQ WORLD NEWS
2115 – FELLOW SHIP
2130 – GRAND OLE OPRY
2200 – ONE NIGHT STAND

CONCERT AT GIFU

The 24th Infantry's 291st Army Band of Camp Gifu, played a concert for the Japanese nationals on August 5th at City Hall, Gifu, Japan. The highlights of the program were the playing for the first time, by an American Band, of the "Cormorant Fishing Song" and a duet "Lover Come Back To Me" sung by Mrs. Donna H. Doyle of Des Moines, Iowa, and M/Sgt. Wilbur G. Flowe, New York City.

The audience was most appreciative and received with thunderous applause the many selections of the two-hour program which included the classics and semi-classics, marches, ballads, ballets, operas, and comedy. M/Sgt. St. Elmo Johnson is the band leader, a graduate of Julliard Institute, and makes his home in New York City.

TROPIC LIGHTNING is published in Osaka, Honshu, Japan, for free distribution to the troops of the 25th Division, under the supervision of the Troop Information and Education Office, Headquarters, 25th Division. News features, photographic and art materials are solicited from personnel of the Division, but publication depends upon available space and general interest value. No payment will be made. Telephone: Lightning dial 339 or 239. News and features of the "Tropical Lightning" are cleared by the 25th Division Public Information Office. Division T.I. & E. Officer: Major P.E. Kline; Editor: Pfc. Charles F. Jacks. "Tropic Lightning" receives Armed Forces Press Service material. Republication of credited matter prohibited without permission of AFPS, 641 Washington St. N.Y.C. 14.

10.8   SYRACUSE NY, MAY 1967 – VETERAN'S AFFAIRS HOSPITAL – OLD WAR WOUNDS – LITTLE BOOK 78 (intended)

I was admitted to the VA Hospital in April of 1967 after a car accident caused by fainting spells. Doctors placed me in the psychiatric ward for a couple of weeks for observation. I had to put up with a lab rat schedule of medical tests intended to find out what was wrong with me. I could go home on any day I didn't have a test.

I started getting dizzy spells around 1963 when I was working for the Tidewater Oil Company, a subsidiary of Getty Oil Company. In 1954, I answered an ad in the newspaper and got an accounting job with Tidewater. The pay was only $2.57 per hour, but that was good money in those days. Nine years later, I was working with three other men in a regional office. Don Gaylord, Ronald (Woody) Woods, and Warren Mosher. We answered to a District Manager named John Paul Jones (not kidding!) whose home office was in New York City. Not a bad setup.

Tidewater paid for me to take courses at Syracuse University in my spare time. I got an accounting degree in 1959 and a promotion to Junior Accountant in 1961. An auditor position opened up and fell into my lap. I drove around upstate New York dealing with clients. Covered Albany, Utica, Syracuse, Rochester, Pittsford, and Buffalo. It was a good job, but a heck of a lot of travel. I got tired of motels and restaurants.

Once the dizzy spells started, I had to rest part of every day. Driving became difficult and I had to stop a lot. I felt sick all the time, but nobody could figure out why. It got so bad I was afraid I would lose my job. Then fate stepped in.

In early 1965, Tidewater announced an austerity budget with heavy cutbacks. The company closed several New York plants and consolidated everyone in Syracuse. Since I was the youngest guy, my position was first on the chopping block. Tidewater offered me a choice: go to New York City; go to Vermont; or resign. Norma and I checked out Vermont. No way. Vermont is located at the end of the world. I decided to resign.

I left Tidewater in 1965 with a healthy chunk of money from company stock. The company matched my investment dollar for dollar. Since I was an accountant, I knew where every penny was and how much interest it was making. I took some much-needed time off.

After I started working for Prudential and got my NYS Insurance license, I had a fainting spell while driving from Eastwood to Liverpool. I went home after my fender-bender and told Norma to take me to the VA Hospital. The VA doctors kept me for almost six months. They diagnosed me with severe anxiety disorder and nerve damage in my back from that Chinese grenade [WW II German potato masher. -ed.] all those years ago. The VA doctor gave me medicine for the pain in my back. The dizzy spells went away temporarily. The VA psychologist told me my anxiety would be lessened if I ran around the house naked. I didn't think Norma would go for that, so I settled for talking about life with my psychologist instead.

Eventually, the VA awarded me 100% disability status and put me out to pasture. I had to visit the VA Hospital on a regular basis, but otherwise, I stayed home as instructed. Good strategy. As I got older, every wound I suffered in Korea came back to haunt me.

10.9   PYUKTONG PRISON CAMP FIVE, WINTER 1951 –
        DYSENTERY AND CHARCOAL – LITTLE BOOK 17
        (intended)

NOTE: Details in this passage merged from Email sent to
[LON-----] and to [VLW---] regarding Captain Douglas
Anderson.

I just came across your posting regarding your grandfather on
the Korean War anniversary page. I do not know how long you have
had it posted or if you have had other people answering your
inquiries, but I did know your grandfather for a short time during
the winter of 1950-51. We were POWs at Prison Camp Five on the
Yalu River in North Korea.

There were no medical supplies or doctors and your grandfather
was the only medical man in camp. During that extreme winter, he
would come around on regular rounds doing what he could for the
sick and wounded. I remember one time when I was having
problems with constipation and mentioned it to him. He replied
"Well, don't worry about it. I've never known anyone to blow up."
He kept his sense of humor even in the worst of conditions.

Later, when I was suffering from dysentery and pneumonia, he
came by and convinced the Chinese to give me some charcoal to try
and alleviate the dysentery, which they did. At first, the Chinese
doctor [American educated Chinese Doctor Ye. -ed.] refused to give
me any kind of medication because he said I would be dead by
morning and he wasn't wasting charcoal on me. That pissed me off.
I told him I would bury him instead of the other way around. Didn't
do that, but I survived anyway.

The last time I saw your grandfather, as best I remember, was
around Feb or Mar 1951. It seems it was a short time later (don't
know exactly when) I inquired as to his whereabouts and was told
that he had died of dysentery and other illnesses. He was a fine man,
an honor to his profession, and an honor to the United States Army.

Paper Lions

11.1   6 NOV 2001 – BOB HICKOX EMAIL TO BECKY
CHILDERS (excerpt) – Regarding brainwashing
techniques used against Korean War POWs.

Becky,

*Something I did notice in reading his article was the effect of the
years of "brainwashing". He talks of Games, Basketball, Olympics,
etc.* [the 1952 Inter-Camp POW Olympics photographed by
Associated Press photographer Frank Noel. – ed.] *I know these
things took place in 1953 after I left and that things did noticeably
improve between the time I was released and the final release (Big
Switch), but* [the Games] *were for show only and the guys were
being used. The fact he can talk about how "well" he was treated
shows the usual effects of brainwashing.*

*Once someone is beaten, starved, berated, and threatened with
death; once they are given something better, there is a tendency to
praise their captors and* [compliment] *their care.*

None of these things occurred prior to my release [Little Switch,
April 1953 – ed], *although the food did improve considerably in the
last six months. I understand why he talks about imprisonment the
way he does. It is basically the old "Manchurian Candidate"
syndrome. Something is so pounded into your head you begin to
believe it after a while. I suffered from some of this for a while, as
did most of the POWs. However, not being there until the end, I was
not subjected to the "good cop" side of my captors. Believe me,
things were not as good as he makes them sound.*

Bob

11.2   25 JUN 2003 – ROBERT HICKOX EMAIL TO ROB
        YOUNG – GUNFIGHT AT OK CORRAL – WHITE
        PHOSPOROUS BURNS – LITTLE BOOK 10 (intended)
        – Regarding events that occurred between Bob's release
        from hospitalization and rejoining his unit somewhere
        between Pusan and Pyongyang.

When I returned to Korea and my company, I went back on an
old Japanese boat of some kind. Maybe it was a Japanese Troop
Transport. Her name was Something-*Maru*. Below deck, it was all
open with straw mats on raised platforms so you could sit or sleep.
Most of the guys going over to Korea were first-timers, so I was the
"big guy on campus" because I had already been there.

After landing in Pusan, I caught a train and chugged north to my
company. Had some really wild guys on board, a few from my unit.
A couple of these guys got in a pissing contest. When the train
stopped for something, they got out and decided to draw on each
other. One was a Mexican and the other was a black guy. I stepped
between them and told them they'd have to shoot me first. (One of
my more stupid moves.) After about a half hour of threatening each
other with me in the middle, they called it off and got back on the
train. They must have got ahold of some bad hooch or something.

I got back to my company by slow-moving train. I expected it to
run off track at any moment. We stopped in Seoul. I think I rejoined
my unit. Don't remember. I got drunk with a couple of guys.

They had a fire in an ammunition dump in Seoul and MPs were
rounding up everyone who wasn't doing anything to help move
105mm and 155mm shells. I got "volunteered". We worked all night
carrying the damn things out of burning buildings. [SEPARATE
EMAIL: I got hold of a hot one and it burned my arm. Still have the
scars from it. I was damned if I was going back to the hospital, so I
went to an aide station and they fixed it up.]

11.3   JUN 2020 – INTERVIEW WITH MARY HICKOX

Q: In Bob's working notes he mentions an explosion in Seoul in which he was burned by white phosphorous munitions. Did he ever describe the event? A Purple Heart?

MARY: He never went into detail. I noticed a darker smooth patch of skin on the inside of his elbow and asked what it was. He said it was a phosphorous burn and that's what happens to your skin. He said it always felt funny afterward.
            He never talked about getting his medals. I asked once why he didn't. He said heroes get medals and he wasn't a hero. Some of the medals in his shadow box are replicas because the real ones, along with a bag of black Japanese pearls and two Samurai swords, were in his original footlocker that mysteriously disappeared when he was listed KIA (killed in action).

11.4   2 FEB 2004 – ROBERT HICKOX EMAIL TO CSM TIMOTHY F. CASEY – Regarding an article printed in the Rochester Democrat and Chronicle honoring a local resident who was a POW during the Korean War.

I dunno. What can I say? If he was in solitary confinement for a year at Camp 5, where was he? I was in Camp 5 from Dec '50 to April '53 and I don't recall anyone being held in "solitary" for even close to that length of time. I have no idea where he would have been kept as there were no "prisons" as such and everyone knew who was in the "hole" and how long they had been there.

I'm never going to knock anyone down without reason, but I think the stories get stretched over a period of years. I just don't swallow it.

Here's a little truth I know for fact. I don't know if it has anything to do with this individual or not. That's unimportant. I know that certain so-called "reactionary" persons [aspiring politicians] banded together and got each other medals by "verifying" the [nonexistent heroic] actions of each other after their release [from POW status]. Some of these individuals were in my outfit and are now deceased. I know they "made" each other heroes.

But, as you said, who cares at this stage of the game?

11.5   5 MAY 2003 – ROBERT HICKOX EMAIL TO ROB YOUNG – PURPLE HEART AWARDS – Robert Hickox description.

NOTE: Bob is consistently evasive about awards that appear in his shadow box, especially the Purple Heart. According to Mary, he kept these awards in his footlocker, hidden from the world. When she asked why he refused to display them, Bob answered: "I know I have them." This passage is a rare description of Purple Heart events.

I was wounded in late July for my first PH (shrapnel in the right shin area). I stayed in Korea at a med unit in Pusan for that. Then on 2 Sep '50, I was "burped" in the right thigh and evacuated to Japan for that. The last one was when I was hit by a concussion grenade right before I was taken POW. Man, I was one lucky SOB.

Obviously, they were gunning for me. Ha!

11.6   EASTWOOD NEW YORK, JUNE 1954 – FBI SUBPOENA – LITTLE BOOK 56 (intended)

After working at Tidewater Oil Company for about five months, Norma and I moved to a new apartment on Tyson Place in Eastwood. It was small (what's new) and close to her mother. Norma was pregnant and it was convenient for her to live close by. I found a decent car, a 1949 Dodge, not new but in good shape. I had transportation – but no license. I had never driven in the United States before. Korea doesn't count. Nobody cares in Korea. I learned American rules of the road and got my license in about two weeks. No more buses.

My sister Beverly married her boyfriend Dave. They moved into the apartment behind us. Loads of fun. We used to talk to each other through the walls. Beverly cooks and talks to Norma. Norma folds laundry and talks to Beverly. Not much privacy.

The FBI kept bugging us. I got dragged into the FBI Office in the Federal Building in downtown Syracuse several times. Threats continued. Sometimes in person, sometimes over the phone.

One day two FBI agents came into my office at Tidewater Oil Company and slapped me with a subpoena ordering me to testify in the General Court Martial of Claude Batchelor. I refused to go. They threatened me with arrest and temporary imprisonment until a federal marshal arrived to transport me to Fort San Antonio, Texas. I figured "yes" was a better answer at that point. They left.

Norma was expecting. I thought if I went to Texas to testify (at my own expense!) and got it over quickly, I would be around when she needed me.

I bought a train ticket and headed for San Antonio Texas.

First Subpoena – 1 September 1954

11.7   12 APR 2002 – BOB HICKOX EMAIL TO BECKY
        CHILDERS (excerpt) – Regarding reconstruction of unit
        history for children of Korean War veterans. Bob's
        comments on the 1952 Inter-Camp POW Olympics and
        Associated Press photographer Frank Noel.

Becky,

*I remember Strand. He wasn't a Sergeant when I knew him. I
don't remember Dillow. I see he was a Sergeant also. Hell, too many
chiefs and not enough injuns. That's why we got our tails wupped.
Hahaha!*

*I imagine Thistle or Bowling would remember these guys better
than me. As I said, I didn't spend a lot of time with the company
before Korea even though I slept in camp (sometimes) :-)*

*I remember Capretto by name but can't remember what he
looked like. I know he was on [Hill] 303 with us and got hit pretty
bad. Jim Belcher covered him with his body so the gooks couldn't
hit him more. That was what he won the Silver Star for. And well
deserved. I will tell you this, Becky, when you are in the presence of
Jim Belcher, you are in the presence of a real hero. He went above
and beyond his duty and, in my opinion, should have got the
Distinguished Service Cross.*

*I finished the book I recommended to you. ...the third memoir
was better but seemed a little on the timid side. He was a Japanese
American and didn't seem to get into it too deeply. However, he was
also a "leftover" from WW2 and an older man. Perhaps this gave
him another perspective. He gave a pretty good description of his
trials. ...one thing that could have been left out is those pictures.
They were mostly taken by Frank Noel, an AP cameraman who was
taken prisoner, and are totally propaganda. I think he, more than
anyone, did a disservice to the POWs by taking the pictures he took,
not only in this book but in other publications I have seen.*

All the pictures were posed and orchestrated by the Chinese. Noel shot only what they wanted. For the most part, we refused to participate in any of his "photo sessions". However, a lot of guys felt it was a way to let people know they were still alive, so they participated. I don't condemn them for it. I did my share of participation [during 30 months as a POW – ed.] *to get my name out, as did others. I do condemn Noel for his willing participation in this sham.*

Most of the "good times" portrayed in the book took place after the April '53 Little Switch. That was when I was released. Between then and September, when the rest were released in Big Switch, (when it became apparent the armistice was pretty much a done deal), things appear to have improved greatly. They even got Red Cross packages, something we had never seen previously. It was during [the armistice negotiation period], *when conditions improved greatly and the guys knew they would be going home, that these so-called games took place. They were staged for propaganda purposes and Noel should never have photographed them. It cast a bad reflection on everybody that was a prisoner.*

[SEPARATE EMAIL TO CSM TIMOTHY F. CASEY – What I found out later was that, although they said in the article that it took place in 1952, the picture was actually taken after the armistice in 1953. They would have been lucky to find healthy individuals to take part in anything like that in 1952.]

Nowhere in the book does anyone tell how bad it really was. I don't know if the years glossed things over for them or if they just don't want to remember. I hope I can bring out more of the facts when I write [my memoir].

Well, enough on that. I guess it comes down to what one person said: "You had to be there."

Bob

11.8   25TH INFANTRY DIVISION HISTORY – NOV 1950 –
        BOOK IX – (Public Domain) – Regarding preparations for
        the UN offensive north of Pyongyang.

NOTE: The following passage summarizes the Division
Activities Report for November 1950 as recorded by
Headquarters 65th Engineer Combat Battalion. Included are
excerpts from the unit war diary and daily reports.

COMMAND – Orders received on 1 November required all units
to move north with the Division. The Battalion formed a truck
company of thirty-five (35) 2.5-ton trucks with a wrecker,
maintenance vehicles, and convoy control vehicles. Trucks reported
to ASCOM City 2 November to haul supplies for the 3rd Logistical
Command. Vehicles and personnel remained on this assignment
during the move [of the parent unit] to Kaesong. This necessitated
the use of rail transportation and shuttling of units. While the
Division was located in the Kaesong area, trucks of the Battalion
were used on supply runs to Pyongyang and to assist in the shuttle
movement of the Division to Kunu-ri.

S1 ADMINISTRATIVE – Plans initiated to consolidate the
Personnel Section under Division Rear CP control. During the latter
part of the month, the Personnel Section and Administrative Section
were separated by two hundred (200) miles, causing a loss in
coordination.

S2 INTELLIGENCE – Maps were issued to all units in Kaesong on
4 November. Map overlays obtained from EUSAK Engineer
Section. Information on these overlays incomplete. The Turkish
Brigade came under control of the Division and was supplied with
Kaesong maps. Arrival in Yongbyon on 22 November necessitated
reconnaissance of all roads in the area. Further information gathered
by interviewing prisoners of war.

S3 OPERATIONS – Reconnaissance and repair started upon arrival
at Kaesong. On 17 November, the 25th Division issued Operations

Instruction #16. This document ordered units to move to the vicinity of Suncheon in North Korea. Companies A, C, and H & S moved together while Company B remained attached to 27th RCT. All units arrived in Kunu-ri instead of Suncheon on 22 November. Reconnaissance and work assignments delegated to companies. Company A responsible for construction of a one thousand (1000) foot airstrip.

S4 LOGISTICS & SUPPLY – Parkas, pile caps, and wool gloves issued to all members of the provisional truck company. Turkish Brigade inspected for equipment shortages. Requisitions submitted to cover these shortages. Issue of back-ordered winter clothing completed by the Division Quartermaster on 15 November. These included the issue of shoe packs and ski socks. [Not all back-ordered winter clothing reached C Company attached to Task Force Dolvin. Robert Hickox had a sweater while other men had nothing. See Hickox Memoir 5.44. -ed.]

11.9   27 NOV 2002 – BILL BOWLING EMAIL TO ROBERT HICKOX – Regarding Thanksgiving Dinner 23 Nov 1950.

Have a good Thanksgiving. I remember our Thanksgiving on November 23, 1950. The dining table was a little cold. We had snow and no fire in the foxhole. We didn't have too many clothes to worry about. A hell of a lot less after you guys were captured. Best to all. Bill and Joyce.

11.10   10 FEB 2003 – ROBERT HICKOX EMAIL TO [GEN---] – Regarding Thanksgiving dinner 23 November 1950.

I hobbled back to the Company around the 10th of November '50 (I think) in the area of Pyongyang, North Korea. We had moved north while I was in the hospital courtesy of the Inchon Invasion. The North Korean Army was beaten at this point, so there was very little activity. Some guerilla and sniper fire but nothing major.

From there, we moved north, met with some resistance, and managed to get about 60 miles north of Pyongyang, in the area of the Chong'chon River near Ipsok/Kunu-ri. We had Thanksgiving dinner in this area. First hot meal in Korea and it was raining cold, hard rain. My turkey floated into my mashed potatoes.

We were [defending] a box canyon. The North Koreans started throwing mortars in on us, so, all in all, it was a lousy dinner.

11.11   25 MAR 2002 – ROBERT HICKOX EMAIL TO BECKY CHILDERS (excerpt) – Regarding "Wimpy" Harold Soyars and Bob's battlefield encounter with him.

I got a call from "Wimpy" Harold Soyars last Sunday. Had a nice chat. I don't really remember him, but he remembers me. He said I gave him my rifle [with KITTEN written on it in yellow letters. - ed.] after I was wounded [by the Russian PPSH-41 Burp Gun] on 2 September 1950 because his M-1 was jammed with Cosmoline and I didn't need mine. He seems to know quite a few guys in the company and he called most of them on Sunday. From what he said, he joined our company in August '50. He wasn't in Japan with us.

I sent Bob McKinney a picture I found on the web of the 65th Engr installing a bridge over the Han River in March 1951. I found it interesting and I wasn't even there. We never did any engineering while I was with the company. We were committed as infantry for most of the first few months until 27 November 1950. I don't think our guys knew how to build anything. We just blew shit up. Ha!

11.12   2 MAR 2002 – BILL BOWLING EMAIL TO BECKY CHILDERS (excerpt) – Regarding reconstructing service history for Kenny Kenoian.

Becky,

I would call you, but my ears are plugged up from a cold. I can't hear a damn thing.

Yes, I knew Kenny Kenoian. He was Armenian. I knew him in Japan in fact. We were in the same squad. Kempfer and I were in the same foxhole together next to Kenny and Oscar Morales when they got hit. Oscar died. [4 Sep 1950] *They didn't think Kenny would live. He had a bad head wound. I think it was our own mortar that got him and Oscar.*

We took that hill the day before, but we were cut off because the other outfits did not reach their objectives. The enemy attacked us the next day. They assigned a forward observer for the mortar, but he lost his map. The CO told him to call in mortar anyway. The first rounds landed in our positions. That was when they got him [Oscar]. *Thistle said he went to see Kenny a few years ago. Said he had memory trouble.*

Thistle was squad leader that day. He and Sgt Harper kept checking foxholes the night before the attack. In fact, our medic at the time, James Seidel got wounded that day. If I remember right, he got some of his foot blown away. I happened to notice him when he ran over to work on Kenny. You can't find medic Corpsmen like Jim Seidel. I don't know if Seidel is alive or not.

...Ask your Dad about that hill. I know he was there. You can send this on to Thistle to see if he agrees with it. The mind gets worn. I could have made mistakes. I should have sent this to Al also, but I just sent it to you because I don't know how to work this machine that well to go back and put your Dad's name in [the email header - ed]. *Dave's body was never recovered. His family installed a stone for Dave in their cemetery. Be good and say Hi to* [your husband] *and* [daughter] *for us. It took me fifty minutes to write this with my one-finger typing.*

Bill

War Trash

12.1　12 OCT 2004 – ROBERT HICKOX EMAIL TO PATRICK SHAUGHNESSY – Regarding prison camps other than Pyuktong Camp Five.

That was an interesting book review you sent. [War Trash, by Ha Jin, published by Pantheon.] Much of what he says regarding the POW camps in the south is true. They were indeed brutal places, as brutal as the north, but in the south, it was between their own people, between radical Communists and those who would have preferred to stay out of it. I do know from my own experience that for the most part it is true that the average Chinese soldier was fighting to protect his country, not to further the cause of Communism. I had many discussions with the guards in my camp at Pyuktong, and this was the general perception I received. They had been told that if they did not fight us in Korea, McArthur would invade China proper. Although this is a novel [the book reviewed], it comes very close to the factual. I can see why the author, Jin, would not be a welcome writer among the Communist hierarchy.

...In my prison camp at Pyuktong, I found most of the common soldiers, the guards, to be quite congenial and relatively easygoing. It was the political cadre and their people [like Commissar Lin], and the North Koreans, that were not so congenial, to put it mildly.

12.2　30 AUG 1954, SAN ANTONIO TEXAS – CLAUDE BATCHELOR TRIAL – LITTLE BOOK 56

Claude Batchelor was a former United States Army soldier convicted in military court of collaborating with his Communist

Chinese captors during his confinement in a North Korean prison camp. Batchelor is alleged to have written a letter urging United States withdrawal from the Korean Peninsula. This letter recommended normalizing relations with Communist China, a government not recognized by the United States due to US support of Chiang Kai-shek, Nationalist leader of China ruling from Taiwan. Witnesses claim Batchelor carried a copy of The Communist Manifesto and actively attempted to convert fellow prisoners to Communist ideology.

On 30 August 1954, Batchelor was convicted by court-martial at Fort Sam Houston, Texas, and sentenced to dishonorable discharge and life in prison. He was represented during trial by civilian attorney Joel Westbrook. Batchelor's defense team offered forced political reeducation (the legendary "brainwashing" excuse as it is commonly known today) as an explanation for his activity.

12.3   12 DEC 2002 – EMAIL EXCHANGE BETWEEN COMMAND SERGEANT MAJOR TIMOTHY F. CASEY U.S. ARMY (RET) POW COORDINATOR AND ROBERT HICKOX – Regarding the General Court Martial of Claude Batchelor.

CASEY: At Batchelor's court-martial, Frank Noel testified for the defense along with Conley Bennett, Robert Collette, Fred Brown, John Owens, Cliff Simmons, Joel Adams, Edwin Clevenger, Robert Vincent, and John Wells. Noel testified that he and Batchelor planned an escape in April 1953 just before Little Switch. They decided not to go in July 1953 because they knew they would soon be released.

HICKOX: Regarding Batchelor's court-martial, it would seem with all that defense testimony, especially Noel's, he would have gotten a better break. It's a wonder they didn't try to destroy Noel too. If I had stayed to testify [in Batchelor's defense as subpoenaed], they would have used that against me. I'm not paranoid, just practical.

CASEY: At the [alleged 1952 POW] Olympics there were [US military] photographers taking pictures.

HICKOX: You say Noel got his camera and film from UNCOM through Wilfred Burchett and Alan Winnington? I assumed the Chinese were furnishing the equipment. I thought Noel was captured with his camera (or that his camera was captured with him. Ha!)

12.4   6 MAY 2001 – ROBERT HICKOX EMAIL TO PATRICK SHAUGHNESSY – Regarding the General Court-Martial of Claude Batchelor.

I hope I did not mislead you regarding the [many] Courts-Martial that did take place. I knew most of the individuals involved and their main crime was not returning [stateside] when the war ended. Batchelor was a quiet individual who spent most of his time reading. He did not preach his so-called Communism to anyone else, if it even existed at that time. Dickerson was another quiet individual, not too intelligent by standards, but not a troublemaker.

I was called as a witness to the Court-Martial of Claude Batchelor in Fort Sam Houston, San Antonio, in 1954. I do feel these courts were warranted based on their [repatriated prisoners] professed activity after the Armistice, and on their refusal to return [to the country of their origin], although a refusal to return could not have been the grounds for a Court-Martial because of the provisions of the armistice.

The only other I recall, offhand, was Col. Schwable. I felt he got a raw deal, as did several of the officers. I do think the author [of the book shared & reviewed] leaned much too heavily on the information derived from the [Courts-Martial] records and the individuals involved. Certainly, the indoctrination of Communism was not as widespread as he would like to have the reader believe. Most of us looked upon the so-called "reeducation" as a joke, always keeping in mind the constant [Chinese] threats of trial as war criminals. This was a very heavy sword they held over our heads for the entire period of imprisonment, and may, in truth, be what happened to many they claim were not returned. Speculation only! [If you were tried and convicted of being a war criminal by the Chinese, you spent your life in a Chinese prison and were not eligible for repatriation as a POW. -ed.]

12.5   HICKOX WORKING NOTES – GENERAL COURT-MARTIAL OF CLAUDE BATCHELOR

I took the train [to San Antonio to testify in the General Court-Martial of Claude Batchelor]. Surprise of surprises! I met Don Disney [veteran 1st Cav] on the train. He got a subpoena too and was on his way to Texas also. It helped to have someone I knew to travel with. This was about September 1, 1954. I was afraid I would lose my job [at Tidewater Oil] as I had only worked there for about five months.

[We] reported in at the post. [After signing in with the] Military Police, [we] took a hotel room at the San Carlos Hotel in San Antonio. Not too fancy but clean and accessible to post. Met a lot of guys who were POWs with me. Some [were] friendly, some not so friendly.

[I] almost got killed in a bar. [I] decided to face down about six of them – wrong move. Reported it to [the] MPs – no investigation. [Unfortunately], it was released to the press and ended up in Syracuse papers.

12.6   24 SEP 1954 – SYRACUSE HERALD JOURNAL NEWSPAPER – LOCAL POW WITNESS ATTACKED IN TEXAS – Newspaper coverage of the early September bar fight mentioned in Hickox working notes.

A prospective defense witness in the court-martial of Corp. Claude Batchelor said he was cursed and abused by several other witnesses in a San Antonio tavern.

Robert Hickox, 144 Stafford Ave, Syracuse, reported yesterday he encountered several witnesses in the Merry-Go-Round Bar in San Antonio. Hickox, a former POW, said he walked into the bar and saw John H. Owens, [illegible]; Sgt. Bernard [Baby Face] Buli, Wilkes Barre, Pa.; Sfc. John W. Fields, Galax, Va.; and Sgt. Clarence Peterson, Media, Pa., at a table. Owens is to be a defense witness, while the others all testified for the Army.

"I walked over to the table at which they were sitting and said 'Hello, boys, how are things going?' Hickox said. "Peterson, I think it was, replied, 'Get out of here, we don't want your kind around.'

"About five minutes later," Hickox said, "Fields, Peterson and one of the others whose name I don't recall came to my table and began to curse me as being a 'Commie -------.'

"Peterson and Fields were both cursing me. At this stage, one of them, I don't know which one, threw either beer or whiskey in my eyes." Hickox said. "It temporarily blinded me. Someone then grabbed my necktie and started to choke me with it. Because I couldn't see, I am not sure whether Fields or Peterson did this."

"A policeman (the bar's bouncer, a special deputy) came over and held Fields and Peterson off me, and I left the Merry-Go-Round. Before I left, I heard Fields tell the policeman I was a progressive and no good," Hickox said in the statement.

12.7   18 SEP 1954 – HOLDING PATTERN – LITTLE BOOK 56
        – While waiting to testify in Texas, Bob grows impatient
        after two weeks of sitting idle.

HICKOX WORKING NOTES:
Waited over two weeks to testify and was told, basically to "sit down and shut up". I told them my wife was expecting a baby and I had to get back home. The Provost Marshall said I had to stay although I probably would not be called to testify. I told him "I'm leaving on the next train out". He says if I leave, I will be brought back under arrest. I told him "goodbye" and "catch me if you can". I got on the train…"

29 AUG 1999 – (LEO---) EMAIL TO ROBERT HICKOX –
Regarding Military Police duties in Japan.

I hated being an MP. I only wrote two DRs while on patrol. The only reason I wrote those is because the OD was standing at my side! Did you ever have an MP hide you in the storage room just off the women's restroom in the train station? I hid many a GI there to keep the OD from catching him. Not that I was such a good guy...it bothered me to write a DR on a fellow soldier! That's the primary reason I became a Company Clerk at the MP Company.

I really got a big bang out of your telling about the MPs walking through the trains [in occupied Japan], but the Japanese would usually hide the GIs. Many a time I walked through a train – knowing there were GIs hidden – but I and my buddies simply walked through, acting like we were searching. Many times, [after we exited the train] just as the train would pull out, some youngster would start hollering GI, GI! HaHa. Obviously, they knew there was no way we could stop the train to check. Loved it!

12.8   6 APR 2003 – ROBERT HICKOX EMAIL TO ROB
        YOUNG– Regarding alleged war crimes performed by UN
        Troops.

You said war is hell. As far as atrocities are concerned, I guess they are in the eye of the beholder. Did we kill civilians? Yes. Did we kill prisoners? Yes.

In most cases, in the units in which I served (27th Regt, etc.), it was generally a case where the "brass" in charge either would turn prisoners over to the South Koreans [who would ensure those prisoners vanished], or tell someone to "take them for a walk down the road". This was pretty much SOP during the early months of the war (July, August). Our backs were against the wall in [Pusan] Perimeter and we had no choice – or time for prisoners.

As far as civilians go, sometimes we got hit by guerilla groups who walked through our lines [the day before] as refugees and then hit us from behind. We received orders not to let any civilians pass.

It was enforced. We had civilians come through our lines carrying concealed grenades and other weapons. Later they would attack us from the rear.

In July '50, we got ambushed at night outside Taegu and nearly overrun by civilians. Even women and children would carry burp guns, machine guns, and mortars. It got so bad [that when] we were [being pushed into the sea along] the Pusan Perimeter, we had no choice but to eliminate the [civilian] danger. We received these orders from [General Walton] Walker's HQ.

23 MAR 1999 – EXCERPT SELECTED BY ROBERT HICKOX FROM PUBLIC MESSAGE BOARD – Regarding killing women and children.

We in Korea faced streams of refugees coming from the north. Some of them were FORCED to come down the roads [as human shields] with [North Korean] soldiers dressed in civilian clothes mixed in with them. Women had machine guns strapped to their backs in a manner that made it look like they were carrying a baby. When they were within killing range of US troops, they dropped to their [hands and] knees and two TEENAGERS dropped with [her] and manned the machine gun [while it was on her back]. Women and children carried grenades and USED THEM.

12.9   4 JUL 2001 – ROBERT HICKOX EMAIL TO JIM BELCHER – Regarding repeated USAF bombing of Pyuktong Prison Camp Five.

Mary and Meg [Bob's family] got the jump on [Fourth of July] last night by going to the ball stadium and watching the county [fireworks] display there. ...Mary was afraid [tonight's festivities] would get rained out and she promised Meg fireworks, so she decided to go to the one last night. Me and the hound [Spike] hid under the bed. I can't take that stuff.

The sound of rockets going off or explosions turns me into a "quivering ball of shivering shit". I think that would be a good way to describe it. Always been a little shy of anything that sounds like a mortar or a 155mm shell. Don't know why (Ha!). Or anything that sounds like bombs falling.

Our eager U.S. Air Force felt it was necessary to bomb the shit out of us every night in the POW camp. God! You cannot imagine what it's like, every night, night after night. And then getting strafed by our F-86s [Sabre jet aircraft -ed.] in the daytime. Sometimes you wondered who the enemy was.

Nope, I can't take fireworks. It's a good thing Mary took Meg, or the poor kid would never see any. Just call me "chicken shit". :)

12.10   3 FEB 2000 – (LEO---) EMAIL TO ROBERT HICKOX –
         Regarding "Kyoto Red", a leading black-market Dragon
         Lady in occupied Japan.

One Saturday afternoon, about six of [us] commandeered bicycles and headed out on what became a seven-mile [MP] trip into the countryside. As [we] approached the foot of the mountain, [I] was about to panic as [I] sure didn't want to ride a damn bicycle into the mountains! Fortunately, the old sarge leading the way stopped at a place enclosed by an eight-foot wall. As we opened the gate, a burglar alarm – a wire run between the gate and house with cans tied to it – made quite a commotion.

   The house was a huge, beautiful Japanese mansion [owned by Kyoto Red]. [My buddies and I] straightened ourselves up, scratched, and urinated in a ditch that ran along the road (a Japanese custom at the time). The [house] door slid back and there stood an honest-to-god carrot red-headed old Japanese woman! (I was a naïve seventeen-year-old and the old woman was probably thirty-five to forty years old.) With an extremely high-pitched voice, she called out: "Haro Joe-san, rong time no see!" The old sarge bounded up the steps, grabbed her up in his arms, and spun her around. After greetings and introductions, the old sarge ordered everyone to remove their shoes before entering the house. [I] was reluctant. [I] remembered the frequent drilling about catching athlete's foot if you went barefoot. This was a Japanese house – you might catch anything, even crotch rot.

The old lady ushered the men into a room, excused herself, bowed, and withdrew. A few younger women (not hardly her maids) came into the room and served cold Japanese beer (good stuff!) [We sat cross-legged in a circle on our cushions, six tall, lanky American GIs.] The younger women with the beer glided across the floor mats as they served. [They never stood up, yet they never sat or knelt on the floor.] Wow!

[Description of drinking and gossip.]

One of the wall panels slid back and there stood a beautiful Japanese woman. Geisha makeup, Geisha hairpiece, gorgeous silk kimono. [I] didn't recognize her. [I] didn't know if it was the beer, [my] youth, or both, but she looked like a porcelain doll. Absolutely ravishing!

The old lady [Kyoto Red] played scratchy pre-war records (78 RPM) on an old Victrola record player. China Nights. [She began playing a samisen. We drank, sang, danced, and drank more.]

...In [another] room, were small tables that barely cleared the floor. ...shrimp, rice, and ??? Dinner! [I] admit [I] ate things that day and had no clue what they were. With close personal coaching from one of the pretty girls, [I] managed to corral those to ivory chopsticks (they really were ivory).

After dinner, everyone returned to the other room... A few minutes later, [Kyoto Red] returned and placed a record on the [Victrola]. [Her] strip tease dance consisted of pulling off a half dozen kimonos as she humped and bumped. As she slid off the last kimono, she yanked off the hairpiece and began gyrating wildly. Judging from her expressions and actions, [I] thought the old broad must have reached orgasm!

[I] sat transfixed and completely petrified. That old carrot-red-headed Japanese woman had shrapnel wound scars all over her body. (I later learned that during the war, she had been working in a defense plant when it was bombed by the Americans. She had been seriously wounded and almost died from numerous shrapnel wounds.) She continued to bump and grind around the room. As she reached each of Leon's buddies, she would sit in their laps, bump, grind, and wipe her [ass] all over them. (yes, her pubic hair was also the same bright red.) The old sarge got off watching her dance.

By the time she got to [me], [I] wanted no part of her. She sat down in my lap and [I] told her: "Ochi-ka!" Get away. She ignored me. [I] jumped to my feet and told her in no uncertain terms [I] would knock her damn ass out into the yard if she didn't get away and leave [me] alone. [My] buddies calmed [me] down and persuaded her to continue dancing...

After that long, seven-mile bicycle trek back to Osaka, [I] got the full story on the old read-headed woman. She was known as Kyoto Red and was the leading black-market Dragon Lady in that part of Japan. During the next couple of years, [I] found myself selling my chocolates and cigarettes to Kyoto Red's [black-market] organization.

Numerous times, [I] saw her walking down the street in Osaka, but [I] would cross the street to avoid her. (She was easy to see – [I] was considerably taller than the average Japanese person, and looking down a street of black hair, her red hair stood out like a red bird in a burned and blackened swamp.) At times [I] worked the MP duty desk when she was brought in on charges of black marketeering. [I] always managed to get someone to work the desk for [me] until she was taken away.

Has anyone ever seen a pendulating, banana-shaped, pock-marked boob flapping in the breeze?

12.11   20 SEP 1954 – ROBERT HICKOX WORKING NOTES – TRAIN WRECK – LITTLE BOOK 58 (intended)

NOTE: Extant Robert Hickox email includes no explanation of the Mattoon train crash. The account presented here is cited directly from Robert Hickox working notes and edited for clarity.

16 JUN 2002 – ROBERT HICKOX EMAIL TO BECKY CHILDERS – Regarding a train wreck.

I just got off the phone with Don Disney. Remember, he was NOT a member of the 65th, but he was a buddy from the POW camp and the one I went to and returned from Texas with in 1954 and we got in a train wreck. We have a common bond there. Actually, I spent longer with him than I did with any of the guys from the 65th. (Except those who were POW with me.) Disney has a computer, so we'll be able to email each other.

HICKOX WORKING NOTES:

I got on the train out [of San Antonio] that night and, to my surprise, Don Disney was on that train also. It was going to prove to be a fateful trip...

*Re: my watch and the Mexican! Also, trip to Mexico (Nuevo Laredo) [No extant explanation of this apparent watch theft. Timing of the trip to Nuevo Laredo is uncertain and may have occurred at any point in Bob's life. -ed.]

We (Don & I) caught the train out of San Antonio about Sept. 18, 1954, headed for St, Louis and home. Don lived in the Midwest (Indiana I think). As we headed out of St. Louis, we were doing about 95 miles an hour and hit a milk truck broadside. It destroyed the truck and derailed our train.

Our car rolled down a steep bank and landed upside down. Several of the cars ended up upside down. There were several deaths and many injuries. We heard the train brakes lock and both of us made a dive under the seats and braced ourselves on the seat braces. When the car came to rest, we were hanging from the bottom of the car. We dropped down and started checking people and helping where we could. Thank goodness Don had been a medic in the army and knew more than I did. He helped a lot of people. I used my suit for pillows and bandages (It was a new suit too!)

The railroad put us up in a hotel for the night. Don and I got a room together. A man we took care of was a judge somewhere and we got a knock on our door. It was his daughter and she thanked us for our help. [She] said the judge thanked us and would make it up to us...last we heard of them.

[We got] on another train the next morning. [I] said goodbye to Don at his stop. [The train] chugged on home.

What a surprise when I arrived home. It seems Norma had had the baby the day before (Sept. 20, 1954) and I missed it because of the accident. [We named her] Barbara.

Norma had a rough time [during the delivery]. Her blood pressure was [very] high and Dr. Kallet was afraid he was going to lose her. [Norma's family] kept the newspapers from her because news of the accident was all over the front page. They didn't want her to see it because she knew I was coming that way. (I called her from San Antonio to tell her I was coming home). Anyway, she was okay, Barbara was fine, and I was home. Everything worked out.

12.12   20 SEP 1954 – SYRACUSE HERALD JOURNAL NEWSPAPER – TRAIN HITS TRUCK, PILES UP – Regarding the Mattoon train wreck mentioned in Robert Hickox working notes.

10 COACHES OVERTURNED

MATTOON, ILL (AP) – At least one person was killed and 21 injured in a train wreck this afternoon, caused by a grade crossing collision east of Mattoon. The dead man was the driver of an asphalt truck that was hit by the eastbound Southwestern Limited of the New York Central System running from St. Louis to Indianapolis. Ten passenger coaches were derailed and overturned and two remained upright. The injured were being rushed to hospitals in Mattoon and Charleston in every available ambulance.

First reports were that a piece of steel from the smashed truck flew beneath the wheels and derailed the coaches. As the coaches plowed ahead of the track, they sheared off utility poles. The truck driver was thrown from his cab and killed.

In New York, a Central spokesperson said the train struck a lime truck, killing the driver and derailing "nine to eleven cars". First reports, the spokesman said, indicated no passengers were killed but that some were injured. Every available doctor and ambulance was summoned to the scene. The Red Cross set up disaster arrangements.

Mattoon is in east central Illinois 224 miles east of St. Louis and 126 miles west of Indianapolis.

A spokesman for the New York Central said the train normally reaches a speed of 70 miles an hour at the crossing where the truck was struck. The truck driver later was identified as Gary Bryant of Mattoon.

Photo- 12-1
CAPTION: None

TRUCK-TRAIN WRECK KILLS ONE. Work crews work to clear right-of-way after truck-train wreck two miles east of Mattoon, Ill. Dead was the truck driver, Gary Bryant, 24, Mattoon. Twenty-eight passengers on the New York Central's eastbound Southwestern Limited were injured as a diesel locomotive and nine cars left the tracks. There were 95 passengers aboard. AP Wirephoto.

Kunu-ri

13.1 27 NOV 1950, KUNU-RI KOREA – ROBERT HICKOX
COMMENTARY – LITTLE BOOK 12

I like the quote from Shakespeare in Henry V that says:
"Whoever lives past today and comes home safely will rouse
himself every year on this day, show his neighbor his scars, and tell
embellished stories of all their great feats in battle. These stories
will teach his son and from this day until the end of the world, we
shall be remembered. We few, we happy few, we band of brothers;
for whoever has shed his blood with me shall be my brother."

I might not have always been the best myself, but I have had the
honor of serving with the best. The battles of 27 Nov 1950 rank
among the fiercest battles in American history. On this date, we lost
a terrible battle but won the war.

ROBERT HICKOX NOTES:

The reason you can't find Kunu-ri on most maps is that it is the
old name for a town that has been renamed and no longer appears
on current maps. Kunu-ri is located in northwestern Korea about
twenty miles upstream from the mouth of the Chongchon River and
seventy-five miles southeast of the Manchurian border.

On the night of 27 November 1950, my unit, C Company 65th
Engineer Combat Battalion (part of Task Force Dolvin), was located
on Hill 222 near Kunu-ri. Other units in the area were the 2nd
Division, two ROK [South Korean] Divisions, the Turkish Brigade,
and the 24th Infantry Regiment. Our front was hit with 30,000
Chinese. My unit was decimated by the Chinese overrun and
suffered eighty percent attrition, mostly killed. Thirteen men in my
company were taken POW. About a dozen managed to escape. The

Second Division, on our left, lost approximately 4,000 men. An entire ROK Division was destroyed.

The battle began around midnight.

13.2   27 NOV 1950 – 0016 HOURS – UNIT HISTORY – 89TH MEDIUM TANK BATTALION – (Declassified) – (excerpt)

At the 2400 hourly report, the Platoon Leader of the Reconnaissance Platoon 89th Medium Tank Battalion reported by radio that an enemy patrol was in his area, about 400 yards to his left front, and he expected contact within 15 minutes. He estimated the patrol to consist of 40 to 60 men.

At 0016 hours, the Platoon Leader Reconnaissance Platoon, 89th Medium Tank Battalion, notified S-3 he was receiving enemy fire and the enemy was attempting to penetrate his position. Shortly thereafter, the platoon was engaged in a heavy firefight.

At 0045 hours, Company B, 1st Battalion 35th Infantry Regiment, reported they were under heavy attack and that two tanks attached to them from Company B 89th Medium Tank Battalion had been knocked out by enemy bazooka fire and satchel charges. The enemy held the satchel charges against the tanks and died in the explosion.

13.3   JAN 2002 – MULTIPLE EMAILS TO BILL BOWLING – Regarding the 27 Nov 1950 Chinese overrun of 65th Engineer Combat Battalion on Hill #222. As seen from Bob Hickox's perspective.

I remember the cold. I sat at the gun [.30 caliber MG -ed.]. My feet were freezing, so I took off my boots to dry out my socks. When the tankers came through, I put them back on. From what I heard, we were going to have company before long. I didn't want to pull out barefoot.

[Chinese parachute signal flares lit up the sky, drifting downward across the battlefield. -ed.]

I remember the tanks getting blown up. It wasn't long after that I saw the chinks across the valley. They came over the hills like ants. Too many. Al Thistle came up behind me and slapped me on the shoulder. He ordered me to disable my gun and get out. Every man for himself.

When Al gave me the order, I had about two or three boxes of ammo left for the .30. Unfortunately, I had to leave it. Earlier, Buli and I secured the ammo at the base of a tree in a little hollow about five or six feet from the gun. I remember Buli going for another box about the time Al came. I made sure [the gooks] wouldn't be using it in the MG. We fired steadily for quite a while. The way the chinks were coming up our hill, it wouldn't have taken much to nail a hundred of them. Lambs to the slaughter. Of course, they weren't doing our health much good either.

After I pulled back, I had one grenade in my harness and an M-2 bayonet in my boot. I picked up an M-1 somebody dropped and moved back about twenty or thirty feet. Then a World War Two German "potato masher" fell out of the sky and blew me ten feet in the air.

I lay there, paralyzed below the waist. I couldn't move anything on my left side. Chinks were everywhere [blowing whistles and trumpets to frighten us. Bob hated whistles for the rest of his life. -ed]. I tried to crawl to cover. The ROK Lieutenant Lee grabbed my shoulder and pulled me up. I noticed my M-1 had been split from stock to forend by the grenade. I grabbed Lee and he dragged me out of there. [Lee was the unit KATUSA interpreter. -ed.]

When we got within sight of a dozen of our guys, Lee set me down at the base of a tree. I didn't recognize anybody because it was dark. I watched the group walk down a hill into low ground between two ridges – and unfortunately, into a Chinese Command Post. I heard someone say: "Take it easy, Boyson. Take it easy." Then he went for his sidearm.

All hell broke loose. Both sides were standing about fifteen feet apart, blasting away. I think Sergeant Harper was part of it.

Lee grabbed me again and dragged me back up the hill. He set me down near the base of another tree and left me. He ran up the hill. Lee covered about a hundred yards before he caught one in the back and went down. I think he died right there.

I stayed hidden in some brush until daylight. It got quiet. I pulled myself to the top of the hill with my elbows. I lay there for quite a while, hoping to see someone I knew or signal a plane.

About mid-morning, a squad of gooks came up the hill, passing within fifteen feet of me. I lay still, pretending to be dead. They walked right by me. Twenty minutes later, another squad came down the hill this time. They all walked by me except for the last straggler, who saw me. Pretty soon, about fifteen of them started sticking me with bayonets to see if I was alive.

I was lying face down when they started sticking me. I started thinking I've got a grenade and a bayonet. What do I do? Do I try to get up, pull the pin on the grenade, and send as many of them to their ancestors as I can, or do I go for the bayonet and try to take out the closest?

At this point, I believed they were North Koreans, who don't take prisoners. I wasn't anxious to surrender. They kept sticking me. I didn't want to start out the day in several pieces, so I rolled over. They grabbed me and pulled me to my feet and held me up. Surprisingly, I still had the grenade in my hand.

Oh, boy. Decisions. I looked down the barrels of all those automatic weapons and realized I wasn't going to do a great deal of damage to my enemy. I opened my hand and let the grenade drop to the ground, pin still in it.

They dragged me around and started going through my pockets. They took my watch, graduation ring, and billfold. One took my New Testament Bible from my jacket pocket. He looked at it and motioned, wanting to know what it was. I made a praying motion. He put it back in my pocket. I have that Bible today.

They dragged me down the hill to a straw hut and placed me with other prisoners. When the Chinese were ready, we began a death march to Pyuktong Prison Camp Five.

HOSTILE DEATHS – 65TH ENGR BN – KOREA

PFC Robert Hickox
CAP   11/27/1950   ENG   E3   Onondaga, NY
AKA: "Little Prick From HQ"

PFC Bernard Buli
CAP   11/27/1950   INF   E3   Adams, PA
AKA: "Baby Face"

13.4   27 NOV 1950 – 0130 HOURS – UNIT HISTORY – 89TH MEDIUM TANK BATTALION – (Declassified) – (excerpt)

The attack on the Task Force CP continued. At 0130 hours, the reserve infantry company, Company E 27th Infantry regiment, plus the Assault Gun Platoon 89th Medium Tank Battalion occupied high ground west of the Task Force CP to reinforce the Reconnaissance Platoon 89th Medium Tank Battalion. The Assault Gun Platoon with infantry [mounted on the vehicles] moved into position from 414212 to 414214. This force moved to the right flank of the Reconnaissance Platoon …taking the enemy fire and holding the position until the remainder of the infantry company arrived and consolidated the ridge.

The intensity of the attack increased at 0200 hours. At 0250 hours, the Eighth Field Artillery Battalion reported that the road to the rear, vicinity 414196, had been cut and an enemy roadblock had been established.

13.5   14 JAN 2002 EMAIL FROM BILL BOWLING TO BOB
        HICKOX– Regarding the 27 Nov 1950 Chinese overrun of
        65th Engineer Combat Battalion on Hill #222. As seen from
        Bill Bowling's perspective.

Robbie had a BAR and Bruneio had an M-1. Bruneio made it
back from being a POW. Did you see him there?

All I heard [Al Thistle say] that night was "Destroy your weapon
and get out." No, I did not get hit the same time Al got hit. The next
night, after we ran the five-mile roadblock [through the gauntlet
between Yongwon and Chosin -ed.] is when I got hit. The shot that
got me fractured my right forearm. I don't know where the hell it
came from.

They sent us [to attack] an eight-man listening post. After we had
been there about an hour, one of our bombers came in overhead at
about one hundred fifty feet. It dropped a flare and opened up with
its fifties. I got ready to fire my M-1 and got hit. I was the only one
hit that night.

They sent me to Japan. I saw a doctor on 27 December. He
informed me I would be in Japan until March. That did not work
with me. I went AWOL and got drunk on New Year's Eve. When I
got back, the doctor called me in. We didn't see eye to eye. I told
him if he didn't like it, he could send me back to Korea. He told me
to put my arm on the table. He cut off my cast.

Three days later, I was back with the company in Korea.

13.6   27 NOV 1950 – 0330 HOURS – UNIT HISTORY 89TH
        MEDIUM   TANK   BATTALION   –   (Declassified)   –
        (excerpt)

The action in the CP area lessened until 0330 hours at which time
the enemy launched another attack against the Task Force CP with
renewed intensity. The 25th Reconnaissance Company had
withdrawn to a line from 418213 to 419215, forming a defense to
the west and northwest. Company B 89th Medium Tank Battalion
sent a section of tanks to 418213 to protect the left flank of the 25th

Reconnaissance Company and deliver heavy fire upon the enemy who was attempting to infiltrate along the draw [low ground between two ridges]. Another section of tanks went up the road to 420207 to form a roadblock and cover the high ground ...which had been formerly occupied by Company F 27th Infantry Regiment.

The attack at 0330 hours lasted approximately thirty minutes at which time pressure [increased] against Company C 65th Engineer Combat Battalion. At 0400 hours C Company 65th Engr reported receiving a strong attack on their position northwest, east, and southeast estimated to be in battalion strength. The Company was forced to withdraw from its position with extremely heavy casualties.

13.7   7 JAN 2002 (POSTMARK) – HANDWRITTEN LETTER FROM BILL BOWLING TO BOB HICKOX – Expanded account regarding the 27 Nov 1950 Chinese overrun of 65th Engineer Combat Battalion on Hill #222. As seen from Bill Bowling's perspective.

On November 26th, we were marching single file up the road. I was behind Lt. Cameron. I was watching the hills. I saw movement on the hill you were captured on. I informed Lt. Cameron. He looked and informed me he saw no movement.

We marched some more. Again, I informed him I saw personnel on the hill. Again, he informed me he did not see anyone. We marched some more and I informed him again that I saw personnel. He halted the platoon and looked as I pointed them out. He ordered me to take two men and check it out.

It took us about two hours to get there. We lucked out. It was men from 25th Recon. We reported back to Lt. Cameron. By that time, the task force had stopped.

That afternoon, they moved us up into a position overlooking a river. Just before dark, orders came to pull back on Hill 222, the hill that 25th Recon had been on. We dug in using foxholes that were already there. The First and Second Platoon dug in. Third Platoon was positioned somewhere else (I don't know where). It was below zero, a full moon, and light snow on the ground. B Company 35th was dug in on a hill across the road from us. They moved four tanks into position overlooking the river. I and Hosea M. (can't spell his name) were dug in on the right flank toward the back of the hill.

I don't know what time it was, but all hell broke loose with B Company 35th. We could not support them because of the distance. I don't know how long the fight went on. Next, they attacked the four tanks. I could see them [enemy] trying to open the hatches on the tanks. Again, the distance was too far for us to support them.

Sometime later, Hosea and I heard movement below us. Someone yelled: "Don't shoot, we're G.I.s trying to get back to our lines!" They were permitted to come up. The old man came over. One of the 35th men said he was Lt. So-and-so and that the Chinese overran their position. The Lt. said he had twenty-four men with him out of two hundred-five men. He asked if he could fall back through us.

He asked our old man how many men he had. The old man told him two platoons. The Lt. suggested the old man call and ask permission to leave the hill. The old man tried to call CP, but the lines were cut. The old man told them we would stay. The Lt. and his men left.

Sometime later, [the Chinese] attacked us. I was down to two grenades and two clips for my BAR. Someone gave the order to destroy our weapons and get out if we could. Robinson and Bruneio were in the foxhole next to us. [Robinson] said he had one clip left for his BAR. I told him to give me the one clip. He, Bruneio, and Hosea threw their weapons in my pit and left.

I fired my clips then threw my BAR in the foxhole. I pulled the pin on a grenade and dropped it in the foxhole. I took off.

I knew the way I came up the hill when I found 25th Recon. I headed for the left flank and ran into ten or fifteen of our guys. Someone asked if anyone knew how to get out and back to the CP. I said I knew. We were heading left on the hill when we heard a fifty-caliber machinegun bolt racked back. We looked and saw one of our tanks about fifty yards away. The guy on the tank was manning the fifty.

We yelled; "Don't shoot, we're G.I.s trying to get back to our lines!"

The guy at the fifty said he didn't believe us. He asked some questions about baseball. I think Thistle answered his questions. If it had been me, they would have shot us. Hell, I didn't know anything about baseball.

We told him what had happened. We suggested he might want to pull out. He said he would stay in it for a while.

We moved to the left flank and then went south toward the CP. We moved to the left side of the road into the rice paddies. Some of Third Platoon must have joined us because Lt. Schmidt was there.

Mortar and small arms fire fell around us. I did not think there were more than fifteen or twenty in our group. Thistle, Wilson, Schmidt, and I were walking four abreast. Mac and Harpo were in the group. We had moved about two hundred yards south when mortar fire hit Thistle, Wilson, Schmidt, and Harpo. Thistle and Wilson were hit bad. Schmidt got hit in the arm. Harpo got hit in the leg. He said he did not know it until we got back to the CP.

We patched up Thistle and Wilson as best we could. I believe they would have bled to death if it hadn't been so cold. We got them patched up and we heard a tank coming down the road from the north. The tank was running full out. The road was about six to eight feet above the rice paddy. We decided to stop the tank if it was ours. We hid along the side of the road until we saw it was ours. We jumped up and waved. Thank God it stopped. We loaded Thistle and Wilson on the tank. Mac went with Thistle. I do not know who went with Wilson. The rest of us moved as close to the CP as possible.

The CP was under attack. We waited until daylight. The Chinese broke off the attack and we made it to the CP.

Bruneio was captured that night and returned. His home is PA.

Bob, I would have sent this email, but I type with one finger. It would have taken me until July. I will make copies of this [handwritten document] and send it to the others. Maybe they saw it differently.

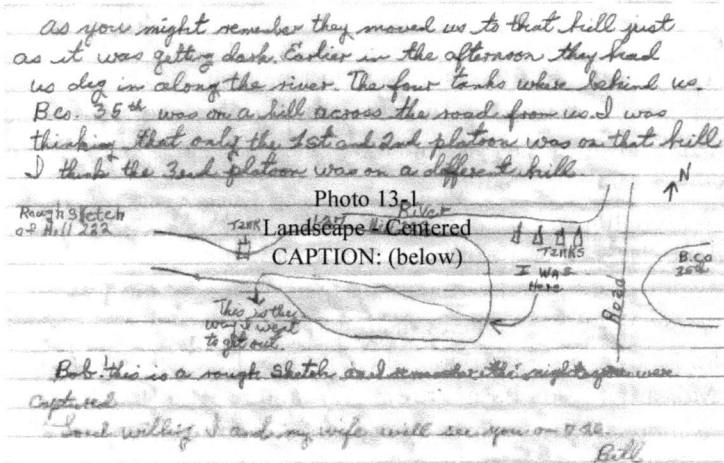

Hill 222 map drawn by William Bowling.

13.8   27 NOV 1950 – 0530 HOURS – UNIT HISTORY 89TH MEDIUM TANK BATTALION – (Declassified) – (excerpt)

At 0530 hours, a third attack was launched against the Task Force CP. This was preceded by the blowing of bugles, whistles, and general catcalling along the entire front. Enemy mortar and artillery fire fell on front-line positions and around the CP area. The mortar fire was very accurate, causing considerable vehicular damage and personnel casualties. The enemy attack, intended to overrun the CP, lasted until 0645 hours. It became necessary to employ every available man, except for one switchboard operator, in the defense of the Task Force CP.

It was imperative the position occupied by the Task Force CP be held at all cost. The defense perimeter [near the CP] included high ground overlooking the Main Supply Route (MSR). If this position had been abandoned to an enemy with superior numbers, [the resulting] enemy roadblock …would have required a large portion of the Task Force to neutralize. [This would have allowed] the enemy to concentrate his efforts on the forward position, [creating] havoc within the Task Force.

Casualties in the Task Force were increasing to a level that normal channels could not evacuate. The Task Force Commander had no intention of leaving them at the mercy of the enemy...

HOSTILE DEATHS – 65TH ENGR BN – KOREA

SFC William E Akers
CAP   11/27/1950   ENG   E7   Accomack, WV

PFC Anthony J Bruneio
CAP   11/27/1950   INF   E3   Adams,   PA

CPL Harrison O Harper
SWA   11/27/1950   ENG   E4   Oconee,   SC

SGT William H Bowling
SWA   11/27/1950   ENG   E5   Warren, IL

SFC Alfred D Thistle
SWA   11/27/1950   ENG   E7   Middlesex, MA

SGT Stanley M Wegrzyn
CAP   11/27/1950   ENG   E5   Adams, IL

SFC General John Wilson
MIA   11/27/1950   ENG   E7   Claiborne, TN

Thirty-Seven Additional Casualties   11/27/1950
        (See Appendix)

13.9   21 JAN 2002 – EMAIL FROM DK MORGAN TO BILL
          BOWLING – Regarding the 27 Nov 1950 Chinese overrun
          of 65th Engineer Combat Battalion on Hill #222. As seen
          from DK Morgan's perspective.

The 3rd Platoon was on the CP side of the hill toward where we regrouped in the morning. The other platoons were toward the Yalu River side of the hill as far as Lt. Schmidt's [position]. My recollection is somewhere around 3 am, Lt. Schmidt, instead of sending a runner to a nearby position, hollered out loudly: "Sergeant Birch, Sergeant Birch!" I remember him getting hit and begging for water. Someone carrying two canteens on his belt grabbed the wrong canteen and [Schmidt] got a mouthful of gasoline.

When the attack came, we saw the 1st and 2nd Platoons firing at the enemy [who was] hiding behind the mounds of graves.

The retreat plan for that hill: In the case of a problem at the listening post, 3rd Platoon was to leave first, then 2nd, then 1st. When the shit hit the fan, 3rd Platoon vacated the hill. We were running alongside the Chinese. Nobody knew who anybody was. I made it to the bottom of the hill [and concealed myself].

At daybreak I ran across a rice paddy to a hut near our staging area. [Near] the farmhouse, [I met] everyone else. The retreat started from [the farmhouse].

General Kean was there.

On the retreat out, I remember the Chinese had set up about three miles of roadblock. It seems that every third vehicle got blown off the road. And the f------ politicians say no one got left there.

General Kean contacted me at Camp Roberts and asked me what I knew about the 65th. They lost contact [with the unit]. I told him exactly what is written here. I didn't know who had gotten out alive.

I am glad to know that we are all still alive. I can't dispute anything you wrote in your letter. You have a good memory. My son-in-law brought the letter by yesterday and I read it. Becky [Childers] is going to make a copy of it.

13.10 6 NOV 2001 – ROBERT MCKINNEY EMAIL TO
ROBERT HICKOX – Regarding 27 Nov 1950 Chinese
overrun of 65th Engineer Combat Battalion on Hill #222.
As seen from Robert McKinney's perspective.

I read the POW material you sent. You guys went through pure
hell. We didn't run out on you guys. We were overrun by the
[Chinese Communist Force] for the next three nights until we got
reorganized. We fought rear action for the next three months. To be
truthful, Bob, I don't know how any of us got out of that mess.

Shall Brothers Be....

AN ACCOUNT, WRITTEN BY AMERICAN AND BRITISH PRISONERS OF WAR, OF THEIR TREATMENT IN P.O.W. CAMPS IN KOREA.

For a' that, and a' that,
  It's coming yet, for a' that,
That man to man the world o'er
  Shall brithers be for a' that.
  ——Robert Burns

The Chinese People's Committee for World Peace

American Communist

"In the camp, I decided to keep my mind busy. If it meant reading
Karl Marx, so be it."

– Robert Hickox

14.1   28 MAR 2003 – BOB HICKOX EMAIL TO BECKY
CHILDERS (excerpt) – Regarding an item Bob posted on
a community message board previously and the firestorm
of comments generated.

Dear Becky,

I did not post that item to provide amusement for myself or to
make you angry. It was not directed at you, only mailed to you and
to others without regard for political leaning. I received answers,
pro and con, from several people. You are still my friends.

Nowhere in my post did I state my opinion. I was trying to
achieve a consensus, and I believe I have found one. If you could
see the intense hate, both pro and con, being thrown around on the
various message boards, I'm sure it would give you reason for
concern. The person who posted the article I sent has been told to
"leave the country, go to Iraq, etc." and threatened with bodily harm.
Regardless of political stance or personal opinion anyone has
regarding this matter, this is not the type of behavior I want to see
in my country.

It seems irrational that one can mouth off, producing hate and
bile, without risk. If the other side offers something rational
(PLEASE: Omit the terrorist comparison – I should have crossed
that out.) they are pillared and stoned. You are young, Becky, and

did not live through the McCarthy witch hunt of the 1950s. This is what I fear when I see the divisions that exist in our country.

I am searching only for a middle ground where there is balance and justice in this time of national turmoil. I am NO tree hugger, although I respect the environment. I am damn sure not a hippie. I have not seen marijuana since I was a prisoner of war and I have never used it.

I support our troops. Every day I send an email message to them. Mary knits hats for the troops to wear under their helmets, slippers for them to wear aboard ship, and neck coolers to keep them comfortable in the desert heat. We have been making lap robes for the patients in the local VA hospital. My flag is flying as I write this – as it has every day since I bought my first house 49 years ago. Please do not classify me with the rabble-rousers. If someone speaks against my flag and country, they tread on very thin ice.

I will not blindly vote Democrat, Republican, Liberal, or any other party. I will vote for the individual I feel most qualified for political office, whether it be a dog catcher, Senator, Congressman, or President. That said, I have one reservation. I do not and cannot, in good faith, support the current resident of the Oval Office. I feel our current war has nothing to do with terrorism. It is an unjust and illegal war being perpetrated and carried out without the support of the just offices of the United Nations and against the will of most people in the world. I believe this war has nothing to do with the terrible 9-11 attack on our country but has been in the works for some time. It is being waged as a personal vendetta of longstanding by a group of people who have planned it for years. I feel many of our Constitutionally given rights are being eroded daily through such proclamations as the "Patriot Act" and soon-to-be "Patriot Act 2". I will not easily give up the rights we have fought and bled for.

During the years you have known me, my patriotism and my reasons for querying a subject have never been questioned. At this time in our country's struggle, I see no reason why I should be questioned now. I never feel I have the right to question others.

What I sent out yesterday was simply another "Fwd, Fwd, Fwd" of the type I receive every day from people who are mostly pro-war, pro-Bush. Yet when I send one (perhaps wrongly, without the "Fwd" heading) I get chastised. I don't see any rationality in this. Am I supposed to accept everything others say without expressing my opinion? This is not what my country stands for.

I am not directing this at you, Becky. I am trying to state another opinion, another idea. I value your friendship, that of your family, and the closeness that our families have found over the years far too much to jeopardize these things over a misunderstood posting.

I hope your family is well. I hope your Dad is holding in there. I know it has been a difficult period for you, and probably will not get better in the future.

Sincerely,
Bob

14.2   15 MAY 2001 – JIM BELCHER EMAIL TO ROBERT HICKOX – Regarding Hill 303 and Hill 222.

You know as well as I do who yelled "Bug out!" [during combat on Hill 222, 27 Nov 1950] It had to have been that young, green, asshole, chicken shit, 2nd John. The nights I remember in Korea, we couldn't see our outstretched hand in front of our face because of the blackness. How the hell did they know which way to run? I'm in no position to second guess that night, but you damn well are owed some answers. I would have never left Johnson, Byers, Harp, Akers, and any of you guys and I wouldn't be sittin' here tonight. You're right about Cameron because I don't remember ever seeing him in any field training and he sure wasn't on 303. Between all of us, we should work out a deal for [remembering events that occurred] that last night.

14.3   5 APR 2003 – EMAIL EXCHANGE BETWEEN ROB
         YOUNG AND ROBERT HICKOX – Regarding snow and
         enemy footwear.

ROB---:   Man, if only we had [sand] instead of rocks and frozen
          ground. Most of the time I was there, we dug slit trenches
          only. On frozen ground, it was mostly finding snow-ice-
          trash or whatever to hide a little bit. Remember the snow
          flying when the bullets hit? The time we had to boogie out,
          I remember [bullets] scattering snow and ice behind us. The
          chinks could not keep up with us, as they kept slipping and
          falling. IN OUR SHIT. Scared it right out of us. He-He-
          Heeeeeeeeeeeeeee.

HICKOX: I remember bullets hittin' all around my ass. I don't
          know what weapon you were on, but when you're on a .30
          MG, you're the "belle of the ball" as far as the enemy is
          concerned. Everyone wants a piece of your ass. Ha! The
          reason the chinks couldn't keep up with us [on snow] was
          because all they had was those little rubber-soled sneakers.
          They could sure run over the damn mountains faster than
          we could though.

14.4   13 NOV 1953 – COMMITTEE ON UN-AMERICAN
         ACTIVITIES SUBPOENA SERVED ON ROBERT
         HICKOX – LITTLE BOOK 70 – Regarding a series of two
         subpoenas served on Robert Hickox by a Western Union
         Courier. Interview with Mary Hickox.

Q: Bob's files contain a second subpoena document from
          Harold Velde, Chairman of the Committee on Un-American
          activities, postponing his appearance. Tell me the story
          about the first subpoena.

Second Subpoena – House Committee on Un-American Activities.

MARY: Bob received a subpoena. He was so pissed off at the
         FBI for following him and calling at all hours he tore it up
         and said he wasn't going. He was tired of the press talking
         badly about POWs who stayed overseas, claiming they
         were traitors and were afraid to come home because they
         would go to prison. Bob said: "No. The reason they didn't
         come home is because they didn't want to put up with this
         shit." He said he wasn't going. They could drag his ass to
         prison if they wanted. Norma taped the subpoena back
         together. She convinced him it was probably a good idea to
         show up before Congress.

14.5   4 FEB 2003 – ROBERT HICKOX EMAIL TO
COMMAND SERGEANT MAJOR TIMOTHY F. CASEY
U.S. ARMY (RET) POW COORDINATOR – Regarding
the McCarthy era inquisition of Hollywood celebrities.

I take it you must be somewhat younger than I, and never had
the experience of the McCarthy era. That was a sad time in our
history. I remember when Garfield testified. It was on TV. He had
probably three-fourths of the actors and producers in Hollywood
blacklisted. The only ones who didn't get raked over were John
"Marion Morrison" Wayne and Ronny "Raygun" – and that speaks
for itself. McCarthy was an evil, self-centered, vicious man who
ruined many lives and was the instigator of the Army hearings. If
you remember, I told you I had my stint before the committee too. I
was accused of associating with known Communists. I replied: "No
shit, I lived with them for almost three years". They threatened me
with contempt. I informed them I could never be as contemptible as
they were. I was lucky I didn't get burnt there, but I came away
clean. Clean enough anyway.

14.6   22 AUG 2002 – [SERP---] EMAIL TO ROBERT HICKOX
– Regarding Garabed Kenoian. Conversation with his sister
about McCarthyism.

Well, I come from a staunch, died-in-the-wool, Republican
Anarchist family, but somehow, I went astray. I used to be middle
of the road, but in my later years, I can't quite accept the way
Republicans are handling things.
    I returned from Korea in 1953, right in the middle of the
Eisenhower, Joe McCarthy witch hunt period. What I saw when I
came back scared me. People were being persecuted for
associations they had years earlier. I could see the Constitution and
Bill of Rights being stomped on and thrown out the window. Then,
what really capped it off, I received a subpoena to appear before the
House Un-American Activities Committee.

When I appeared before the Committee in D.C., I asked: "Why was I subpoenaed?" The answer I got was: "For associating with known Communists." Those known Communists were the Chinese and North Koreans who held me POW for nearly three years.

To me, this was one of the most asinine things I had ever heard of. They primarily wanted me to squeal on other POWs who might have [collaborated]. They got nothing out of me and even threatened me with contempt. I remember telling one of the members of the Committee that I found them far more contemptible. [SEPARATE EMAIL: At one hearing, I was held in contempt. I replied that I found the questioner contemptible. That did not win me points.] I walked out on the subpoena. They never pursued me.

Later I received another subpoena from another committee. I refused to appear. After threats of contempt, imprisonment, etc., they finally gave up and never pursued it. I still have the subpoena in my memoirs. I guess they had bigger fish to chase and bigger lives to ruin. But they never hurt me. I look back on it now and smile. What fools they were. And how dangerous. I'm still here. Where are they?

14.7   19 DEC 2002 – EMAIL EXCHANGE BETWEEN TIM CASEY AND ROBERT HICKOX – Regarding the book A Thousand Days On Hold by ex-POW Arden Rowley, who specifically mentioned Robert Hickox and a POW group who frequented the Communist Chinese library.

CASEY: Rowley wrote a book about his experience. He likes me, so he gave me a copy at one of the reunions. I read it over that night in the hotel room and noticed quite a few errors. [I have the original reports he based his story on.] For instance, [...ten citations].

HICKOX: I read Rowley's book. [Discussion of several chapter items.] The so-called "Library" at Camp Five was an old wooden building with a couple of tables in it and a shelf with a few books. There were copies of newspapers such as the London Daily Worker, New China News, and other publications with Communist or Socialist leaning. They were generally several months old and of little value. The impression I got from [Rowley's] book was that the library in Camp Five was somewhat similar to the Library of Alexandria. Ha! They can call it what they want, but it was a barren, cold shack. There were some good books, and he acknowledges this, but [he gives] people the wrong impression.

The [library] study group individuals you mentioned were not all listed in the alleged group. I say it this way because I don't remember any type of organized group. And how the hell I got to be secretary of anything, I'll never know. Maybe that was some of Dunn's [Rowley's source] daydreaming. The book listed about twenty individuals, including me. Dick Grenier's name was on it. So were [Don] Disney, Adams, Morrison, [Paul] Schnur, Copeland, Smith, Dunn, Lex, Pinkston, Stotts, Douglas, Brezee, Laurie, Dickenson, Ward, and Hinkle. I don't remember Stotts or Hinkle at all. The book also listed Batchelor and Skinner. As surmised, this list was headed by ASCIR #5452, no testimony of which was shown.

This is my problem with the book. A million references from where things were researched, but no text or transcripts of interrogation or testimony. Without that, it's just something somebody wrote. I know the material exists, but unless I want to devote my life trying to get ahold of each item, it's just a story in a book, relating little to fact.

14.8   4 MAY 2001 – ROBERT HICKOX EMAIL TO PATRICK SHAUGHNESSY – Regarding McCarthyism.

I had a chance to get the book "Broken Soldiers" from the library. I found it interesting, but stand by my previous critique.

I know that most of those convicted of collaboration were victims themselves. I believe it was primarily the McCarthy cry for blood and the general political mood of the time that created a need for court martials. We were not covered under the UCMJ at the time, and had no military chain of command to follow due to segregation of ranks [in the camps]. I know the last order I received was to tell them [Chinese & North Koreans] anything they want, sign anything they tell you to, etc. because it won't make any difference anyway. I made a recording in the winter of '51-'52 so I could get a message out to my parents that I was still alive. Of course, it had to concur with what the Chinese wanted. But it got out. Perhaps not proper for a soldier, but I felt it was necessary. A year and a half being classified as MIA is long enough.

For the most part, under the circumstances, we did the best we could and tried to walk the thin line between right and wrong.

14.9   PYUKTONG PRISON CAMP FIVE – CHINESE PROPAGANDA PUBLICATION – (excerpt) – Regarding Christmas messages sent by POWs to their families in the United States. On 2 December 1951, Radio Peking broadcast POW messages on three English-language radio stations. In his working notes, Robert Hickox discusses the two-edged sword associated with recording a Christmas message for your family. If you were MIA, a Christmas message containing necessary Chinese propaganda would let your family know you were still alive. Unfortunately, if you uttered Chinese propaganda, you could be accused of collaboration with the enemy.

SHALL BROTHERS BE... Published by the Chinese People's Committee for World Peace, 1952, Page 19

POWs Broadcast Christmas Greetings To Families.

PRIVATE FIRST-CLASS JAMES R. YOUNG, RA 18334686, TO HIS MOTHER, MRS. A.L. YOUNG, QUEEN CITY, TEXAS:

"Mother, I received a letter from you on the 30th of October, so I am going to tell you just how friendly the Chinese Volunteers treat us here in the POW camps. I am telling you this because in the letter I received from you, you seem to be worried about how they treat me here and you wanted to know if I am in friendly hands or not. Well, you might have heard a lot of propaganda about us being maltreated. We are not maltreated in any way. The Chinese Volunteers treat us as friends."

CORPORAL FRED W. PORTER, RA 19360788, TO MRS. BENNIE L. LINK, LOS ANGELES, CALIFORNIA:

"The Chinese Volunteers and the Korean People's Army have set up wonderful recreational facilities for us, in fact, our Company has the championship team. Mother, please don't be fooled into thinking that we are being treated badly. No doubt this is what you have heard, just like at first I thought when I was captured I would be killed. But, instead, I was told to lower my hands, and was extended a handshake and patted on the back. I am safe and sound far behind the lines. I want you to read my words to the family and friends of our community and tell them all to do everything they can in the interest of peace."

14.10   SPRING 1951 – PYUKTONG PRISON CAMP FIVE, KOREA – LITTLE BOOK 18 – Regarding the visit of Chinese Premier Lui Shaoqi. Interview with Mary Hickox.

Q: In his working notes, Bob mentions a conversation he had with Lui Shaoqi shortly after the Chinese resumed control of Pyuktong Five from the North Koreans. No details are given. Did Bob ever tell you the story?

MARY: No, but I'm sure Lui Shaoqi started the conversation. Bob wasn't in a position to walk up to the premier of China and say hello. He was probably in the office typing prisoner lists when the premier walked in. [The Chinese had resumed control of the camp and] he probably wanted to check the records. Bob might have requested better conditions for the prisoners if he said anything.

14.11   14 AUG 2004 – ROBERT HICKOX EMAIL TO PATRICK SHAUGHNESSY – Regarding Australian newspaper correspondent Wilfred Burchett.

I was listed as MIA first and then my parents received a "presumed" KIA telegram. It was over a year before I could get word out that I was alive and that was only through a Communist Correspondent for "Ce Soir" by the name of Wilfred Burchett, who came through the camp. He was quite helpful to many of us and managed to get my name to Peking [Beijing], and then on to Paris, London, and finally to the USA and my parents. It took about three months to get the message delivered. Then it was several months later that the Chinese allowed us to make a recording (propaganda) to let the people at home know we were alive. We faked it as best we could and the Chinese did send them to the families through the CPUSA and some "Peace" outfit. ...there were times we had to walk a thin line to get info out or to get anything done in the camp.

As an aside, during the period I was listed as MIA & KIA, everybody had written me off as dead except for my girlfriend and high school sweetheart [Norma]. She kept telling my mother "he's all right, they can't kill Bob" She and I were married two weeks after I came home. We had 28 wonderful years and three terrific kids. She passed away in 1981 from cancer, shortly after we moved to Florida.

14.12   12 DEC 2002 – EMAIL EXCHANGE BETWEEN
         COMMAND SERGEANT MAJOR TIMOTHY F. CASEY
         U.S. ARMY (RET) POW COORDINATOR AND
         ROBERT HICKOX – Regarding Wilfred Burchett.

CASEY: Wilfred Burchett was a party hardliner right to the end.
          He also covered the Vietnam War – naturally from the other
          side (VC). From all that I've heard about him, he was a fair
          guy and didn't hide his leanings. The one I heard was a jerk
          was the Englishman, Alan Winnington, London Daily
          Worker Correspondent. They were responsible for Noel
          getting a camera and an unlimited supply of film from the
          UN Command in Kaesong. Doubt if Burchett was KGB.
          [Probably] just a Commie reporter. I heard Burchett and
          Winnington "refined" all the germ warfare confessions
          before they were published.

HICKOX: I got the story about Burchett from an article I read
          some time ago, regarding the KGB. Just happened to come
          across it again on the John Birch Society web page (not that
          I frequent that) but could never swallow it. There was no
          doubt which side he leaned to, but from what I saw, he was
          generally fair and honest, as honest as his profession would
          allow him to be. As has been said of him: "He was the most
          loved and the most hated." I think that rings true.
              As for Wilmington, I couldn't stand the guy. Two-faced
          liar. Definitely a wannabe. I met him a couple of times and
          took an instant dislike to him. In the surroundings we were
          in, he came across as too much of an aristocrat. Typical
          Englishman. Even some of the English POWs hated him.
              As for the germ warfare confessions, I don't know
          enough. I never saw any publications at the time. The
          Chinese were foolish about the whole [bioweapon] thing.
          Maybe Burchett and Winnington smoothed off some of the
          silly notions the Chinese had so they didn't look like fools.
          I'm certainly not denying anything. I talked with the pilots,
          but some of the Chinese claims went a little beyond the

confessions and "evidence". Didn't care. As long as I caught my quota of flies to qualify for a cigarette, I was happy. [See Memoir 15.2 -ed.]

14.13 5 JAN 2003 – ROBERT HICKOX EMAIL TO ROB YOUNG – Regarding American General Douglas MacArthur and his plan to drop nuclear weapons on Manchuria.

I agree that we should have stayed at the 38th [parallel] instead of trying to push to the border. China warned us they would come in if we got too close, but I guess ole Mac didn't believe them. I guess Mac figured if he could push to the Yalu, he could be the "Emperor" of both Japan and Korea.

I'm awful darn glad Truman didn't push the idea of nukes in North Korea. I would be toast if he had.

NOTE: According to Robert Hickox's working notes, Pyuktong Prison Camp Five was located in McArthur's planned nuclear retardation target zone.

14.14 30 NOV 1950 – PRESS CONFERENCE WITH U.S. PRESIDENT TRUMAN – Regarding the use of nuclear weapons to halt Chinese intervention in the Korean Peninsula. This press conference occurred four days after the destruction of Task Force Dolvin at Kunu-ri.

Q: Mr. President, I wonder if we could retrace that reference to the atom bomb? Did we understand you clearly that the use of the atomic bomb is under active consideration?

TRUMAN: Always has been. It is one of our weapons.

Q: Does that mean, Mr. President, use against military objectives, or civilian—

TRUMAN: It's a matter that the military people will have to decide. I'm not a military authority that passes on those things.

Q: Mr. President, perhaps it would be better if we are allowed to quote your remarks on that directly?

TRUMAN: I don't think—I don't think that is necessary.

Q: Mr. President, you said this depends on United Nations action. Does that mean that we wouldn't use the atomic bomb except on a United Nations authorization?

TRUMAN: No, it doesn't mean that at all. The action against Communist China depends on the action of the United Nations. The military commander in the field will have charge of the use of the weapons, as he always has.

14.15   25 JAN 1954 – DOUGLAS MCARTHUR INTERVIEW WITH JIM LUCAS AND BOB CONSIDINE – Regarding McArthur's plan to deploy and use nuclear weapons against Communist China.

MCARTHUR: I could have won the war in Korea in a maximum of 10 days.... I would have dropped between 30 and 50 atomic bombs on his air bases and other depots strung across the neck of Manchuria.... It was my plan as our amphibious forces moved south to spread behind us—from the Sea of Japan to the Yellow Sea—a belt of radioactive cobalt. It could have been spread from wagons, carts, trucks and planes.... For at least 60 years there could have been no land invasion of Korea from the north. The enemy could not have marched across that radiated belt.

14.16   16 AUG 2003 – ROBERT HICKOX EMAIL TO
COMMAND SERGEANT MAJOR TIMOTHY F. CASEY
U.S. ARMY (RET) POW COORDINATOR – Regarding
American General Douglas MacArthur and his plan to drop
nuclear weapons on Manchuria.

I just finished reading the book MacArthur's War, Korea and the Undoing of an American Hero by Stanley Weintraub. It was very interesting and detailed. A slow read, small print, but very comprehensive.

It covers the first years of the war [through] MacArthur's dismissal. The thing I found most interesting was that MacArthur wanted to lay a line of nuclear bombs the length of the Yalu River, along the Korean border on the Korean side of the river. Basically, in MacArthur's thinking, [he would] make a corridor of "no man's land" of radioactive material from Sinanju on the west coast to Vladivostok, USSR, on the east coast, with the idea no one would be able to cross that area and invade from the north (China or USSR) for hundreds of years because of radiation. As crazy as it sounds, he had tentative approval for this from JCS and Truman. The bombers to carry out this were sent to Okinawa and were awaiting MacArthur's order to commence bombing. MacArthur overstepped his political authority and was fired by Truman.

While I was reading this, I could only think how close I came to being "toast". It would have incinerated everything from the Yalu back about thirty miles, forming a radioactive buffer. Sounds pretty sick to me and shows how desperate our brass and leadership were during that period.

If you get a chance, pick up the book at your library or a bookstore. It's paperback, about 400 pages, and covers every aspect of the war during that first year period.

Freedom

15.1   13 NOV 2002 – ROBERT HICKOX EMAIL TO TIM
        CASEY – Regarding conspiracy rumors in Pyuktong Camp
        Five.

I realize most things in my POW dossier will not be flattering. I
was not working for POW of the Month. I went through some rough
debriefings, some nightmare interrogations, and got worked over at
Valley Forge Hospital by an Army CIC officer who posed as a
psychiatrist.

I could name those who did not speak well of me for the times I
spent at the Chinese HQ. One thing none of them knew though was
what I was doing there. I was doing the best I could to convince
"Screaming Skull" to lighten up, to give us more and better food,
and to let us use the river to clean our clothes and bathe in. I never
mentioned any POW names. That's in the past and my conscience
is clear. What has been said about me is in someone else's
imagination. I know there were men alive who wouldn't have been
if I hadn't talked to Lin. Screaming Skull was willing to discuss
conditions although he sometimes reacted badly. I tried. When it
was said and done, years later the Army saw fit to give me an
Honorable Retirement. I feel vindicated.

15.2   17 JUN 2001 – BOB HICKOX EMAIL TO JIM BELCHER
        – WANTED DEAD OR ALIVE – Regarding the fly killing
        spree in Prison Camp Five.

My daughter got me the book Chicken Soup for the Veteran's
Soul for Father's Day. I was perusing it and came across this short
story I had forgotten all about. (It's a collection of short stories and

anecdotes from veterans of all wars) Anyway, this story was related by a person who was a prisoner with me. I didn't recognize [his] name but think he was a Turk. Had to chuckle. [Lord of the Chinese Flies by Akira B. Chikami, page 125 -ed.]

It seems in the spring and summer of '52 the chinks went on a fly-killing spree. They told everybody who wanted to participate they would receive one cigarette for every two hundred flies they turned in. I had forgotten all about that. You had guys making nets to catch them around the latrine and guys were playing poker with them. [Using the flies as poker chips -ed.]

Thinking back, it was terribly ridiculous, but it's pretty funny now. I think back on all of us running around killing flies, stealing them from each other, and numerous other ways to get them just for a lousy chink cigarette. Ha! Goes to show that even in the worst situations there can be a little humor. This whole thing was all tied in with the chinks' idea we were using germ warfare and using bugs to carry the germs. Oh well! [If you kill all the flies, you kill all the American biological weapons. -ed.]

15.3   13 NOV 2002 – ROBERT HICKOX EMAIL TO TIM CASEY – Regarding POW use of the camp river for bathing.

In the spring of 1951, after I almost died of dysentery and pneumonia, I watched several good friends of mine die horribly [from the same things]. I saw twenty or more buried each day. I sat on a stone wall next to the compound and cried – and prayed. I was going to try to connect with our captors and I prayed God would show me a way. [After that], I started talking to Lin every chance I got. I know it helped. I could get away with things others couldn't.

One time, the Chinese closed off the river to us and said we couldn't use it anymore. I went down to the river and started to wash. [Mary Hickox interview: "Bob said he expected to feel a bullet in his back, but it never happened."] A guard came up and motioned me away. I walked the guard up to Lin and told Lin we had to use the river. The next day we were allowed to wash in the river again. This is an example of what can be accomplished if you take a chance and not always be a hard ass.

15.4   28 JAN 1952 – CHINESE PEOPLE'S VOLUNTEER ARMY HEADQUARTERS – Regarding a reported smallpox outbreak southeast of Incheon followed by additional disease outbreaks near Pyongyang and in Manchuria. Chinese claims of biological warfare activity in Korea are summarized in public domain record: Report of the International Scientific Commission for the investigation of the facts concerning bacterial warfare in Korea and China, Peking, 1952.

PLAGUE INCIDENTS IN KOREA – Page 24, 25 - …the classical method of bacteriological warfare involving plague, that adopted by the Japanese during the Second World War, consists in delivering, whether by container or spray, large numbers of fleas infected with plague bacteria. Since the beginning of 1952 numerous isolated foci of plague have appeared in North Korea, always associated with the sudden appearance of numbers of fleas and with the previous passage of American airplanes. Seven of these incidents, the earliest dating from 11th Feb., …and in six of them the presence of the plague bacteria in the fleas was demonstrated.

    …Tests carried out by the Korea-Chinese Services showed that these fleas were infected with plague bacteria, and that they were human fleas [Pulex-irritans]. …Analysis shows that in these circumstances some of the normal links in the epidemiological chain of plague, in which Pulex-irritans participates, are missing. [Suggesting that the insects were purposely introduced into a Korean environment by external means.] In light of all these and other similar facts, the Commission had no option but to conclude that the American air force was employing in Korea methods very similar to, if not exactly identical with, those employed to spread plague by the Japanese during the second world war.

PHYTOPATHOLOGICAL DATA – Page 22 – Several references were made in the earlier [report] literature to the dropping of packets of plant material from American airplanes. They were usually seen by the eye-witnesses to burst at about 1000 ft. and scatter the leaves or other parts of plants over a wide area. Incidents of this kind occurred at Chong-Ju in Korea on 20 March …and at more than ten other localities in Northeast China and North Korea. …It was established that the stalks and pod of [air dropped] soya-beans were infected with purple spot fungus, Cercospora sojini, …which could cause serious damage and loss to soya-bean crops.

15.5   18 NOV 2002 – ROBERT HICKOX EMAIL TO TIM CASEY – LITTLE BOOK 18 (intended) – Regarding a conversation with USAF "germ warfare" pilots and the book Broken Soldiers.

Also, sometime in the Fall of '52, I was called into the "theatre" (our lecture hall) by Lin, the Screaming Skull. He asked me if I would like to talk to American pilots. I was taken to a small room where I was introduced to Lt Quinn and Lt O'Neill. I remember them because of their Irish names. We joked about all pilots being Irish.

They were relaxed and did not hesitate to converse with me about their capture and their participation in germ warfare. They answered all my questions regarding the subject. I was extremely skeptical of the Chinese and North Korean claims. I found both men amiable. After an hour, we shook hands and they departed.

I returned to my compound terribly confused. We had seen the so-called "bug bombs" that had been dropped. [Lin showed Bob pieces of salvaged ordnance. -ed.] We saw photos of sickness supposedly spread by these weapons. Still, we could not believe our country would do such a thing. Despite this, my talk with Quinn and O'Neill greatly shook my belief on the subject. It could have been a massive propaganda ploy. In view of the deposition by Schwable [in Broken Soldiers], the whole thing was pretty difficult to ignore. After all, I spoke with American officers.

15.6   23 SEP 2001 – EMAIL EXCHANGE BETWEEN DUANE MORGAN AND ROBERT HICKOX – Regarding current health issues stemming from Korean War injuries.

MORGAN: I keep busy, but it's getting to where my legs hurt so bad I don't think I will keep it up much longer. I talked to the Vet Officers today and I have an appointment with the VA clinic in October. I'll see what they can do for me. Hope your MRI turned out okay.

HICKOX: Just a suggestion, Duane. Check with the DAV (Disabled American Veterans). They have terrific service officers. Let them work your case through the VA for you. It'll take time but not as long as if you try to fight it on your own. The VA is recognizing leg and foot problems as a result of Korea. You shouldn't have much trouble if you're represented by one of the service organizations.

Won't know how the MRI came out until a doctor looks at it and sends me an appointment. Hope they can fix it. I haven't been able to walk much or even stand for long because of the pain. It must be leftovers from the POW experience or the concussion I received on that night [I got hit with] a chink potato masher. Just have to wait and see. Thanks for your concern.

15.7   6 MAY 2001 – ROBERT HICKOX EMAIL TO PATRICK SHAUGHNESSY – LITTLE BOOK 18 (intended) – Regarding germ warfare and the book Broken Soldiers.

What I wanted to mention in my reply to your letter was regarding the "accusations" by the Communist [Chinese] of germ warfare. I think you might find this interesting. Do not dismiss it out of hand.

In the winter/spring at some period, I had the opportunity to interview Lieutenants Quinn and O'Neill two pilots who professed to the dropping of "germ bombs". I was alone in the room with these two officers for quite a period of time and in my discussion with them, they both openly admitted dropping such weapons. I must say, hearing this from United States Air Force Officers, plus the so-called evidence that the Chinese had, such as bomb casings, reports of various diseases breaking out in areas where they had been unknown, and the affidavits of other individuals, certainly made me think very seriously about the possibility of such a happening. To this day, I still have not reconciled this area of my imprisonment entirely to indoctrination [slang "brainwashing" – ed.]. After reading the affidavit of Lt. Col. Schwable in the book, I'm afraid I remain all the more unsure of my position on this particular issue.

15.8   24 APR 2003 – EMAIL EXCHANGE BETWEEN BARB SOYARS AND ROBERT HICKOX – Regarding the erroneous DD-214 belonging to "Wimpy" Harold Soyars.

BARB SOYARS: Do you remember anything about where you knew Wimpy in Korea (places, vicinity, etc)? Wimpy got turned down for the cold injury [because he was never in Korea]. Our congressman told us to appeal it and see if any of you guys could state that you knew of him being in the Chosin and Yalu River area in the winter of 1950. He was there, but nothing in his records shows it. His records were in that fire in 1973 [in St Louis. -ed.]. They sent him [what was left] but most of them are unreadable. Anything you or any of the others could do to help us would be appreciated. I don't want anyone to tell a falsehood, but anything you can remember would help.

HICKOX: I don't think I can be a great deal of help regarding Wimpy's cold injury claim. The last I recall seeing him was

August of '50. I was wounded in September '50 [I don't remember handing him my rifle with "Kitten" painted on it] and spent a couple of months in the hospital. …I will put a query out to the others that were there during that period. Maybe someone will remember something that will help.

He's not alone as far as his records. Mine were all lost too. I've been fighting for three years to try and locate something. There are several medals and awards due me that I no longer have any record of since the fire. [Apparently, I was never a POW.] It's one of those things I never thought important until I got older and decided I wanted them. Oh well! I'll see what I can do.

15.9   15 MAR 2002 – ROBERT HICKOX EMAIL TO ROB YOUNG – Regarding typing a POW list for UN Armistice Negotiators.

I was conscripted by the Chinese because of my typing ability. I had to type the roster of POWs held in all camps during the winter of '51-52 for release to UN Command for accountability through the Armistice Commission. Aided by four Chinese assistants, I typed for four days straight with little rest to complete the list on time for delivery to UN Command. I do not know how many names in total were on that list, but I do not recall coming across any names that were not repatriated, other than those who opted to [remain in Communist hands after Operation Big Switch].

I spent nearly three years as a "guest" of the North Koreans and Chinese. During that period, I [met] many …fellow prisoners. I know of hundreds in [Camp Five] that did not survive the first winter. I am aware of 2600 who died ...during the first winter when conditions were the worst. Men were buried on a distant hill – barely covered – and very few or no records were kept. We were intermingled from different units and different countries. We did not make close attachments and seldom knew the individual lying next to us. [That person might be dead tomorrow.] On the death march north, hundreds died and remained where they fell, unburied. On 27

November 1950, our company was overrun and decimated. The 2nd Division, on our flank, lost approximately 4000 men during that period. For the most part, they are still lying there [unburied]. Only recently have recovery units been allowed into the Chongchon River area at all.

I do not know of, nor do I believe, there are any American Service men held prisoner in North Korea, China, or Russia. I would not overlook the possibility of one or two or several "technical personnel" or pilots [black ops?]. I find no evidence from my experience or from the comments of others to support allegations of anyone being held in these countries against his will. In my mind, I have accounted for all 8100 missing.

15.10   14 AUG 2004 – ROBERT HICKOX EMAIL TO PATRICK SHAUGHNESSY – Regarding Bob's loss of the family photo memorabilia.

Sorry, that was the only photo I had. Unfortunately, I didn't get anything back from Korea. I had many photos and movie films of my return when I came home. My father took rolls of film and 37mm pictures. They gave them all to me in the '60s and I had them for a while, splicing the film together and getting it all in order. When I moved to Florida in 1979, I gave it all to my sister for safekeeping. Unfortunately, she did not have the same feelings for family records that I did.

When she moved to a new house [after our parents died] she destroyed all the family photos because she didn't want to be bothered with them. I could never forgive her for that. Some of those pictures, particularly the film, were priceless because [they included] my wedding pictures to [Norma] (she passed away in 1981), as well as all my "homecoming" pictures and newspaper accounts.

So, you see, there were an awful lot of pictures available. And not a single one survived. They were all in a box together and, I suppose, burned up. Many times, I wish I had them to put on a tape or CD for my current wife [Mary] and daughter.

15.11 11 MAY 2002 – ROBERT HICKOX EMAIL TO TIM
       CASEY – regarding typing a POW list for UN Command
       at Panmunjom.

It was not hard to get stigmatized in the camps. I went through the same crap yet never did anything except sign a damn paper so people on the outside would know I was alive [Christmas Greetings to relatives via radio Peking. See 14.8. -ed.] and try to drive the camp political officer [Screaming Skull] crazy, which I took great delight in.

Most of my problem came because the Chinese recruited me to type POW lists during the winter of '51-52 for exchange with the UN Command at Panmunjom. That was a job I was honored and anxious to do, but it took quite some time. While I was working on the lists at the Chinese main HQ in Pyuktong, everyone got the idea I was wining and dining with the chinks. Nothing could be further from the truth. I returned to my compound each night and ate the same food everybody else did. I never even got a damn cigarette out of it. But I got the satisfaction of knowing I was getting a lot of names out there into the right hands. I made damn sure my name was on that list.

I think my record speaks for itself. I was investigated and interrogated for months and then retired with full benefits. That speaks clearly.

15.12 21 OCT 2001 – ROBERT HICKOX EMAIL TO BILL
       BOWLING – Regarding Bob's desire to write a memoir of
       his experiences.

Bill, I've spent the last three years trying to format my ideas for these memoirs. It will probably end up more of a biography than a war story. I've had a few unusual things happen in my life that most people don't run into. I want to leave as complete a record as I can, so, hopefully, others won't do some of the stupid things I've done.

I'm going to write about the war because we were in the wrong place at the wrong time and in many ways, we were [sacrificial] goats. Most of the physical wounds have healed, but some only get worse with time. The real wounds, the loss of dear friends like Sergeant Harper, and Sergeant Terry – of course, we could go on and on. Those wounds never heal.

[I remember] when I held Kenny Johnson's head in my lap when he was dying in the POW camp. I couldn't do anything to help him. [Memories of] hundreds like him that I helped take "across the ice" will live with me forever. [In Korea, I saw] man's inhumanity to man. [I saw] how war can dehumanize a person and wipe away [our] thin veneer of civilization and turn us into animals.

These are the things …I want to write about because you'll find no record of [them] in any book or official record.

And of course, I want to write about the good times, the crazy times in Kanaoka, at Fuji, and on amphibious maneuvers. Me sitting in the lap of the Great Buddha of Kamakura. All my crazy, comedic, AWOL times and good ole (Ha!) Sgt Francard trying to get me court martialed. [I want to write about] getting drunker than a "hootie-owl" in Kanoaka with Bob Jones and Harold (Sgt) Terry.

Heck, I could go on forever.

15.13   12 APR 2003 – EMAIL EXCHANGE BETWEEN TIM CASEY AND ROBERT HICKOX – Regarding Little Switch.

CASEY: One of the Little Switch returnees brought some memorabilia to a reunion. His name was Shinagawa. Captured July 1950. Had a banged-up arm that wouldn't heal, so they turned him loose in Little Switch. He brought the [eating] bowl you spoke of, a green metal enamel cup, flat brass spoon, and a Russian watch. They gave him the watch because he told them his watch was taken when he got captured.

HICKOX: I do not recall anyone by that name (Shinagawa) in Camp #5, although he may have been there. If he was in another camp, he may have had other eating utensils/arrangements. All I had was that one little, metallic, silver bowl. Wish I'd saved it. I'd have it gold-plated.

By the way, didn't General Dean have some pretty nice eating utensils? I guess he had something to eat.

Perhaps one reason I didn't bring anything out was because I had no inkling I would be released. There were no rumors or mention of it by the Chinese cadre. One day I was told to go up to Lin's office. He bluntly told me: "Hickox-soo, you go home tomorrow." I was stunned and didn't think much about getting souvenirs. They put me on a truck the next morning.

That was it, cut and dried. I had nothing with me except the clothes on my back, the blue issue uniform. I also had a "little red book" and a "little blue book", one with excerpts from books I had read, the other with names and addresses I managed to get before I left. I still have those books. CIC wasn't interested in them. I also have a watch (Swiss-made) with a cheap plastic band that was given to me because they had taken my watch when I was captured.

15.14   19 DEC 2002 – ROBERT HICKOX EMAIL TO TIM CASEY – Regarding Little Switch and his final meeting with Comrade Lin (aka "Screaming Skull").

Just before I got on the truck at Camp Five headed for Panmunjom, I went to see one of the men who was sick but not scheduled for release. I told Lin this man was sick and should be released. He said he couldn't release him. I told Lin I refused to go if he didn't put this man on the truck with me. Well, Lin told me the man would be released so I left. Unfortunately, Lin did not, or could not release him. I believed Lin was serious (as was I) but couldn't get approval. The man was later released. (Can't think of his name right now. Brain fart.)

I got a laugh out of Cavaganaro's description of how Lin chewed him out [for not calling Formosa Taiwan]. That was a bone of contention between Lin and me. I had been taught in school to call it Formosa. I pissed Lin off to no end because I would, even in our private conversations, refer to it as Formosa. I can picture what Cavaganaro went through.

Picture Lin, about five foot two inches, and eighty pounds soaking wet (the book says 135, but it would never happen), with big horn rim glasses. The moniker "Screaming Skull" fit him perfectly. When he got excited, his head seemed bigger than the rest of him. He was so thin, he looked like a skull with glasses and big teeth. Ha! But he was reasonable. [And you could bum a cigarette off him on most days. -ed.]

15.15   PANMUNJOM KOREA, 24 APRIL 1953 – LITTLE SWITCH DAY 5 – LITTLE BOOK 20 (intended)

"Hickox-soo, you go home tomorrow," Lin told me without warning.

Prisoners had been exchanged at Panmunjom for four days and none of us knew it. The Chinese remained quiet about the matter and told only those who needed to know. One hundred prisoners per day were selected from among the sick, the dying, and those with political allies in America.

Our North Korean guards woke us at dawn to board trucks headed to Panmunjom. I was selected for exchange because the Chinese thought I had tuberculosis. During the previous winter, I got sick again with bronchitis. It was so bad, I coughed constantly. As far as my captors knew, I was a walking dead man.

I gathered my things quickly. I didn't have much. You could scoop it up in your arms and run if you needed to. I left my prison behind, a hut with a mud floor and thatched roof that needed repair after every storm and headed for the trucks.

I saw Pyuktong Camp Five for the last time. I saw the parade field where we assembled years ago, where the Chinese divided us into squads and read us the riot act. Kenny Johnson, Akers, Buli, and me. I saw the mountain where we buried our dead, men I helped carry across the ice. I saw the Yalu River for the last time, the river so many of our soldiers died trying to reach.

As I climbed on a truck, I looked at the other guys who were going. Compared to men dying in huts behind me, some of these guys looked pretty healthy. We said nothing. No more greeting each other as *comrade*. No more of our old life.

The trucks drove through barren Korean hills that all looked the same. We stopped near the exchange point and were met by other North Korean soldiers. Our guards ordered us out of the trucks and into a field. They pointed out the way to the United Nations lines and released us.

We traveled on foot, helping weaker guys walk. We were nervous, scared it was a trap. I had been placed in front of North Korean firing squads more than once in Pyuktong. After the order to fire was given, nothing happened. They needed to break you.

After a while, we realized it wasn't a trick. When we saw friendly troops waiting for us across a bridge, some guys started to run. Ahead of me, I could see the bridge. I could see freedom.

REUNION

16.1   23-28 JULY 2001 – WASHINGTON, D.C. – 17th
ANNUAL KWVA REUNION – 65TH ENGINEER
COMBAT BATTALION – Summary of hotel arrangements
and events scheduled for Korean War veterans and their
families.

Dear Korean War Veteran:

It is time to plan for another reunion and get-together of Korean
Veterans, their families, and friends. For those who are members of
the KWVA, the January/February issue of the Greybeards gave you
a good insight and introduction to the Crowne Plaza Hotel.

A word about the dates 22-28 July: We are bringing in veterans
as early as 22 July to accommodate those who wish to attend the
special ceremony at Arlington Cemetery to honor the Afro-
Americans who served in the Korean War. There will be a wreath-
laying at the Tomb of the Unknown Soldier and also a tree-planting
and placement of a plaque in the area of the cemetery with
ceremony. This is a 50th Commemoration event sponsored by the
DOD 50th Commemoration Committee.

24 July   Full Registration and hospitality. Evening of 24
               July, our special Welcome Party.

26 July   Buffet Dinner and entertainment.

27 July   Breakfast. [Busses available] for the ceremony at
               the Korean War Veterans Memorial. Lunch.
               Ceremony at Arlington Cemetery. President's
               Reception at 5:30 PM Crowne Plaza with open bar

until 8 PM. Banquet served at 7 PM with music by
Army Band/Joint Color Guard, Military District of
Washington.

28 July   Departure breakfast.

Door prizes will be given away at dinners and meetings
beginning 24 July.

We look forward to seeing you in July 2001.

16.2   27 NOV 2020 – INTERVIEW WITH MARY HICKOX –
Regarding the KWVA reunion from her perspective.

MARY: Bob, Meg, and I left for Washington D.C. We took a bus
instead of driving. We got to the Crowne Plaza and checked
in. Bob started calling the front desk to find out who else
was there. He was really excited to get together with
everybody. Really excited. I could see it. It was like he was
a little kid again. He kept telling me different stories about
him and his friends out on the town in Japan and all the
nasty things they shouldn't have been doing. (Mary laughs.)
        At dinner, we were waiting on two other guys, but the
main crew was there. It was Bill [and Joyce] Bowling, Al
[and Carol] Thistle, Bob McKinney, Jim and Betty
[Belcher]. We sat down and had dinner. [Afterward], we got
Meg situated in our hotel room with her new video games
[then] Bob and I went down to the bar for a nightcap with
the guys.
        Al only drinks Guinness. Oh, god, in the glass it looks
like mud. (Mary laughs.) Everybody was drinking and
having a few laughs and a good time. Bob turned around
and he said to me: "Do you know what these guys used to
call me?" Bill and Al, together in perfect unison, turned
around and said: "the little prick from headquarters!" I
thought I was going to pee my pants. Honest to god, it was

so funny to hear them say that. "Yeah, we just thought he was a little prick because he was up in headquarters all the time. He didn't have to get up in the morning for reveille, he didn't have to sleep in the barracks…

FROM LEFT: (front) Robert McKinney, Alfred Thistle. (rear) Robert Hickox, Harrison Harper, James Belcher, William Bowling.

Mostly it was a night of those guys starting to talk and it was like they were never apart. It was so good to see them get along like that. Conversations they hadn't had in forty years. Now all of a sudden, everybody is talking. They're laughing, and they're joking. The wives quietly went to the side and exchanged our own war stories while the guys had their chest-beating bigamy. (Mary laughs.)

It was a great weekend. We went to Arlington National Cemetery and took the tour. The funny thing was listening to Jim [Belcher]: "Oh, my god, I can't get in and out of this trolley because my knees hurt so bad." But he did. After the tour, Bob and Meg and I went to the Smithsonian. We got together for dinner again [on] Saturday night. We weren't there the whole week. We were only there for the weekend. It was great.

The final day we had breakfast together. Everybody exchanged addresses and pictures and everything. The only one who was missing was Becky [due to schedule conflict]. Becky was the one who got all these guys together. It was a big hole that she wasn't there but… it was great. It was great just watching the guys sit together and bullshit. (Mary laughs.)

16.3   SELECT CORRESPONDENCE BETWEEN FAMILIES WHO ATTENDED THE REUNION

ROBERT HICKOX: I told Stumpy [Leonard Stamper] he should plan on making the reunion this year [in Reno], if possible. He said he can't plan that far ahead at his age. He says he won't even buy green bananas…

BECKY CHILDERS: I understand you "New Yoikers" got hit with an earthquake. [It's pronounced: "New Yawkers". -ed.] We usually have 5.0 [in California], you get used to them, but when they come out of the blue, they are pretty scary.

ROBERT HICKOX: I've been in a lot of earthquakes in my life, in Japan almost daily. They are no big thing. I didn't think we would have one here. By the time I figured what was going on, it was over. I went back to sleep. …No damage here. A few roads in the area buckled, but nothing major. Mary never knew about it until she got home at 7:00 pm. Ha! According to the news it was about a 5.1. Just a little shake, rattle, and roll.

16.4   10 JUN 2002 – ROBERT HICKOX EMAIL TO ROBERT
        MCKINNEY – (excerpt) – Regarding West Virginia
        flooding and errors in Robert McKinney's DD214.

Glad to hear from you, Brother. I was getting worried. I checked
with Becky and she said she talked to you. She said you were
"lounging around on your deck and enjoying life" now that you got
your mess cleaned up. I told her that maybe you should have a boat
under your deck with all that flooding.

...Have you heard anything on your claim or all the letters [See
Bio-7] we sent in support of it? Probably take a few months, the
way the VA moves. I hope you get what they owe you before it
becomes posthumous!

...Had a long talk with Bobby Arnette the other day. I don't
remember him, but I do recall the name. We had a good talk and he
remembers me. I told him the story of how we got our butts in jail
when you came to visit me in '53 [See Memoir 1.4] and how we got
out of it. Thought he'd split a gut laughing. I told him: "If you don't
believe me, ask Mac." Ha!

16.5   29 NOV 2001 – HARRISON HARPER HANDWRITTEN
        LETTER TO ROBERT HICKOX – Regarding Christmas
        preparations, shared service history, and the events of 9-11.

Just a line to let you know I got the pictures. Thistle sent me the
history on the 25th Division. Said he was doing fine. Haven't heard
from Mack yet.

What do you think about the terrorist attack? We might have to
get the guys together and go over there and handle Bin Laden. What
do you think?

Have a Merry Merry and a Happy Hippy. God bless you all.

3 DEC 2001 – ROBERT HICKOX EMAIL TO HARRISON
    HARPER – Regarding Christmas preparations and his
    general opinion about the events of 9-11.

Everything is fine up this way. We're still looking for snow (not
really). Haven't had any yet. It's most unusual for up here not to
have had a few inches by now, but I'm not complaining. [Mary's]
busy with her craft stuff. She had a Christmas order for ten knitted
sweaters and has been busting her hump to get them done.

As far as this terrorist crap, I just think [our] group might have
to get into it. Only way I can see to take care of it. Kind of like
"Charlie's Angels". Ha! Or would that be the "Magnificent Seven"?
(We'll get DK too!) I posed the question to the rest of the guys. I
told them Harp wanted to know if we should get involved. Haven't
got any answers back yet. Heck, if nothing else, that $25 million
reward looks mighty good.

Take care of yourself and God bless.

16.6   16 FEB 2003 – ROBERT MCKINNEY EMAIL TO
        ROBERT HICKOX – Regarding a blizzard.

MCKINNEY: Hi, Bob & Family. I am fine. We have about a foot of
        snow here. And one inch of ice on top of that. And rain and
        sleet. So, everything is okay. Ha, ha! Old "Auther"
        [arthritis] hurts in this weather. How is everything with
        you?

HICKOX: Thanks for the Valentine gift for the girls. You're gonna
        spoil them, Bobby. [Regarding a picture attached to an
        email] – You were quite the "baby", weren't you? Yo daddy
        musta been a horse. I thought the picture was legit until I
        scrolled down. Ha! So well hung, kid.

16.7   8 SEP 2001 – ROBERT HICKOX EMAIL TO PATRICK
        SHAUGHNESSY – Regarding events that occurred at the
        50th Anniversary Reunion.

As for the reunion, it couldn't have gone better. Only if we could have found more people. [Unfortunately], I believe we would have had to dig them up, literally. As it was, there were six of us from all parts of the country who hadn't seen each other in 51 years. We brought our wives, and in my case, my thirteen-year-old daughter, and we had a great time.

We were in D.C. for five days and renewed old camaraderie. During the day, we did the tour thing. Arlington, the Korean War Memorial, etc. In the evening, we would sit around and retell old tales and, in some cases, make up new ones. I had my big question answered. I wondered for fifty years how some got out and I didn't. It seems the Chinese attacked the hill in a way that cut me off before I [could have escaped] as did a majority of the company. Ha! We sat around in the hotel restaurant drawing war maps on napkins and trying to figure out what went wrong.

It was a great experience; one we all look forward to doing again.

I felt fortunate that my old squad leader [Al Thistle] showed up. The last time I saw him was on 27 November 1950 when he tapped me on the shoulder and told me to disable the gun and get out. He was severely wounded getting out, but he made it.

The whole thing was a very moving experience.

16.8   25 APR 2003 – ROBERT HICKOX EMAIL TO ROBERT
        MCKINNEY

Good to hear from you. Thought you got lost. Hope everything is alright. Haven't heard from you for a while.

I got a call from Stamper [Stumpy] last Sunday. We had a nice long talk. First time I've heard from him by phone. He had me confused for a while. I thought it was you. All you darn hillbillies sound alike. Ha!

...Sally Costigan (Kenoian) called me this noon. She called Becky to find out what they were doing for DK. I guess they're going with cremation and nothing special. I sent cards, but didn't know about flowers or where to send any. Too bad it happened.

Weather gradually getting better. It's sunny and a little warmer today. Cripes, we had snow again Wednesday.

Take care, brother, and keep in touch.

16.9   20 MAY 2002 – JIM BELCHER EMAIL TO ROBERT
        HICKOX – Regarding wounds Jim suffered in Korea.

The gooks took one more shot at me and missed again. April 25th, bad flu bug, heavy coughing, and scar tissue on the left lung from August 23, '50 and it blew. Really collapsed. Spent the next 17 days with tubes hanging out all over the place. I decided no cheap NK scar was going to take me out. Took 10 days to get it inflated and 7 days to heal the hole. Almost as good as new. Home May 10th.

16.10   17 FEB 2002 – HANDWRITTEN LETTER FROM AL
        THISTLE TO ROBERT HICKOX – Regarding events of
        27 November 1950.

THISTLE: Lt. Wyman – I believe they stuck him in as a PX officer or something like that (after the horseshit incident). Pecoraro took care of that bastard.

Pecoraro was a 1st Lt when he took over. Made Captain in Korea by kissing Col. Michaelis's ass. He [Michaelis] had the Wolfhounds and a good press agent. Female at that. It almost cost Jim Belcher his life. He [Pecoraro] made Captain when he got hit on that ridge in the beginning of our [Chinese] indoctrination. I can't believe you didn't know or see the eager little bastard. He got the name "We can do it!" from all of his NCOs.

In November, when we caught [Chinese] hell, it was Pecoraro, Cameron, and Harper who showed me and the other NCOs how to get out in case of an [overrun]. I had a good bunch with me until Lt.

Third Platoon Schmidt appeared. I was all for going straight down the road, but he insisted [we take] the left side of the road (in the rice paddy). That was the end for me and [General John] Wilson.

In '49 we got a shitload of Korean vets. Ones that had plenty of time left on their enlistments. Anyone who came from Korea then knew it was about to happen, but they didn't know when. A lot of little things people brought up in my "off duty" time (which I have plenty of NOW). I laugh, I cry, I curse the stupid waste of men and time that [Korea] was. I can't blame anyone, but… I remember J.D. because of the things he did.

You've got your thoughts and ideas, I got McKinney and a damn tank [See memoir 13.7 -ed.] to thank for mine.

Then, of course, there's Becky. Without her and her persistence, I would still be sitting and looking at the stone walls as before.
I was talking to David Frye's sister on Wednesday the 14th and she is sending me some of Frye's pictures she has. I'll boot them over to you and the others after I get them.

I'm sending you two pictures. I want them back.

Whatever happened to Wegrzyn, Stanley Sgt, from [Adams] Illinois? You can see him in the battered picture. In between Wilson and Hormann. In the second picture – who is that G.I. sitting on the left? It was taken in the [Asiah?] beer hall in '50 right after Frye and I made staff. King was another training NCO. You can see he and Frye had some time in service. Looks like nine years for King and one wound stripe. Am I right?

I can't take time to think [about things]. If I don't do it right away, on the spur of the moment, [it won't get done]. With the pictures. Send this [letter] back also. I keep [copies of] all my mail.

HICKOX: Received your letter and pictures today (snail mail). Rest assured, all will be returned to you after I scan them and make a photocopy of your letter.

Your letter gave me a wealth of information about …the company. It was with nostalgia I looked at the pictures. Damn, we were all so young.

I'm glad they found a place for Wyman. I would have suggested Leavenworth. At least we got him out of our hair. The damn fool would have got us killed early on for sure. [See Bio-8.1]

Pecoraro sure made rank fast if he went from Lt. to Captain in Korea. Was he one of the West Point Wonders also? I never met him. Generally, the only time I met a CO was after I'd been AWOL. Ha!

Ninety percent of the trouble we got into in Korea was the result of somebody kissing Michaelis's ass. Ole "Iron Mike" just loved us. He said once he'd rather have C Company 65th with him than an infantry company and he tried to prove it every chance he got. We spent so much time with the 27th that the Wolfhounds Association offered to make me an honorary Wolfhound. I liked Michaelis, though, because you always knew where you stood with him – generally on the front line or on a hilltop. Who was his press agent? Maggie Higgins? Now there was a gal. She had more balls than most of the men there.

You guys from Korea to Japan knew something was going to happen? We that were already in Japan and had come from the States were naïve. I don't think we knew where Korea was. It's too bad our upper echelon brass didn't realize the same thing. They might have trained and equipped us a little better.

It's ironic. Pecoraro, Cameron, and Harper showed you guys (NCOs) the way out (in the November Fiasco) and they ended up getting taken POW. Maybe they should have followed you guys out. Hell, maybe I should have followed you guys out. Apparently, they were expecting an attack if they were laying escape routes. Sounds like you should have overruled Lt. Schmidt and you'd have been better off. ...Let me say that I am awfully glad that damn tank and McKinney were there for you.

Regarding the stripes on King's sleeve: The diagonal one is for every 3 years (one complete enlistment) and the short yellow ones are overseas marks, one for every six months. In your picture, King has one complete 3-year enlistment and 18 months of overseas duty. Of course, he would have been on his second enlistment so he might have four or five years in, but less than six.

God Bless You and Carol.

16.11   21 MAR 2002 – EMAIL FROM BILL BOWLING – 50TH
            ANNIVERSARY FOLLOWUP – Another installment of
            the ongoing saga: "The Perils of Bill on the Hill of Death".

HICKOX: That's about it for now, brother. Write soon with another
            segment of "perils of Bill on the hill of death" or something
            like that.

BOWLING: Ongoing story on the same hill, or mountain. Two days
            later, I'm in my foxhole. I looked at the hill on our left flank.
            About 3000 yards out, I saw a puff of smoke and a mortar
            lands about 1000 yards from our position. We were told it
            was our crew. I looked again and another round fell short of
            our position. I grabbed my BAR and headed for the CO's
            foxhole to tell him.
                When I was even with the CO's foxhole, about fifty feet
            behind him, I shouted: "Incoming mail!" He was sitting on
            the back side of his foxhole. He shouted: "Incoming mail!"
            and fell forward in his foxhole. [I hid behind a little
            embankment where I was.] The mortar hit about three feet
            from me on the other side of the embankment. It threw
            rocks and dirt all over me. My pant legs were warm, like
            blood running down my legs. I thought I've got the million-
            dollar wound. I'm out of this shit!
                I dug myself out of the dirt and rock. Hell, there wasn't
            anything wrong with me, just [piss] and a dirty BAR.

16.12   ROBERT HICKOX MEETING WITH USAF OFFICERS
            DURING THE 50TH ANNIVERSARY REUNION

    I found my perfect forum in Washington. We were all in the
dining room and Bob McKinney was out at the bar. He came in and
told me there were a couple of guys out at the bar who wanted to
talk to me. It turned out they were Air Force Officers in charge of a
program designed to train men to be POWs. Well, that was
something I wanted to talk about for a long time.

There is no way to train men to handle being POWs. I told [the officers] you can't beat trainees, you can't kill them, and no matter how much you threaten, come morning the sun will rise. They will put on their uniforms and walk out of there and they know it. You can't do that when you are a prisoner.

I talked with the Air Force Officers for about an hour. I hope I made an impression. I have heard about those programs and they don't work, can't work, because they fail to do what the enemy easily does every day.

16.13   EMAIL EXCHANGE BETWEEN JIM BELCHER AND ROBERT HICKOX – THE LEGEND OF JIM'S MIATA

BELCHER: Did I tell you I lost my beautiful, sweet little Ranger? Yep, she's gone. I plead guilty to abandoning her for the Miata, but I felt good because she was always there.

HICKOX: Gosh, Jim. Sorry to hear about the loss of your dearly beloved ole Ranger. Ha! …and you deserted her for one of those little foreign gals. You oughta be ashamed.

BELCHER: Yep, still kickin' and wheelin'. Wish I'd owned the Miata 50 years ago. I've had more fun in this sucker than any vehicle. I can take mountain curves at 50 and she hugs the road like the Roadrunner. Fun, but nearing time for the hard top as we seem to be moving into the 70s.

HICKOX: I thought you would drive up to Reno. Not that far from you is it? You could drive into town in that Miata with a big cigar and they would think you was one of them thar oil barons.

BELCHER: Put the hard top on the other day and it still looks and drives great.

HICKOX: Sorry it's so cold you had to put the cap on the car. What is it now, in the 70s? Ha! About 42 degrees outside here…

BELCHER: Betty drives the van. The Miata is MINE! Wondering if I can use it as my casket.

16.14   21 OCT 2001 – EMAIL FROM BILL BOWLING – 50TH ANNIVERSARY FOLLOWUP – Regarding Bob writing his memoir.

Write your book. Let the world know the hell all of you went through as POWs. Let them [hear] about your wounds. Let them know the good times we had. Let the world know what we laughed about. Let them know we hurt when we lost one of our buddies.

Praying this finds you and your family in good health.

APPENDIX 1
MEMOIR EXTRAS

This section contains the balance of Bob's narrative not included in the main memoir. Structurally, the information presented here is secondary to the memoir and is presented for completion. Robert Hickox felt his childhood experiences and the cruelty shown to him by his parents shaped the man he became.

EASTWOOD NEW YORK, 1930 – GROWING UP

I was born in the year 1930 in a little village known as Eastwood, a small community outside Syracuse, New York, during the height of the Great Depression which devastated the whole United States. Hunger was widespread and work was nonexistent. People resorted to crime – or starved to death instead.

My grandfather worked for twenty-five cents a day. A man who could make four or five dollars a week was envied by his neighbors. Bread lines stretched for blocks when the trucks handed out loaves to the crowd.

During that time, my father, who had studied to be a barber under his uncle, opened a small barber shop on James Street in Eastwood. Throughout the later years of the Depression and into the end of the 1930s, we, as a family, fared better than most. My father's business did well and he made good money, considering the times. He bartered with other businessmen for goods in exchange for haircuts. He made enough money to purchase a new car and a house during this time, something few people were able to accomplish during this period. Compared to others, our life was good.

I had a sister born in 1935. Her name was Beverly. She quickly became the family favorite, as girls have a way of doing. In 1939, my parents were blessed with another son whom they named after my father and paternal grandfather, Charles Durwood Hickox, Jr., or Chuck for short.

I did well in school. I went to Grade School on Nichols Avenue, just a few blocks from home, and later to Junior High and High School. There was no separate Middle School then. I like school and my grades were good.

It was plain I was not the favored son from the beginning. My parents were restrictive with me, my father being quite restrictive from the beginning. On many occasions, I became the victim of his razor strop, a tool he used in barbering and on my rear, even when undeserved. My mother was a psycho and satisfied with nothing, despite having more material possessions than most women of her time and ilk. At home, she picked on my father continuously and checked on him at work since the barbershop was close to our home. They fought continuously and I often bore the brunt of their hatred. I wanted to run away but realized it would only cause me more grief.

At age eleven, I was forced to work in the barbershop shining shoes. At that time, this type of work was considered demeaning. I kept the shop clean, the floors swept, and the windows and mirrors sparkling. Although I made good money, I did not like the shoeshine business. A shoeshine went for ten cents and generally carried a tip of one dime. Some weeks I could make twenty dollars or more. Unfortunately, I had to turn over most of the money I made to my mother for room and board. I didn't get to spend much. She said she would put my money in the bank for me, but I never saw any of it.

In December 1941, the Japanese attacked Pearl Harbor, our biggest and only naval base in the Pacific, and destroyed most of the fleet anchored there. Shortly thereafter, Congress declared war on Germany, Japan, and Italy. Things changed rapidly in this country. Everyone became patriotic and began taking classes on spotting enemy aircraft. Young men flocked to recruiting stations by thousands to enlist. Everyone flew the old forty-eight-star flag. (Alaska and Hawaii didn't come into the Union until years later)

Everything was rationed. You couldn't get gas for your car without ration stamps and you were allowed only so many gallons per week. The same held true for foodstuffs, meat, milk, sugar, and most staples. Here we were lucky because my father was wheeling and dealing with local businessmen, trading haircuts for gas and food stamps so we had everything we needed.

My paternal grandparents also helped us. They owned a big dairy farm close to us. We used to take weekly trips to pick up gallons of fresh milk and fresh meat from butchered cows and hogs. We were eating good, war or nor war.

Another thing we did was cover all the windows in our house with black curtains. Several nights a week, we obeyed the air raid drills. We turned off all the lights and hid until we heard the all-clear. Certain people in our neighborhood were designated Air Raid Wardens. They came around and checked all the houses to make sure your lights were off. Violators could be fined or arrested.

It seems my father didn't want to go into the service and pulled every trick imaginable to stay out. One time, when the draft board was getting close, he got a job in a casket company polishing caskets. His job was considered draft-exempt because America needed many caskets due to war deaths. He polished caskets for a while and let one of the other barbers run his shop.

In 1942, the Draft Board caught up with him. Rather than go into the Army, he enlisted in the Navy because he found out they needed barbers to shave the heads of enlisted men. After Boot Camp, he was sent to an East Coast base where he worked in a barbershop. Eventually, he transferred to Cape Cod.

Throughout this period, my life remained the same. When I was older, I got a job working in a silk factory where they manufactured silk on huge looms. My job was to roll and pack the silk as it came off the loom. I worked about three hours a night. I had a paper route I shared with another kid and had to deliver papers before I went home for dinner.

I was glad my father was gone because there wasn't much fighting in our home, and I wasn't getting whippings. Even so, my mother rode me all the time. There was no pleasing her. I stayed out later at night so I wouldn't have to deal with her. And I was getting into trouble. Nothing bad, just feeling my oats.

It was now about the middle of 1943 and my father was stationed at Chatham Massachusetts on Cape Cod... (see Memoir Chapter One – 1.3)

CHATHAM HARBOR 1944

The local fishermen would go out of Chatham Harbor every morning for their daily fishing run. They would go several miles out to sea, and if fishing was good, they would come back around four in the afternoon with a full load.

Some of the local kids and I would get down there in time to help them unload. Generally, we got paid with cash or fresh seafood. It was dirty, stinky work but the fishermen were generous, and we could make a few dollars a week for spending money. I liked working on the boats because it was "manly" work and pretty much the only work available for a kid in Chatham. Portland is where I learned to love the sea.

On weekends, a group of us would build a big driftwood fire down on the beach and broil up clams, fish, and corn (in season), using seaweed that washed up on the beach. Those were good times. Those are times I like to remember.

The only thing we knew of World War Two was what we heard on the radio. One time I heard that the Navy or Coast Guard sunk a German submarine a few miles off the Chatham coast. Other than that, the war seemed far off for us. My father went to work in the base barbershop every day, just like he did before the war. Life seemed good.

About the middle of 1944, my father received orders transferring him to Portland, Maine to work in a barbershop at the Naval Base there. He had earned enough rank to oversee the barbershop. Quite a promotion. This, of course, brought my idyllic life on Cape Cod to an abrupt halt. My mother, my siblings, and I packed up our belongings and returned to Syracuse while my father went on Portland. My eternal "Summer of 42" came to an end.

***

We settled back into our old house in Eastwood and life resumed as it had been before we left. I was almost fifteen and was entering High School. I had been put ahead a half year while on Cape Cod.

Since I had always been rather athletic, I became involved in gymnastics. I got to be quite proficient at this sport, thanks to the interest of my gym teacher and competition provided by my best friend at the time, Bob Mulherin. I worked out in the gym every chance I got and managed to make the gymnastics team. I could not participate as much as Bob and the others because my mother demanded I get a job.

She tried to make me go back to shining shoes, but at my age, I would have none of that. I got a paper route and worked for several months at it. I made enough money to pay for my room and board, so my parents were happy. I managed to keep a few dollars in my pocket for spending money which led me into some bad habits.

I learned the addiction to tobacco and started smoking. I also stopped at a local bar and had a beer now and then. Laws on serving minors were not as strict then as they are now, and your local barkeep would gladly set one up for you if you had a dime to pay for it. My parents raised hell over this. I never figured out if they were concerned for my health or angry they didn't get the money I was spending on cigarettes and beer.

I began running numbers for one of the bookies in Eastwood. It paid better than my paper route, but eventually, the police shut him down and I lost my lucrative, highly illegal position.

Throughout all this, my school marks stayed good and I attended several local gymnastic meets. I enjoyed the competition and it got me out of the house, so I didn't have to hear my mother tell me what a bad person I was. I acquired many good friends and we hung out at a local diner after gymnastic meets or evenings after school. I did my best to stay as far away from home as possible.

***

Sometime in the winter of 1945, around February if I remember correctly, a friend of mine who worked at the New York Central Railroad roundhouse said he could get me a job working there. The roundhouse is a huge building where they repair steam engines and get them ready to travel. It sounded interesting and the pay was good, but it would be full-time. I had to work from three in the afternoon until eleven at night, sometimes later. It was also a full day on Saturday. It would cut into my gymnastic schedule somewhat, but I worked out a compromise and took the job. My bosses at the railroad were lenient and allowed me to take time off for gymnastics. When we weren't busy in the roundhouse, I got my homework done for school. It was hard, dirty work, but it was "man's" work and it kept me away from my mother and her continual bitching.

The war was grinding down. We had beaten the Germans and the Italians. By the early months of 1945, Germany had surrendered and Japan was on its way out. In August 1945, we came up with a new weapon called the atomic bomb which we dropped on the cities of Hiroshima and Nagasaki, Japan, destroying both cities and causing horrible, widespread death along with the immediate surrender of Japan. Hundreds of thousands of deaths resulted from these two bombs and thousands more were horribly burned and disfigured. Japan surrendered to prevent its annihilation. The war was over. We had won peace.

Peace was a word that would teach me a hard lesson in the future.

With the end of the war, all the boys came back home from the far reaches of the earth and times became good again. No more rationing or air raid drills. Sugar, meat, and gasoline became plentiful again. My uncle, Ray McGann, who served in the Seabees, the Combat Engineer section of the U.S. Navy, and took part in the Normandy invasion and fought his way across the Pacific, came home to stay, his part of the war finished. My father crawled out of his barbershop foxhole, returned home, and picked up his barbershop business right where he left off. My life remained the same except for the fact I now had both my parents around to beat me. I prayed for the day I could leave home and never see either of them again. Little did I realize how soon that time would come.

I kept my studies up in school, kept working on the railroad, and tried to keep up with gymnastics. My grades remained good. When I entered my junior year in High School, I arranged my schedule so all my courses were in the morning and I could leave school at noon. Since my marks were good and I had accumulated most of my required credits, I had only the basic sequence of four-year courses to complete. This worked out well because it gave me time between school and work to complete my homework.

By this time, I was sixteen and had become involved with a gang. When I came home from work at eleven each night, I showered, changed clothes, and met up with the guys. Heavy drinking, fights, cruising around in cars looking for trouble. We started stealing cars and stripping them for parts... (See Memoir Chapter Two – 2.1.)

CAMP PICKETT VIRGINIA, 1947

NOTE: Bob describes Basic Training (Boot Camp) at length and ends this section with the following entry: "I have interjected this tale to give the reader some idea as to what my life in the military would be like. In many ways, it turned out to be most unconventional."

Basic Training moments described by Bob, although at times colorful, duplicate experiences shared by decades of soldiers in many nations. Highlights found in Bob's account appear in the main memoir. In the balance of the text, which involves drill, mess hall etiquette, and chain of command, I found this curious entry:

"After breakfast, it was usually close order drill, marching, and on occasion a hike of several miles with full field equipment. We also underwent hand-to-hand combat (something that would come in handy later), bayonet practice, our turn through the gas chamber to acquaint us with our gas masks, and our turn qualifying on the rifle range. Since I had never fired a rifle too much, only a .22 cal. pop gun on the grandparents' farm, I wasn't too skilled. However, under the watchful eye of our drill sergeant, I improved rapidly.

"We also did quite a bit of basic combat training such as scaling high walls, climbing ropes, and crawling along the ground while caressing an M-1 rifle with .30 caliber machinegun bullets flying thirty inches over our heads.

"There was, of course, the continuous daily close order drill and marching, designed to make you work as a single unit. At the time it seemed stupid, but later I found out how important it was. At the end of our training, we capped it off with a fifty-mile march under full field pack."

Taken at face value, Bob's account records live fire exercises with a safety margin considered unacceptable in today's world. Most unconventional.

CROSS-COUNTRY BY TRAIN, 1948
20th Century Limited, Super Train of the Forties

NOTE: In Memoir Chapter Three (3.3), I summarized this portion of the trip in a single sentence: "Cincinnati, Chicago, Deadwood, Reno." My decision was intended to maintain the narrative pace leading to Chinatown. Bob's account of his journey appears below.

"As we pulled out of Syracuse and gradually gained speed, I saw the countryside fly by. Quite an experience for an eighteen-year-old on his first long trip. As we rolled along toward Buffalo, I found a lounge car and settled down for a few drinks before lunch. The staff was cordial and friendly to anyone in uniform. During the period after World War Two, the soldier was still respected.

Several of us "service types" were onboard, all headed for the West Coast. Naturally, we got our little card games and crapshoots going. I was never good at either, but I sat in for fun. The stakes weren't too high and it was a jolly group, getting jollier with each round of drinks. I don't recall ever getting lunch. They had a good snack bar, so I didn't go hungry.

We pulled into the station at Buffalo, exchanged a few passengers, and were on our way again. "Go West, Young Man." Before long, we heard an announcement that Cincinnati, Ohio, was our next stop. If we wanted more drinks, we should order them now because Ohio was a dry state and no alcohol could be served after we crossed the state line. We hit several dry states during our trip. Naturally, everybody ordered up and went back to the game.

During the entire trip, I believe I lost only a couple hundred dollars, which was small compared to some of the bets that started flying around. Being a man of small means and smaller talent, I knew when it was time to leave a game. Besides, I enjoyed watching the world fly by, and seeing as much of this beautiful country as I could. At each stop, I would get off, stretch my legs, and look around. We stopped in such places as Chicago, Deadwood South Dakota, and Reno Nevada. We made many interesting stops and I saw things I had only read about in books. America is indeed a beautiful land.

The place I was most intrigued by was Reno, Nevada. We had a two-hour layover there and I wanted to see the city. I left the train and headed for the bright lights.

I remember a big banner across the main – and only – street, stating "Reno Nevada, the Biggest Little City in the World". The lights, glitter, and razzle-dazzle were more than this poor boy could handle. I checked out a few casinos, lost more money in the bandits, drank, and marveled at everything I saw.

One thing that amazed me was the silver dollars. We paid for everything, received change, and won money in silver dollars. Silver dollars (made from real silver) were a big thing back home, so I collected as many as I could before I realized I had to carry them. I ended up blowing most of them in the slots and kept about thirty for souvenirs.

One thing that struck me as odd was all the gals hanging around the casinos, streets, and bars. They were dressed really fancy like they were going to a party or something and seemed very friendly. Girls kept asking me to buy them a drink, which I did sometimes, and then they'd ask me if I wanted to see where they lived. I thought that was downright friendly, but I was on a tight schedule. The train was leaving soon, so I declined. Later I found out these fine ladies were working girls, that is, whores. Prostitution was, and still is, legal in Reno. These girls were just trying to relieve a poor soldier boy of all that heavy money.

CAMP STONEMAN, 1948

With the help of a few MPs (military police), we found our reporting office and got in line (yes, there is a line at Camp Stoneman for everything), ready to present our orders and be quickly on our way. When my name was called, I stepped forward and saluted the lieutenant in charge of new arrivals. He gave me a barracks number, and a diagram of the camp, then pointed toward a truck that would carry me to my assigned quarters.

After they loaded the trucks with fresh souls for the grinder, we rolled out. We rode around the camp for several miles before we pulled up in front of a large, clean barracks. Outside, guys were picking up cigarette butts and trash discarded by less caring individuals. As I would soon learn, this was one of the many duties I would be assigned.

My favorite duty was KP, or Kitchen Police. KP is normally the scourge of an Army base, but here at Stoneman, we fought to get assigned to KP duty. As Kitchen Police, our duties included preparing and serving meals under the supervision of the regular cooking staff. The work wasn't hard and the upside was you could have anything you wanted to eat – anytime you wanted it, twenty-four hours a day. If you were peeling spuds at three o'clock in the morning and you got the urge for a steak and some ice cream, it was there for you. I've never seen so much food in my life.

The downside was the ever-present inspections and close order drill, neither of which happened too often. The main purpose of Camp Stoneman was to house men awaiting formal orders to ship out and to keep them busy at mealtime. The usual layover was about three weeks, so nobody got stuck with bad duty for long. I found my stay at Camp Stoneman to be quite enjoyable.

One day I checked the roster board and saw a familiar name. Bob Ivison. My old friend who helped me drive a stolen car through a gas station… (See Memoir Chapter Three – 3.3.)

KANOAKA JAPAN, 1948
DAILY GRIND WITH 65th ENGINEER COMBAT
BATTALION

Note: The following section describes unremarkable aspects of daily life in the 25th Infantry Division of that period. A reader with modern military experience may appreciate the details Bob recorded simply for completion.

I reported to Battalion HQ and was tentatively assigned to B Company. The Battalion consisted of three field companies, A-B-C, and Headquarters company. There were also various sections and details such as Medical Attachment, Motor Pool, Mess Hall, and so forth. I was billeted in B Company for a time because C Company had been deactivated at the end of World War Two and was now being reactivated. This is where I enter the story.

Despite its paper strength, C Company contained almost no personnel. I was assigned as Company Clerk, chief cook, and bottle washer. I was in charge of the entire company as far as paperwork, daily reports for Battalion and Division, and receipt of supplies. It was "seat of the pants" type of work because I was unfamiliar with Army forms and regulations. My only saving grace was I could type – nobody else could. Rumors of my typing ability followed me from Basic Training to Japan. No sin goes unpunished. After an initial period of disaster, things straightened out and ran smoothly.

I would like to mention that Camp Kanoaka was the nicest, best-groomed camp in Japan. It was a beautiful camp. I understand it was previously a Japanese Army training camp, either cadet or officer, during the war. It was a pleasure to serve in a country club atmosphere run by a congenial Army cadre.

The village of Kanoaka was a short distance outside the main gate and the natives were very friendly, a bonus that allowed me to study *beeru* and *Suntory* during my time off. I discovered I got along well with Japanese people and, due to being a clerk in a ghost company, I had plenty of time to fraternize with the locals.

I would like to mention that Japanese culture and landscaping techniques take some getting used to. Your first impression is that Japan is a dirty, stinky country. This is because the Japanese use human excrement for fertilizer and the smell hangs in the air. Also, buildings in most towns and villages were run down due to the war. People were extremely poor. The American dollar was welcome and the Black Market flourished.

During the next few months, the Army filled out C Company and I got moved into an HQ building so I would have direct contact with command. We got a new Company Commander, Captain Schmidt, a career officer and a fatherly type who was easy to get along with. Captain Schmidt gave me his signature stamp and turned the operation of the company over to me. I consulted him only on matters of protocol and discipline.

As Company Clerk, I had a great deal of leeway in handling company affairs and assigning details. I issued passes to all personnel (including myself), a function that made me well-liked or hated, depending on who you were.

Most of the men assigned to C Company came from "Lightning University", the Division stockade. A few came from South Korea where they served with KMAG, Korean Military Augmentation Group. The Army phased out KMAG and reassigned personnel to occupation duties in Japan, often with 65th Engr Combat Bn. For the most part, they were a good group. A little rowdy though, probably from their easy living lifestyle in Korea. Graduates from Lightning University were good soldiers but couldn't handle garrison duty. Overnight they were in trouble again. Eventually, guys from both groups turned out to be my dearest friends. The infamous ones I will never forget. The heroes I will always remember.

Finally, we were assigned a First Sergeant and a few administrative personnel to take over most of the duties I had been doing. This cut back on the work I was responsible for and made life more pleasant. I had many run-ins with my new boss who had "all the stripes" and was always right. As time went on, senior Sergeants, NCOs, and old-timers leftover from World War Two joined our company. When we attained effective combat strength, training programs began.

As Company Clerk, I was not required to participate in training, reveille, retreat, or inspections. I worked in the office and went on pass, to the PX, or to the beer hall. I worked from eight o'clock in the morning until four-thirty in the afternoon then did what I wanted. It was a much easier schedule than most of the guys had and many of them resented me. Some did not trust me because I handled their records and worked with the brass. They had nothing to worry about. I was as big a screw-up as they were. Some never warmed up to me. Others became lifelong friends.

I didn't learn this until fifty years later, but I earned a nickname at Kanoaka. I was known as "the little prick from headquarters". I think about it now and smile.

(See Memoir Chapter Six – 6.3, Teahouse Wisdom.)

10 OCT 1999 – EMAIL TO STACEY [MED---] – Regarding Bob's attitude toward his father's medical care.

Just wanted to clarify my father's VA treatment. He is now about 89 years old (WWII) and fought the war [entirely] in Portland Maine and Cape Cod as a Navy barber. (Grrrr.) He has no SC at all but in the last 20 years or better he has received all kinds of medication from the VA (he has regular VA appointments) and has had two hernia operations, and is currently on his third pacemaker for a heart condition, all at the expense of the US taxpayer. And he has always had insurance coverage. Go figure. This is why I thought anybody would be eligible for anything. He did not retire, has no service-connected problems, and never went to the VA until he was in his sixties. I'm glad he got help, but it's situations like this that I think clog up the system for the service-disabled vet.

C Company 65th Cmbt Engr Bn

Mt Fugi 1950

C Company 65th Cmbt Engr Bn

Mt Fugi 1950

BIOGRAPHIES

This section contains information about men and women mentioned in the memoir.

65th ENGINEER COMBAT BATTALION

https://www.koreanwar.org/html/units/65en.htm

1. Belcher, James	MOS: 00-405	00 Support + 405 Medical Clerk/Typist
2. Bowling, William	MOS: 03-729	03 Infantry + 729 Pioneer
3. Buli, Bernard	MOS: 05-729	05 Equipment + 729 Pioneer
4. Donovan, Lawrence	MOS: 00-861	00 Support + 861 Medical Tech
5. Francard, Leroy	MOS: Unavailable	
6. Harper, Harrison	MOS: 03-729	03 Infantry + 729 Pioneer
7. Hickox, Robert	MOS: 00-189	00 Support + 189 Rigger
8. McKinney, Robert	MOS: 00-345	00 Support + 345 Lt Truck driver
9. Morgan, Duane	MOS: Unavailable	
10. Saloway, Aldin	MOS: 05-729	05 Equipment + 729 Pioneer
11. Shaughnessy Michael	MOS: 02-110	02 Intelligence + 110 Adjutant
12. Soyars, Harold	MOS: Unavailable	
13. Stamper, Leonard	MOS: 00-078	00 Support + 078 Electrician
14. Thistle, Alfred	MOS: 00-572	00 Support + 572 Seacoast Gun Data

OTHER UNITS

15. Ivison, Robert	MOS: Unavailable	25th Div, 35th Regt, E Company
16. Young, Robert	MOS: 04745	2nd Div, 38th Regt, K Company

James Thomas Belcher
Bio-1

Rank - SGT   MOS: 00-405   RA15416789
                           Muhlenberg, KY

SERVICE: Japan Occupation Army
                Korean War

OBITUARY
https://everloved.com/life-of/james-belcher/obituary/

HIGHLIGHTS

BIO 1.1   9 MAR 2003 – JIM BELCHER EMAIL TO ROBERT
               HICKOX – Regarding attempts to commission a
               reproduction of the 65th Engr Cbt Bn Crest.

I've never even heard of a crest. I remember seeing the logo "First In, Last Out". Did you mention a bulldozer? Never saw one at the 65th and didn't think combat engineers would use them. [They spent too much time as infantry -ed.]

Photo B-1
Landscape – Column Width
CAPTION: (below)

25th ID *Tropic Lightning*
over bulldozer with Mt. Fuji. Four colors: Red, black, gold, white.

5 JAN 2002 – ROBERT HICKOX EMAIL TO PATRICK SHAUGHNESSY – Regarding the 65th crest.

Thank you for responding to my request regarding our battalion crest. I've been trying to track this down for some time. It must have been an officially "unauthorized" badge. I recall something to that effect being mentioned at the time, but we were allowed to use it. Our Battalion CO even promoted it at the time. We wore them on our uniforms and caps, so there must be one "alive" out there. They were quite attractive. Wimpy [Harold Soyars] won't give me his.

BIO 1.2   1 JAN 2004 – ROBERT HICKOX EMAIL TO PATRICK SHAUGHNESSY – Regarding Jim Belcher's Silver Star citation.

I'll ask Jim Belcher regarding his S/S citation, but it's doubtful he has it. I do not believe he even has the medal anymore. He did not put a great deal of interest in those things. I've been trying to get him to apply for the Combat Medic Badge and he won't bother with that. Stubborn ole' coot, but a great guy just the same. I don't think he even kept his Purple Heart. I'll check with him.

I referred to the August 23, 1950, War Diary and it pretty much describes Jim's actions. It omits much of the actual happenings though. Jim's platoon got overrun. Sgt. Harper and Sgt. Akers organized and led an attack to recapture the position. There were twenty-nine of us in the attack. Once we regained the position, we secured the area. My best friend Sgt. Terry was killed along with Scott.

Jim had taken over Bill Capretto's machine gun and was protecting Capretto from enemy fire. Jim killed several of the enemy, more than the six mentioned. Jim was shot seven times. We never thought he would survive. Me and two others (forget who) were sent on a recon of the hill to see if there were more wounded or dead and to find enemy troops. All in all, it was quite a day.

I believe the Company received a Presidential Unit Citation for that action.

Capretto suffered severe head wounds and still carries the bullet in his brain to this day. He functions pretty well. Paralysis in his left arm. He was at the group reunion in Vegas. He and Jim had a chance to get together for the first time since the incident.

BIO 1.3   4 FEB 2001 – JIM BELCHER EMAIL TO ROBERT HICKOX – Describing hazards associated with combat engineering in an enemy-contested area and the friendly fire death of Curtis A. Fair on 4 Aug 1950.

BELCHER: I remember exactly when and how it happened. The company had just laid a "daisy chain" across the road. We were climbing up an adjacent hill. It was afternoon and supposedly no friendly vehicles would be using the road. Someone forgot that three guys in a jeep had gone out on recon. Fair was one but I don't remember the other two. [Cpl James C. Shaw and Pvt Emil J. Kieth. -ed.] [We] saw the jeep coming and started screaming and shooting at it even though we were five hundred yards from the road. It kept coming and hit the chain which cut the jeep in half and bodies flew. It set off at least three of the mines.

I started down the hill but [Sgt. Harper] called me back because he knew there was nothing we could do. …It was a shitty feeling watching that jeep coming and knowing it was going to hit the chain.

HICKOX: I did not send this to the Fairs [family research request] because I thought it might be a little too graphic. If you think they want this eyewitness account, you can send it to them.

William H Bowling
Bio-2

Rank - SGT   MOS: 03-729   RA16275082
                              Warren, IL

SERVICE: Korean Military Advisory Group (KMAG)
                Japan Occupation Army
                Korean War

OBITUARY
https://www.legacy.com/us/obituaries/theherald-
news/name/william-bowling-obituary?id=29325715

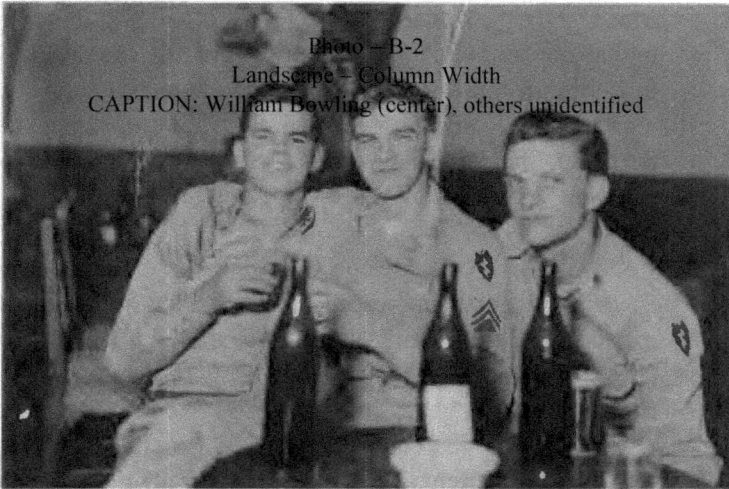

Photo – B-2
Landscape – Column Width
CAPTION: William Bowling (center), others unidentified

William Bowling (center), others unidentified

HIGHLIGHTS

BIO 2.1   ONGOING EMAIL CONVERSATION BETWEEN
           WILLIAM BOWLING AND ROBERT HICKOX.

BILL BOWLING: "You can see why we [KMAG] were so wild
    when we got to Japan. Hell, in Korea, we could fall out
    naked and no one said anything. When we got to Japan, they
    tried to make soldiers out of us. Couldn't do anything with
    us until Sgt Harper took over. He was a soldier's soldier."

BOB HICKOX: "Really? [KMAG?] I thought [Chief] Saloway was
    born in Lightning University!"

BILL BOWLING: "I still think [Lawrence] Donovan made a
    mistake about service stars. My DD-214 shows three
    service stars: PH, AO of Japan, Korea. Korean Service
    Medal – they cheated me. We [KMAG] should have got a
    medal for going AWOL, getting drunk, caught out of
    uniform, off limits, fighting, black marketeering, and court-
    martials. Hell, my uniform wouldn't hold all my medals.
    Sergeant Francard [Frankfurter, or so we called him -ed.]
    said that wasn't the sign of a good soldier."

BOB HICKOX: "I like your idea on why medals should get issued.
    Heck if we got them for all those things, (fighting, black
    market, AWOL, off limits, stealing Lt. Hayward
    Cameron's uniform and going around performing bed
    checks) we'd have to hire somebody to carry them all.
    HAHAHA!" [Lieutenant Cameron, nicknamed "Shorty",
    was the same height as Bob so the uniform fit. See Memoir
    6.3. -ed.]

BILL BOWLING: "You were lucky they didn't catch you in the Lt.
    [Cameron's] uniform, or when you caught the guys with the
    girls [during bed check]. A few might have decided to beat

the hell out of an officer. Good thing you didn't run into *Chief* with firewater in him. You two would have gotten into a fight and both ended up in the stockade.

BOB HICKOX: "From your description of [KMAG], it's no wonder I thought everybody was fresh from the stockade. The wild bunch. ...I was naïve as to what was going on around me. No wonder I seemed like such a prick to you guys. I wore clothes. Ha!

BILL BOWLING: "Mac told me he enjoyed Korea in '48 and '49. I sure as hell didn't like it. Nothing to do but get drunk and fight. And get court-martialed. I got two. What fun. Hell, everything was off-limits, but as you know [as HQ clerk in charge of our files], we followed the rules.

Thistle was in Korea in '47 and '48, I think. He must have been a good boy, or smart enough not to get caught. He was a sergeant in Japan. Good NCO. I think Saloway got time from Korea. He got shipped to the stockade straight from Korea. I can't remember what the hell he did to get six months.

It was spit and polish when I was there. The first three months in Japan, I went AWOL for three days every time I got paid. Remember Cpt. Schmidt? He was CO when I got to Japan. When I got paid in the fourth month, he handed me a three-day pass. Told me he might as well make it legal. He told me I was one of the best twenty-seven-day soldiers he ever had.

I think Saloway got the stockade when he came in [after AWOL]. They gave him a hard time, so he [physically] battled them.

Sometimes, I would run into Sergeant Harper while I was AWOL. We would have a couple of beers. He told me to come see him FIRST when I came in. I don't know if he talked me up [defended me] or not, but I think he did. I would get restricted for fifteen days. I could do that standing on my head.

...Remember when the gook got hurt? Woolard and I and our squads went AWOL. Woolard and the rest came in after a while. I stayed out. Woolard and I were mad because they made a guy in the Motor Pool Corporal and we were acting squad leaders.

I came in a couple of days later, around sick call. Sgt. Francard told me to take [the sick] to medical. I refused. I told him to get his new Corporal to take them. He told me he would tell the CO I had refused. I told Francard to go to hell. He ran into the CO's office. A few minutes later, he came out and told me to report to the CO.

I reported to the CO, who at the time was the infantry Lieutenant. We got into a bad discussion. He said: "You think you're a smart-ass SOB?" He came out of his chair and put one knee on the desk. I backed off and was going to bury him behind the desk if he put his other knee on the desk. He saw what I was going to do. He backed down behind the desk and told me to give him my pass. He tore it into a hundred pieces and reduced to Private.

Broke my heart. I had a little score to settle with Francard, which I did on Fuji.

I've bored you with enough. God Bless."

BOB HICKOX: "You took your squad AWOL? Wonder you didn't get the book thrown at you for that. ...I agree that [Arden] Strand and Thistle were the two good soldiers in Japan. I wanted to be like Thistle, but I couldn't stay sober – or ranked – or in camp long enough."

***

That's about it for now, brother. Write soon with another segment of "perils of Bill on the hill of death" or something like that.

- Robert Hickox

BIO 2.2   30 MAR 2002 - WILLIAM BOWLING EMAIL TO
             ROBERT HICKOX – Describing a firefight where
             he received no support from fellow soldiers.

"The Perils of Bill on the Hill of Death"
(latest installment)

I will [continue] with my story of the mountain. We were tied
in with [another unit]. They sent two [men] out on patrol. They
came under fire and came running back to their lines. They ran
into a minefield and were both killed.

They sent Kempfer and me up to clear the mines. We got down
on all fours like they trained us to do [when clearing Bouncing
Betty mines]. We found them all and got rid of them. Little hairy
finding them on our hands and knees. They were trip-wired [and
booby-trapped to discourage removal].

[Two] days later, the [tied-in unit] came under smalls fire and
they sent some of us to help out. I don't know who brought up the
water-cooled .30 [but] they set it up on a bare spot. The gunner sat
down on the five-gallon can of water and was firing the .30. I was
about fifteen feet away from them, standing [!] and firing my
BAR. [When] I looked at the .30, two holes appeared in the water
can. Then they shot the water jacket on the .30. We went looking
for holes [to hide in].

I saw a foxhole and jumped in. I landed on top of two guys
[from the tied-in unit] lying on top of each other. I rose up and
fired a clip. The enemy had me zeroed in. One of the [soldiers I
thought were dead] looked up at me and said: "Man, get out of this
motherfucking hole. You know Mister Kim is looking for you
motherfuckers with BARs." They never [complained] about me
sitting on them [while returning fire].

I jumped out of that hole and into another hole about twenty
feet away. Same thing all over again.

Later, I couldn't help but laugh at them and me standing up in
the open firing. It's a wonder any of us made it back.

Bernard Buli
Bio-3
"Baby Face"

Rank - PFC   MOS: 05-729   RA13334990
                            Adams, PA

SERVICE: Japan Occupation Army
                   Korean War

HIGHLIGHTS

BIO-3.1   3 JUN 2001 – ROBERT HICKOX EMAIL TO
              ALFRED THISTLE – Regarding Bernard Buli.

I'm sorry I had to be the one to tell you about Buli. I know you
were friends with him. He turned into a good soldier. You would
have been proud of him.

I don't know how he died, whether illness or accident, but he
was young, only 42. Lt Cameron was only 59. A lot of ex-POWs
died young. But then, our experience was not conducive to a long
life. [Buli died in Wilkes-Barre, PA in August 1978. He was 46
years old. -ed.]

[SEPARATE EMAIL] I don't have Buli's address. He was from
somewhere in PA. Last time I saw him was in Fort Sam Houston,
San Antonio. We were witnesses to a court martial of an ex-POW.

BIO-3.2   22 DEC 2000 – ROBERT HICKOX EMAIL TO TIM
              CASEY – Regarding Bernard Buli.

Sorry to hear about him. He was always treated as the "baby" of
the company. He was smaller than everyone else and
[inexperienced]. He had a bad situation shortly after we arrived in
Korea. His squad had been on a motorized deuce-and-a-half patrol

(mine laying). When they pulled back to the company area, [Buli] went to get off the back of the truck. As he did, his Platoon sergeant reached up for his weapon and Buli handed it to him barrel first. It went off and killed the sergeant instantly. I forget the sergeant's name, but it was a bad situation for a while. They let Buli stay in the Company and he soldiered it out pretty well.

BIO-3.3   1 AUG 2002 – BILL BOWLING EMAIL TO ROBERT HICKOX – Regarding the rifle misfire incident discussed in Hickox Memoir 8.7.1.

BOWLING: I think you will remember Don Wrightson. Remember when Brenna was killed on 7-29? Don's rifle fell over when they were getting off a truck. It killed Brenna.

HICKOX: I do not remember Don Wrightson... I remember an instance where a sergeant (I thought) got killed when someone handed him their rifle while getting off a truck. They handed it to him barrel first and the safety wasn't on. I thought Bernard Buli did that. Unfortunately, I don't remember Brenna either. Was he a squad sergeant? I always thought that was the first fatality in the company, but I think we had fatalities before that. I guess this is one of those matters I'm confused about. I remember something, but I don't remember the people involved.

HOSTILE DEATHS – 1950
CPL   Brenna, Odell C   KIA   29 Jul 1950   RA17218585   E4
                          Marshall MN

***

I had about two or three boxes of ammo left for the .30. I remember Buli going for another box about the time Al came... We fired steadily for quite a while.

                                              - Robert Hickox

Lawrence E Donovan
Bio-4

Rank – CPL   MOS: 00-861   RA13309915
                          Adams, PA

OBITUARY

https://warcholfuneralhome.com/tribute/details/279/Lawrence-Donovan/obituary.html

NOTE: Lawrence E. Donovan's writing was published in the book: The Korean War (Uncertain Victory) by Alfred Coppel.

UNPUBLISHED EXCERPTS

BIO 4.1   6 NOV 2001 – HANDWRITTEN LETTER FROM AL THISTLE TO ROBERT HICKOX – Regarding Lawrence Donovan POW [Hickox Memoir 5.42].

I got a letter and pictures from Larry Donovan. Seeing I don't have a scanner yet, I thought maybe you would kick them out to the others. I am sending you the letter also. I would like it back after you have done your thing.

No problems between you two, is there? [From Pyuktong Camp #5. -ed.] I don't want old fires to smoke again. Whatever is back there, let's hope we can leave it back there.

HICKOX: There were a lot of bad memories coming from that POW camp. I can understand the reluctance of many who don't want to get social. I felt the same way for years. Recently, I realized it was time to renew old acquaintances. Time is running out. I'm not interested in forming alliances with any ex-POWs. As I said in D.C., there are things better left unsaid as far as things that took place [at Pyuktong #5].

<u>BIO 4.2</u>   13 OCT 2001 – HANDWRITTEN LETTER FROM
               LAWRENCE DONOVAN TO ALFRED THISTLE –
               Regarding Donovan's general situation since Korea.

Al, we received your letter and were glad to hear from you. Hope
all is well with you and Carol. Certainly, the war news [Al Qaeda –
7 OCT 2001 invasion of Afghanistan] has us in shock. Who would
have thought someone could strike US soil?

You wrote that some of the men from C Company 65th were
getting together but you didn't say where. I belong to the
Greybeards... and the 25th Infantry Association.

Last year, two men from C Company passed away. They were
both captured with me on Nov 27th of 1950. Master Sergeant
Charles Cuccaro and Sgt Raymond Hess. I provided a full military
funeral for Cuccaro. We always stayed in touch. I also visited Ray
Hess in Honaker VA before he died of cancer.

None of us are getting any younger... [medical details]

We formed a Korean War Veteran's Association in Western PA
ten years ago. We have 600 members and I am on the Board of
Directors. We built a beautiful memorial in the city of [illegible
abbreviation – Pittsburg?]. We have great times together. Hope to
hear from you soon.

<u>BIO 4.3</u>   24 NOV 2002 – HANDWRITTEN LETTER FROM
               LAWRENCE DONOVAN TO ALFRED THISTLE –
               Regarding Donovan's schedule conflicts.

Hi friends. We received your letter and I wanted to respond
before the holiday rush. I received Bob Muzzy's letter and hope to
make the reunion, however we have an ex-POW reunion at Valley
Forge PA. I don't know if the dates will conflict. ...if I am able, I
will try to make both reunions.

As we approach November 27th, it brings back a lot of memories
[not all bad]. Life is strange. Believe it or not, my wife's birthday is
November 27th!

I have a lot to be thankful for and it helps me forget the bad times, although my POW memories never fade away.

I do a lot of public speaking at schools, colleges, and television. Recently spoke to 300 veterans on Veteran's Day. Also spoke to city schools at the History Center in [illegible abbreviation – Pittsburg?] It keeps me busy and some of the students will learn what the price of freedom is all about. All the men in C Company paid a high price for the freedom South Korea enjoys today.

...I hope you all read this letter. I must print due to my poor eyesight. [medical details]

Hope your holiday is great.

BIO 4.4   12 DEC 2002 – HANDWRITTEN LETTER FROM LAWRENCE DONOVAN TO ALFRED THISTLE – Regarding events in [illegible abbreviation - Pittsburgh?] PA.

Greetings friends,

It is 7:00 a.m. here in "the burg". I have taken some time to play catch-up answering all your mail. I received three phone calls from men you contacted for me. It was good to hear from them after 50 years. It's hard to believe [50 years has passed] isn't it?

[medical details]

...I would like to meet the guys from C Company. In response to your question about why ex-POWs don't attend [reunions] ...many have been to a reunion. We are a strong, close group. Like family. I have close friends from the 1st Cavalry, 24th Division, and 25th Division. We send out over 100 Christmas cards each year. I enjoy being with veterans and we have been to many reunions.

[extended list of people jointly contacted on behalf of families requesting service history]

I recall two guys by the name of Hanson, a radioman, and Donald Sherik, both in 2nd Platoon. Lt Flynn, a West Point Officer, made me carry Hanson's bedroll up a mountain. When I got to the top, I rolled it back down the hill. It was waterlogged, so heavy I could barely carry it. I told [Flynn]: "The Lt said carry it up the hill. He didn't say it had to stay up here." That guy was a real nut case! He kept a notebook on anyone he didn't like!

I was told Lt Flynn made it out of the firefight. He was in Japan in a whorehouse, got bitten by a rat, and died.

Another officer, Lt Cameron, was captured, [and] stayed in the Army. He came to see me and tried to get me to reenlist. I'm not that crazy! I never disliked the Army until I joined it. Ha, ha!

Best Always,
"Doc" Donovan

25 DEC 2002 – ROBERT HICKOX EMAIL TO BILL BOWLING
      – Regarding Lt Flynn's rat bite.

I don't know as I believe the way Flynn died, but maybe so. If that was the case, I am surprised a lot of us didn't die that way.

BIO 4.5   10 OCT 2003 – HANDWRITTEN LETTER FROM LAWRENCE DONOVAN TO ALFRED THISTLE – Regarding events since Donovan's last letter.

Hi, Al. Just a note to thank you for the pictures. Bob Muzzy puts on the best reunions. He is the most organized man I have ever met. Always enjoy his reunions.

I have stepped down as director [Korean War Veteran's Association], twelve years as an officer. I get a lot of calls to do public speaking on Veteran's Day.
[medical details]
I went to my POW reunion and was the only 25th Division man there. I was surrounded by 1st Cavalry men. All my 65th POWs have died. We hope to make a Division reunion. Always enjoyed them.

Yours in friendship,
Larry Donovan

Leroy J Francard
Bio-5
"Frankfurter"

Rank - MSGT   MOS: 01-331   RA39425352

SERVICE: AUS World War II (unknown)
                Japan Occupation Army
                Korean War

HIGHLIGHTS

BIO 5.1   RECONSTRUCTING LEROY FRANCARD'S
             SERVICE HISTORY – editor comments.

Despite differences of opinion MSGT Francard had with individuals mentioned in this memoir, he proved to be an influential force in the 65th Engineer Combat Battalion. Francard's story is one-sided, his perspective on events lost in time. A brief biography of Leroy Francard is presented here to allow his descendants to reconstruct a portion of his service history.

Concrete data regarding Leroy Francard begins with his RA number, a unique personal identifying number issued by United States Military Organizations. Francard's RA number is 39425352. Conscripted service numbers range from **30 000 000** to **39 999 999**. The first two numbers indicate the geographic area of conscription. Francard's service number begins with 39, indicating he originated in one of the following states: Alaska, Arizona, California, Idaho, Montana, Nevada, Oregon, Utah, and Washington. The next six digits, 425352, compose his personal identifying number.

As Master Sergeant, Leroy Francard likely has eight or more years of service to his credit. This places Francard's conscription date no later than 1942, making him a World War II veteran, as pointed out by Robert Hickox who described him as a "leftover" from that war.

MSGT Leroy Francard is listed as a non-battle casualty [Appendix IV - 25.C.4c] on 3 October 1950 due to a wound in the left hand. No details are given regarding the cause of the wound.

Subjective information regarding Leroy Francard is found in documents prepared by Robert Hickox. Hickox alternates between using the term "Sergeant" and "First Sergeant" when referring to Francard. Given Leroy Francard's administrative abilities as demonstrated in the Hickox manuscript, a rank of E-8 appears likely for him. Francard does not appear in a training capacity in the Hickox manuscript, only in an administrative role. In harmony with this conclusion, the 25th Infantry Division Non-Battle Casualty List for October 1950 records Leroy Francard as Master Sergeant.

The Hickox manuscript (Book 5) describes 65th Engineer Combat Battalion Company C as having been deactivated after World War II. During its reactivation in Japan circa 1948, MSGT Leroy Francard was assigned to the company, along with other "recycled" WW II veterans and KMAG troops, under a career officer named Captain Schmidt. Francard's presence in the manuscript places him in Kanoaka during 1949-50. The casualty list places Francard in Korea along the Pusan Perimeter during the breakout in October 1950.

BIO 5.2   13 JUL 1951 – INDEPENDENT JOURNAL –
            Regarding Marin County Social activities.

"High School Romance Results in Ishmael-Petosa Nuptials"

Delighted were the family members when the bride's [Andre Petosa] brother-in-law, Lt. Leroy Francard, just home from Korea, arrived in time to attend the reception. [Francard received his commission. -ed.]

BIO 5.3   UNDATED NEWSPAPER CLIPPING

Second Lt. Leroy J. Francard, 31, of Sausalito, will return home
after serving in Japan and Korea since March 1950. [Francard was
possibly born in 1919 and was twenty-two years old when the
United States entered World War II after Pearl Harbor. -ed.]

BIO 5.4   4 SEP 1954 – INDEPENDENT JOURNAL –
             Regarding matters of faith.

                 "Sausalito Bible School Closes"

As the Vacation Church School of Sausalito Presbyterian
Church closed August 27, twenty-one students received
certificates for perfect attendance. They include: ...Leroy
Francard. [An unidentified individual of the same name received
an award. -ed.]

BIO 5.5   14 JAN 2002 – BILL BOWLING EMAIL TO
             ROBERT HICKOX – Regarding a battle on Mount
             Fuji between Sgt Bowling and MSgt Francard.

I agree with you about Francard. I think most of the old timers
felt about him the way you and I did. When I got back to the
Company, he was an officer [field commission].
    I had a good fight with him on Mount Fuji.
    Williams and I were drunk in the village below Mount Fuji one
night. We were in a house with a couple of gals. In came Francard
and "Prince" D---. Do you remember D---? They told us the gals
were theirs. We agreed to leave. The room [where the girls were]
was on the second floor. I got to the stairs and stopped. I told
Williams we were here first. [He agreed.] So, we went to the room.
    I opened the sliding doors and told them I was here to stay.
Francard started talking. Then he led me to the stairway. I let him

because I knew he wanted to knock me down the stairs. When we got to the stairway, I knocked him down the stairs and went after him. Williams and D--- were at the bottom of the stairs [fighting].

D--- was Sergeant of the Guard that night and was wearing a .45. Francard hollered at D--- to shoot me. I heard D--- say (not loudly): "I can't he's choking me!" I looked around and saw Williams had D--- by the throat.

In came two MPs. If you remember, we had our own company MPs. One of them was Moose and the other was Dambrose. They broke it up and called a company truck. They loaded Williams and me on the truck and took us back up the mountain [to camp]. After the truck unloaded us, they turned around [to leave]. I jumped back on the truck and went back down into the village.

The next day I had to go to the Orderly Room for something. Lt Perry was the only one there. He asked me if I made a mistake last night. I said: "No, sir." He didn't say anything else.

Lt Perry must not have thought much of Francard. In my mind, Francard did not deserve a field commission. Oh hell, what's fair in war? Have a good night old friend.

BIO 5.6   13 AUG 2003 – ROBERT HICKOX EMAIL TO ROBERT YOUNG – Regarding his visit with war correspondent Maggie Higgins.

[MacArthur's War] covers several exploits of Maggie Higgins, the only female war correspondent in Korea. She was quite a gal. Spent one night early in the war while we were on Hill 303 sitting on the edge of my foxhole talking and taking notes while the North Koreans were shelling the shit out of us. She had a lot of guts. Went on to win a well-deserved Pulitzer Prize.

Maggie was there before any of us. She landed in Seoul the day after the North Koreans crossed the 38th. Quite a story.

EDITOR NOTES: Like Leroy Francard, whose story remains untold, the details of Maggie Smith's foxhole experience are lost.]

Harrison O Harper
Bio-6

Rank – CPL   MOS: 03-729   RA14283255
                              Oconee, SC

SERVICE: Japan Occupation Army
                  Korean War

OBITUARY

https://www.legacy.com/us/obituaries/thestate/name/harrison-
harper-obituary?id=14141889

HIGHLIGHTS

<u>BIO 6.1</u>   11 DEC 2002 – HARRISON HARPER
            HANDWRITTEN LETTER TO ROBERT HICKOX

Just a line to see how you were doing. I hope you are going to have a nice Christmas.

I have a five-year-old [grandson]. When anybody comes to see me, he will run and get the pen you sent me and say: "Look what papa's friend sent him!" …If I get a letter from you, he knows your name. "It's from Mr. Hickox." I am proud of him.

Did you make [Reno]? If you did, I bet you had a good time.

I've been sick for four months. Down in back. Old "Arthur Itis" [arthritis] got me. I have to go to the VA December 13.

…How is your wife and that pretty little daughter doing? I bet the daughter cannot wait for Christmas. Did you ever finish the book you were going to write?

Are you going to the Kentucky reunion next year? I am planning to go to the Kentucky reunion if I can get my brother to drive me. Doctor doesn't want me to drive on account of my heart.

Well, I never was much at writing letters. Have a very "Merry Christmas and a Happy New Year".

Robert H Hickox
Bio-7
"Little Prick From HQ"

Rank – PFC   MOS: 01-729   RA12284788
(several times)   Onondaga, NY

SERVICE: Japan Occupation Army
                              Korean War

Photo B-7a
Portrait – Centered Horizontally
(no caption)

LAST PHOTO—This is the last picture taken of Pfc. Robert Hickox before his capture last year.

HIGHLIGHTS

<u>BIO 7.1</u>   ROBERT HICKOX: A Combat Engineer Company operates a little differently than infantry. We worked in squad units, with a truck (deuce-and-a-half), and usually laid mines (AP and Tank), or blew bridges. In that type of work, a lighter weapon was

more useful because we always had our hands full of something else like mines, detonator cord, C-3, etc.

I was the squad machine gunner, I had a .50 mounted on the cab of the truck for blasting through roadblocks, and a light (air-cooled) .30 MG for when we were dug in somewhere. I was on the .30 the night we were overrun by the chinks. I went through about two-and-a-half boxes of ammo and had just sent my assistant gunner [Baby Face Buli] to get another box when I got orders to destroy the gun and move out.

BIO 7.2   3 MAY 2003 – ROBERT HICKOX EMAIL TO JIM BELCHER – Regarding the latest issue of Greybeard Magazine and Bob's encounter with an infamous North Korean Major allegedly nicknamed Tiger.

If you got the "Greybeard" magazine [March-April 2003, page 4, Tiger Survivors Story. -ed.], read the article by Shorty Estabrook under the President's page. It describes the conditions of the people who were taken POW in early July '50. Mostly 24th Division and civilians.

The Korean Major [Tiger] they refer to is the one who took over our group in Dec. '50 for our death march. He was a vicious little bastard. He was the one I tangled with. I think I told you before, way back when we used to write about such things, that one day during the march while we were resting, I called him [Tiger] a bastard and he heard me and slapped my face. At this point, I hauled off and slugged him. The other guys grabbed me. [Tiger] hit the ground and grabbed for his pistol. He had it halfway out of the holster when he got up but shoved it back in and strutted off. [I was lucky.] I figured he would shoot me for sure. And at that point, Jim, I really didn't give a damn. You get that way after a while.

EDITOR'S DISCUSSION POINT: Robert Hickox's working notes suggest that the Korean Major was known as Tiger because he fabricated tales of Siberian tiger attacks to keep POWs in line.

Q: Did the Siberian Tiger attack on the POW death march group [See 5.8] occur, or was the attack fabricated by North Korean guards to discourage prisoner escape? Was the North Korean Major nicknamed "Tiger" or was he simply known as "the tiger Major" – a phrase whose meaning got lost in translation and was later misunderstood by POW survivors? -ed.]

BIO-7.3   21 SEP 2001 – ROBERT HICKOX EMAIL TO ROBERT MCKINNEY – Regarding Harley Coons, president KWVA.

Hope you are doing ok. Shoulders feeling better? I went into the VA for an MRI on this arm. They were also having a thing at the VA called POW Recognition Day. Harley Coons was there and I got a chance to talk to him for a minute. I missed him when we were in D.C. He and I were in the same POW camp. We were both captured at the same time on 11/27/50. He didn't remember me, but I don't blame him all these years. Hell, I wouldn't recognize him either. He's not the skinny kid I knew in POW camp.

BIO 7.4   4 MAR 2002 – JIM SEIDEL EMAIL TO ROBERT HICKOX – Regarding Hill 303 and the battle of Masan.

I replaced Jim Belcher as Company Medic after he got wounded. I think it was late August 1950. I know we were near Masan on the Pusan Perimeter. Jim says he thinks you were wounded the same day I was on 4 Sep 1950. I was evacuated to Osaka with part of my left foot missing but was sent back to the 65th in late October.

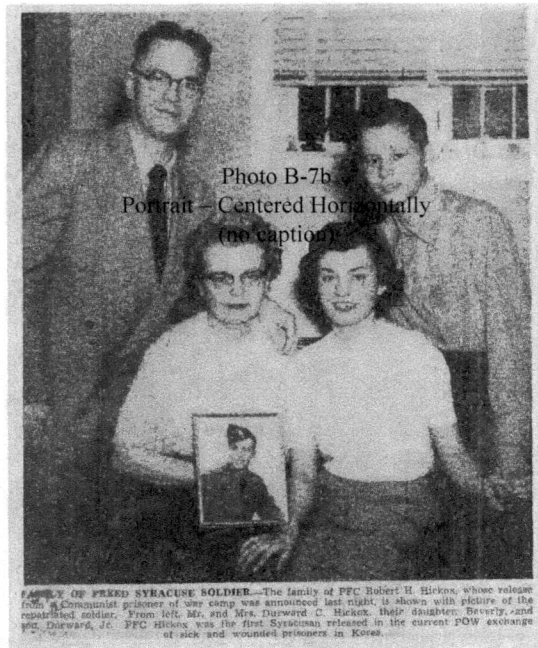

FAMILY OF FREED SYRACUSE SOLDIER.—The family of PFC Robert H. Hickox, whose release from a Communist prisoner of war camp was announced last night, is shown with picture of the repatriated soldier. From left, Mr. and Mrs. Durward C. Hickox, their daughter, Beverly, and son, Durward, Jr. PFC Hickox was the first Syracusan released in the current POW exchange of sick and wounded prisoners in Korea.

I remember telling the medic [Seidl?] *I didn't want any morphine. I told him to save it for himself. He'd need it before the night was over.*

- Robert Hickox

2 SEP 2002 – In reference to your question about your wound, I can only tell you …I [Jim Seidl] could have been the one that patched you up because I think I was the only aidman in the company at that time. I replaced Jim Belcher. I don't know of any other aidman being assigned to Company C. We took quite a few casualties during the 2-4 September period, including me on the 4th, so events aren't clear in my mind. They tell me the second thing to go in old age is your memory. I can't remember what the first thing is.

Robert Lee McKinney
Bio-8
"Mack"

Rank - SGT   MOS: 00-345   RA Unknown
                           Matoaka, WV

SERVICE: None (credited) – bad DD-214

VACATION TRAVEL: Korean Military Advisory Group KMAG
                           Japan Occupation Army
                           Korean War

NOTE: Later in life, Robert McKinney submitted a claim for health care services connected with injuries he suffered while in Korea. At that time, critical errors in his DD-214 (including no credited overseas FECOM activity) disqualified him from receiving the requested services. The men McKinney served with in Korea submitted affidavits detailing their contact with Robert.

STATEMENT IN SUPPORT OF A CLAIM (SUPPLEMENT TO VA FORM 21-4138) – ROBERT MCKINNEY

I [Robert Hickox] served with Mr. Robert McKinney in the United States Army from approximately April 1949 until November 1950, both in the Occupation of Japan and the Korean War.

We were assigned to C Company, 65th Engineer Combat Bn., 25th Infantry Div., Kanoaka Barracks, Osaka, Japan, until the start of the Korean War, June 25, 1950, at which time we were mobilized and sent directly to Korea, arriving there on or about the 5th-10th of July 1950.

Mr. McKinney and I were in the same squad, same unit as in Japan. He served as squad truck driver and I was assigned to the squad machine guns. We were in close contact at most times and were close friends.

As it got closer to fall and winter, the weather turned extremely cold, at times -20 to -30 below zero. Many of the men suffered severe frostbite due to the extreme temperatures and the fact we had not been issued any winter clothing.

On November 27, 1950, our Company, including Mr. McKinney, was overrun by the Chinese Communist Forces in the area of Ipsok, N. Korea, near the Chong'chon River. A few managed to escape, including Mr. McKinney. Others, including myself, were taken prisoner.

[Medical Details]

I CERTIFY THAT the statements on this page are true and correct to the best of my knowledge and belief.

Robert H. Hickox

OBITUARY

https://www.bailey-kirk.com/obituaries/Robert-McKinney,-1091/#!/Obituary

HIGHLIGHTS

BIO 8.1   27 JUN 2001 – ROBERT HICKOX EMAIL TO JIM
                 BELCHER – Regarding Robert McKinney's combat
                 account as it appeared in Graybeard magazine
                 January/February 2001, page 23.

HICKOX: He wrote about saving his whole squad and [I think] he should have gotten the Silver Star, at least, for that. But that asshole Lt. Wyman was another story.

He [Wyman] got us way the hell (about 12 miles) ahead of our lines and we got bushwacked by the gooks and pinned down from both sides. We were laying in rice paddies and stacking up dead gook bodies (from a firefight the day before) for cover from the incoming. We had to leave the [Engineer] truck sitting like a duck on the road [filled] with a couple of tons of high explosives and blasting caps, mines, the whole nine yards.

Bob made a dash for the truck with bullets tearing up the ground around him. He jumped in the truck, started it, and leaned out the door as he backed the thing up for at least a mile through a hail of bullets, mortar rounds, and you name it, to get back to our lines [so we could] get the big guns to open up and give some cover so we could get the hell out. I saw the two .50 caliber holes in the back of the driver's seat that would have hit him if he'd been sitting there [in the correct driving position -ed.] and the truck was shot to shit. But he made it and saved the whole squad's bucket that day.

A BOY GREW INTO A MAN
Graybeards Jan/Feb 2001
by Robert McKinney

EDITOR NOTES: McKinney summarized his six-year military career in the United States and Korea. He described his recovery of the engineer vehicle and driving backward through enemy fire:

"When we got to Korea, my platoon was ordered up to Yongdok on the east coast to clear a minefield. We came under a lot of small arms fire. Lt. Wyman told us to get out of the truck because it had about a ton of mines and explosives on it. We got in a rice paddy. Lt. Wyman told me to get in the truck and get it out of there. I got in and started the truck. I put it in reverse, pulled the throttle out and laid on the running board and backed out of the line of fire. I could see bullets hitting in the rice field. The truck was hit 42 times. I felt something splash on me. Later when I got back around a curve, I stopped to check myself. I was ok. A shell hit the right front fender and ricocheted and hit the fire extinguisher and blew it in half. There were two holes in the back of the seat where I would have been sitting. It looked like it was 50 cal. bullets. Lt. Wyman told me he was putting in for me a medal, but I never got it."

HICKOX: "How many holes did you say were in that truck? Fifty-nine? Man, it's a wonder they didn't hit them blasting caps or detonator wire. You'd have been just a big hole in the ground."

BIO 8.2   7 MAR 2002 – ROBERT MCKINNEY EMAIL TO
             ALL – Regarding a bridge built over the Han River.

Hi, everyone. On this day, March 7, 1951, we were ordered to
build a footbridge across the Han River about 40 miles east of Seoul
so the 25th could cross. I'm sure Bill and DK remember. It snowed
the night before, about four inches, and the ground was white. They
called in airstrikes on the mountain north of the river. There were
spots all over the mountain where napalm and rockets had hit. The
south side was flat and open with sand. No trees, nothing. The river
was swift. Every time we got a footbridge across, the current would
wash it out or the gooks would destroy it with mortars. Private
Fletcher took a direct hit and was killed. I don't remember if we had
wounded, but it was a rough day. We did get the bridges across.
God had to be with us that day.

BIO 8.3   27 SEP 2001 – ROBERT HICKOX EMAIL TO
             ROBERT MCKINNEY – Regarding POW torture.

I got the greatest pleasure talking to those two Air Force guys
down in D.C. you introduced me to at the bar. I've seen so much
crap about training men to be POWs. I saw the training films and
did nothing but laugh. You can't train men to be POWs. Not unless
you can beat them up, or shoot them, or starve them to death, along
with a million other tricks. The trouble with "training", as I told
them, is when the Sun comes up, you take a shower, put on a clean
uniform, and walk out the door – something the enemy [forbids].

BIO 8.4   13 MAY 2002 – ROBERT MCKINNEY EMAIL TO
             ROBERT HICKOX – Regarding local flooding.

I am back online again. We had another flood. This time, the
phone company was underwater. Thanks, guys, for the letters you
sent to the VA. I got $19,620 back pay and I will get $790 a month
until ??? Thanks again old pal.

Duane K Morgan
Bio-9

Rank - CPL   MOS: Unavailable   RA Unavailable

SERVICE: Japan Occupation Army
                Korean War

Photo B-9
Portrait – Centered
CAPTION: Duane K Morgan]

OBITUARY
https://www.koreanwar.org/html/units/65en.htm
Page 2 – Entry 56674
Page 3 – Entry 33844

HIGHLIGHTS

BIO 9.1   22 SEP 2001 – EMAIL EXCHANGE BETWEEN
            DUANE MORGAN AND ROBERT HICKOX –
            Regarding POW Recognition Day and Osama Bin
            Laden.

MORGAN: Just writing a note to recognize you on this POW
Recognition Day. Hope all is well. Just got back from Fire Camp
down at Oroville and have been working nonstop because my
[employer] is shorthanded. I haven't had a day off in eighteen days,
so I am behind on everything. It would be nice to be younger – I
would like to have a lick at Bin Laden. It is so sad for all those
people and families. Anyhow, got to get to work tonight. Talk again
soon. [I got] the version of "Are You Lonesome Tonight?" [you sent
me]. Thanks. Take Care.

HICKOX: Thanks for the thought on POW/MIA Recognition
Day, Duane. You and your wonderful daughter, Becky, were the
only ones who noted it. God Bless.

BIO 9.2   20 APR 2001 – EMAIL EXCHANGE BETWEEN
            DUANE MORGAN AND ROBERT HICKOX –
            Regarding combat along the Pusan Perimeter during
            September 1950.

MORGAN: Engineer Ridge was on the way to Old Baldy. It was
our first hill, the one where Saloway got killed. We went to Old
Baldy after. If you remember – the gooks [ours] with their A-frame
packs carried our ammo and supplies to the top of Old Baldy where
we spent 28 days under attack [nearly] every morning from 3-6 AM.

HICKOX: I know why I don't remember Old Baldy. If Engineer
Ridge is the hill where Saloway was killed, that was the hill I was
hit on and would have spent the time [you were] on Old Baldy in a

hospital in Kobe, Japan. I was shot at the same time, within seconds I guess, of the time Chief was. That's what they told me when I got back in early November '50 – just in time for Thanksgiving and the chinks. Just as glad I missed that one [Old Baldy].

BIO 9.3   26 MAR 2001 – EMAIL EXCHANGE BETWEEN DUANE MORGAN AND ROBERT HICKOX – Regarding Kanoaka Barracks and Lightning University.

MORGAN: Happy Birthday. You have the same birthday as my father-in-law. I will be 70 in July.

I think you are the one who mentioned Lightning University. I remember that [school] well. I spent 28 days there as Prisoner #28 for sleeping on guard in the day room in the middle of the morning in Company C Barracks. Caught by the OD. He was on his way to check B Company next door. [SHORT VERSION: Alcohol may have been involved. The OD removed Duane's boots and socks before waking him up. – ed.]

HICKOX: So, the OD caught you taking a little snooze, huh? Seems like pretty stiff punishment for an in-barracks infraction…

BIO 9.4   24 MAR 2001 – DUANE MORGAN EMAIL TO ROBERT HICKOX – Describing a Kunu-ri firefight from Morgan's perspective.

When the [North Korean] attack hit, we could see 1st and 2nd Platoons firing weapons from behind mounds of [bodies]. The 3rd Platoon ran off the hill [by order]. Every man for himself. Some without weapons, some without clothing. [I was in my sleeping bag.] When daylight broke…we retreated south, fighting through five miles of roadblocks. Vehicle after vehicle blown off the road by mortars. We had to keep moving. They say nobody got left behind, but I say that's bullshit.

"Chief" Aldin B Saloway
Bio-10

Rank - PFC   MOS: 05-729   RA19308014
                    Blackfeet Reservation MT

SERVICE: Korean Military Advisory Group (KMAG)
                    Japan Occupation Army
                    Korean War

HIGHLIGHTS

BIO 10.1   KOREAN WAR PROJECT
            https://www.koreanwar.org/

Comments: Per David Pepion: Alden "Buddy" Saloway was of
mixed heritage. He was White, Metis, French, Blackfeet,
Chippewa-Cree. He was an enrolled member of the Blackfeet Tribe
of Montana, USA. His father's name was Archie Salois (Metis:
Chippewa-Cree) and his mother's name was Lizzie Bullshoe
(Blackfeet). He was orphaned at the age of five and was adopted
and raised by his paternal uncle, Gabriel Saloway (Salois), Jr. and
aunt, Sarah Saloway.

ROBERT HICKOX GUEST BOOK ENTRY
KOREAN WAR PROJECT

Chief, I knew you well. Thanks from the bottom of my heart for
saving my life on that stinking hill. I never got the chance before, it
all happened so quick.

I knew Aldin well. We served together for over a year in Japan
at the 65th Engr Combat Bn at Kanoaka, a small town near Osaka.
We all called him 'Chief' and he was one hell of a guy. I guess the
best way to put it is he just wasn't a garrison soldier. Hard to
discipline and wild as a colt. Seemed like he was always in some
kind of trouble. I guess he even spent a little time in Lightning

University, but he was a great friend. During this period, I was his Company Clerk and got used to seeing his name on my morning report quite often.

Then we got the word that Korea had happened and we were one of the first units to be shipped over. Because of the way our squads were split up I lost track of Chief for a while but when things began to get tight around the perimeter, we were put into infantry duty and Aldin and I were designated foxhole buddies. We climbed a zillion hills together and dug a zillion foxholes together. He was the bravest man I have ever personally known and I was in the company of a lot of them in Korea.

Right in the middle of the fiercest battles, grenades exploding and bullets flying all over the place I'd look up from the foxhole and there was Chief standing on edge bigger than all get out. I'd holler "Chief, get the hell down here! You're going to get yourself killed." He just laughed at me and said "How am I supposed to hit them if I can't see them?" And he'd stand there blasting away at the enemy like a walk in the park. He was completely fearless.

Then came Sept. 2, 1950. It was raining and miserable out and we got orders that afternoon we had to take and secure a hill before nightfall. We marched for what seemed an eternity along a dirt road and suddenly saw this mountain looming before us. We were all dead tired from constant combat and the miles of marching. Cold, wet, and slightly disgruntled, we took the orders and attacked the hill. It was supposed to be lightly defended. I was on right point and Aldin was on my left. I couldn't see him because of the foliage but I knew he there. Suddenly, all hell broke loose and enemy fire was pouring on us from everywhere. I looked up and suddenly saw this bush move but before I could respond this gook cut loose on me with a burp gun and he nailed me across the legs and I was spun around and laying flat out on the ground on my stomach facing downhill. My rifle had been knocked out of my hands and I could still hear that burp gun blasting away. I knew he was going to make another pass at me and would, because of my position, probably cut me in two. Then, just as suddenly as he had started firing at me the firing stopped. I crawled part way down the hill until I ran into some of the other guys and I was then taken down the hill, patched up as best they could, put on the back of a jeep and on to Pusan and hospital in Japan.

Toward the end of October, I returned to the outfit. When I got back to the squad, I was anxious to see Chief. When I asked his whereabouts, I was told what had happened. It seems when the gook opened fire on me on that hill Aldin saw him and immediately dispatched him, which was why fire had stopped so abruptly. However, as I was told, when he exposed himself to get my gook he was hit and mortally wounded with one shot through the heart. I have been all these years trying to find a place to list a tribute to the brave man that saved my life. He was a good soldier, a fine man, and a good friend. Rest in Peace old friend.

Bob "Hick" Hickox, 2 April 10, 1999.

***

One night the gooks put a mortar or rocket into a tree right behind where Chief [Saloway] *and I had our foxhole. Blew the tree all to pieces. Chief and I crouched in our hole for a few minutes listening to* [our buddies offer] *our obits.*

"I hate to rain on your parade," I said, "but we're alive!"

- Robert Hickox

BIO 10.2   24 NOV 2001 – EMAIL FROM ROBERT HICKOX TO JIM BELCHER – Regarding Chief's legendary court-martial.

Bill Bowling told me Saloway was in Korea with him and Mac. He told me how Saloway got a General Court-Martial for sluggin' a Colonel with a rifle butt. According to Bill, the Colonel snuck up on Chief when he was on guard duty and hollered "Gotcha!" At that point, ole Saloway swung around and nailed the Colonel. When the Colonel pressed charges, the court threw it out and told the Colonel he was lucky to be alive. I'm afraid I would have shot the SOB.

Michael A Shaughnessy
Bio-11

Rank: Captain   MOS: 02-110   O-2011055
                                St Louis, MO

SERVICE: AUS – World War II
                Japan Occupation Army
                Korean War
                Viet Nam

Photo B-11
Landscape – Centered
CAPTION (below)

1 December 1950 – in the Korean "wilderness"

OBITUARY
https://www.koreanwar.org/html/units/65en.htm
Page 2 - Entry # 54761

HIGHLIGHTS

SHAUGHNESSY FAMILY SAYING: "What does that have to do
with the situation in the Far East?" – per Patrick Shaughnessy.

BIO 11.1   18 APR 2004 PATRICK SHAUGHNESSY EMAIL
            TO ROBERT HICKOX – Regarding service history
            for his father Michael A. Shaughnessy.

...the 66th moved to England in November of 1944 and onto the
continent on Christmas Eve 1944. The 66th Division took over the
94th Division's mission of containing the enemy in the vicinity of
Lorient and St. Nazaire, France. There were about 50,000 Germans
bypassed in two pockets defending their submarine pens. Actions
in this area were confined to patrolling and artillery duels.

The last time I was at the archives, I looked at his company's
morning reports. Here is a typical entry for 31 March 1945:
"Caudan, France – Heavy enemy artillery fire, approximately 150
rounds in the company area. One EM [enlisted man] wounded." I
remember Dad saying how impressed he was with the Germans as
soldiers and with the [German] positions he examined after the
surrender. Their firing positions were complete with landscape
drawings with tactical annotations. I'm sure he was glad that their
mission was to keep [the Germans] bottled up and not to try to
remove them!

BIO 11.2   MICHAEL A. SHAUGHNESSY SERVICE
            RECORD – Excerpted from Prolegomena to a Life:
            A Work in Progress by Patrick J. Shaughnessy.

My father, Michael A. Shaughnessy, was adjutant of the 65th
Engineer Combat Battalion and was in Korea from July 1950 to
March 1951. He died in 1980.

He earned a battlefield commission in France in 1945 and
received an Honorable Discharge at the "convenience of the
government per Par 3a AR 615-365". After the war, in March of
1946 he was separated per "A70 RR 1-5" but had an appointment
in the Officer Reserve Corps. After he married my mother, Dorothy
C. Kelly, in January 1948, he went back into the Army as his career.
My parents left for Japan after that.

In March 1948, Michael Shaughnessy arrived in Japan and was assigned to 25th Infantry Division, Kanaoka Barracks, and served as Adjutant, Athletic & Recreation Officer, and Special Service Officer. Two children, Patricia Ann and Michael Allen, were born while the Shaughnessy family resided in Japan.

During the Korean War, Captain Shaughnessy served with Headquarters, 65th Engineer Combat Battalion during the Battle of Pusan Perimeter and the United Nations Force drive to the Yalu River. During March 1951, Captain Shaughnessy was transferred back to Japan.

In December of 1962, he was "Relieved from Active Duty per Section V, AR 135-173, SPN 617, Maximum Service – Commissioned Officers". He was a Major at the time. His promotion to Lt. Colonel wouldn't be effective until October 1963 because his time served in a temporary AUS wasn't credited correctly. In order to solve his problem, my father reenlisted in his permanent grade E6 for ten months.

He retired on 31 October 1963 per Title 10 USC 3911, SPN 567 Retirement after 20 years but less than 30 years active Federal Service.

I [got] a copy of my father's service record because he reenlisted in 1963. This action moved his WWII record to a [Federal Records storage area] that survived the "Great Fire of 1973" in St. Louis which destroyed eighty percent of Army enlisted personnel files for individuals discharged November 1, 1912 to January 1, 1960.

***

One night, we got pretty "buzzed". We went over to HQ and... borrowed a couple of uniforms. I took Lt Cameron's uniform. My buddy took Lt Shaughnessy's [the Battalion Adjutant]. *We* [went] *...into the town of Kanaoka and pulled "bed check" on all the guys shacking up.*

- Robert Hickox

BIO 11.3   16 SEP 2001 – JIM COLLINS HANDWRITTEN
            LETTER TO ROBERT HICKOX – Regarding B
            Company and Michael Shaughnessy (excerpt).

Dear Bob,
        …the only person from the 65th that I have seen or heard from
was Mike Shaughnessy. We had a couple of beers together in
Saigon in 1959. He was a great person.
    [2nd Lt] Shorty Cameron I knew real well from Kanoaka
barracks. He was really a class guy. I also knew Tony Pecoraro who
was in C Company. We were so fully engaged all the time in Korea
that I never saw C Company or any of its people. In fact, I only saw
the [65th] Bn Commander twice all the time I was over there.
    I didn't get to know people in the other companies, but I thought
the people in Company B were the greatest group of men ever
assembled. I have great respect for every man in the unit.
    Time has taken its toll on me also. I was at Omaha Beach at "H"
Hour and the action in Korea is beginning to show.
    After C Company was hit up near the Yalu River, we were
attached to the 35th Infantry who was the covering force all the way
down to the Imjim River. We blew all the bridges from [Anjou?]
down to Seoul. We didn't have as many explosives as we wanted,
but we damaged all the railroad bridges as much as we could.
                                                    Jim Collins

BIO 11.4   22 SEP 2001 – PATRICK SHAUGHNESSY EMAIL
            TO ROBERT HICKOX – General conversation.

    Thank you for the information about Dad. I look forward to
reading the letter and writing to Major Collins. Dad was in Vietnam
for a year. March 1958 to March 1959. He was with the Military
Assistance Advisory Group in Saigon.
    I managed to get a photograph Dad brought back with him that
was taken on Christmas Eve 1958 published on the last page of the
December 1996 American Heritage Magazine.

"Wimpy" Harold E Soyars
Bio-12

Rank - Unknown   MOS: Unknown   RA Unknown

SERVICE: Japan Occupation Army
                  Korean War

OBITUARY
https://www.legacy.com/us/obituaries/godanriver/name/harold-soyars-obituary?id=28585088

HIGHLIGHTS

BIO 12.1   15 APR 2003 – EMAIL EXCHANGE BETWEEN HAROLD SOYARS AND ROBERT HICKOX – Regarding the officially "informal" Battalion Crest for 65th Engineer C Combat Battalion.

SOYARS: I will get Mary some seeds off in a day or so. The seeds need to be planted so the vine can grow up on something like a trellis or fence or pole or something. It has a sorta lacy looking foliage and red trumpet bloom (which is not very big). I don't have a picture of it.

.....yes, I do. I just remembered I took a picture of my vine last year. I'll send you the picture when I send the seeds and you can send it back to me.

Any luck with the crest?

HICKOX: No, I haven't got any farther with the crest. The problem is I have three different versions, basically the same but with different colors. I am trying to find out which one is which. I know the one you sent a picture of is the correct one, but the others are the same with different color combinations. I don't want to get them made up until I'm absolutely sure of the colors.

SOYARS: We planted about 20 tomato plants and 18 pepper plants before I fell. [Long story. I had a stroke. I had to get fifteen staples in my head.] I wanted to wait until I got another copy of the vine picture before I sent it to Mary. I will send her one plant when it gets warm so the frost will not kill it.

HICKOX: Mary says to tell you the bird seed you sent never came up, but the tomatoes are crawling along.

TWO MONTHS LATER

SOYARS: I have the old crest. It has a dozer and lightning strike down the middle. I talked to Lt. Grossman of the Military Matters. He says it takes some time to make up a metal crest. He will make them [for us], but he suggested [a cap with a crest] and our unit, rank, name, and [service dates]. Something like that. This will all be on the back of the cap. The crest will be on the front. How would that be? I can get these done before the reunion after I find out who all wants them. [I can get pins too.] Let me know, Bob.

BIO 12.2   24 DEC 2000 - UNIDENTIFIED NEWSPAPER
             CLIPPING – Regarding philanthropy displayed by the
             Soyars family.

Santa Comes To Westover Area
(image unavailable)

CAPTION: Saint Nick arrives on Shumate Street not by sleigh but by lawnmower to pass out gifts to the neighborhood.

Harold "Wimpy" Soyars plays the part of Santa Claus on Shumate Street Saturday riding his lawnmower around the street to deliver boxes…

"Wimpy" Harold Soyars (left) wearing the coveted crest on his cap.
Unidentified man (right).

Wimpy said I gave him my rifle [with KITTEN written on it in big yellow letters] after I was wounded on 2 September 1950 because his M-1 was jammed with Cosmoline and I didn't need mine.

- Robert Hickox

Leonard Deen Stamper
Bio-13
"Stumpy"

Rank - PFC   MOS: 00-078   RA18322835
                    McLennan, TX

SERVICE: Japan Occupation Army
                    Korean War

OBITUARY
https://www.legacy.com/us/obituaries/wacotrib/name/leonard-
stamper-obituary?id=21253912

HIGHLIGHTS

<u>BIO-13.1</u>   ARRIVAL AT PUSAN, JULY 1950 – Described from
                "Stumpy's" perspective.

In June 1950, we were on maneuvers at a base close to Yokosuka
Naval Base. We had Marines teach us how to climb down the side
of a ship. We went out and hit a beach in the afternoon. Rainy and
cold. The ship we were on was the U.S.S. Union.

The next day we were on the ship when we were told to go to
our quarters. They tuned in the radio to the North Korean
[broadcast] at Seoul airport. We went back to Kanoaka to get ready
to go south. We packed all our stuff to ship home and were outfitted
for war.

We were sent to Camp "Nowhere" on the south side of Japan.
While we were there, we blew up a bridge that was on the base
around the 1st of July 1950. All but one squad was sent on an LST
to Korea. There were 10 or 15 left to unload incoming trains
carrying tanks, trucks, etc. We stayed there until the 3rd of July and
then we loaded on an LST and went to Korea.

On ship all night long until the next day. We landed in Pusan.
Don't know what outfit we were with, but road [march] all day and

half the night. We were in a riverbed. The next morning, my 1st Sgt woke us up and we rejoined the Company. As I remember, we went to Taegu. For a while, we were under a bridge. Don't remember the name. We went from there to Taegon and then to Masan. We were in a schoolyard there.

"Bed-check-Charlie" [sniper] came in for about a week until the Marines fired on him a couple of nights. The Marines moved about 10 miles north of us. One day they turned a truck over in a rice paddy and we got their beer. We got a beer ration – three cans of hot beer. We left there and went north again around the 1st of September 1950.

We were in a firefight. The BAR man (Moose) took a wounded man to the medic station. He took my M-1 and I took his BAR. He came back on the 3rd of September. He had lost my M-1, so I gave him the BAR back. [and had nothing.] That was on a Sunday.

Lt. Pecoraro told us that the infantry had been kicked off the hills on each side of us. He made a little speech. He said: "All right you engineers, we are going to take this hill!" [See Alfred Thistle comment, Hickox memoir 16.10 -ed.] Then he called for air support. Sent four Corsairs [WWII – Voight F4U] from the [USS] Boxer [CV-21]. We had to tell them to quit – they were close to us.

It started raining. Very cold and wet. We dug in and took several rounds by mortar. The boy in the foxhole with me was only in the Army for five months. Been with us only 5 days. Seems like the Company had split up as not too many on top of the hill.

Rained all night and about daybreak the next morning, 4 September 1950, took several mortar rounds. One hit in front of the foxhole I was in. Killed the boy with me and I was hit in the right hand. Medics and Akers (who was also hit) pulled me up behind some rocks. My leg was hurting by then. I was also hit in the left leg, knee, and thigh. They took me off the hill on a stretcher about 9 or 10 a.m.

I was taken to a field hospital and operated on that night. The next day, Billy Agee was there. He did not know anything about the rest of the Company. I remember Akers with his head and mouth in bandages. I was sent to Japan and then to the States. Landed in the

States on 15th September 1950. I spent 13 months and 25 days in the Hospital.

Got to our Company in Japan in March 1950. I was 5' 8" tall and 150 pounds. I was small. Some of the guys used to tickle me. They would hold me down to do this. I remember the lake [probably a rain-filled excavation crater or retention pond. -ed.] behind the barracks at Kanoaka. When the tide was out, I could see the "Boom of Dragline" [a large earth excavating machine]. Do not remember what platoon I was in, but I was upstairs, across from the Orderly Room (which was downstairs). We got two new 2nd Lts, who were on the same ship I came over on. Will try to remember more later.

Thanks
Stamper

P.S.   I was in a group all promoted at the same time. We all got a stripe up, but one man. He was a PVT. The rest of the PVTs were promoted to PFC in Korea in late July or August 1950.

My nickname was Spider.

***

I told Stumpy he should plan on making the reunion this year [in Reno], *if possible. He said he can't plan that far ahead at his age. He says he won't even buy green bananas...*

- Robert Hickox

Alfred David Thistle
Bio-14

Rank - SFC   MOS: 00-572   RA31510248
                    Middlesex, MA

SERVICE: Korean Military Advisory Group (KMAG)
                    Japan Occupation Army
                    Korean War

QUOTE: "Time is flying and I don't have wings."

OBITUARY

https://www.chesmorefuneralhome.com/obituaries/alfred-david-
thistle/18508/

HIGHLIGHTS

BIO-14.1   27 MAY 2002 – ALFRED THISTLE EMAIL TO
            ROBERT HICKOX AND GROUP – Regarding best
            wishes for all.

Stand tall, do not bend. You all did your share. You all made it back for one reason or another. Who knows? Not I. I am pleased and proud to know you all.

We may have been called upon during a forgotten time, but we will not forget each other. I thank each one of you for the part you played in my life. I won't forget moments I choose to remember. There are blanks, but I listen and ask. Some answers I hear, others I don't.

Mac, you are special to me. Robert, you gave me another answer. You didn't follow me [that night], but somebody guided you. Jim, they sent you out early – no answer for that. Bill, your turn to remember and share your answer. Harp has his life and answers also. Kenoian, the Arab, has his answers under lock and key.

The new friends we have met [at the reunions] will have the thoughts and answers we all need. Say a prayer for each other.

BIO-14.2   1 MAR 2002 – ALFRED THISTLE EMAIL TO ROBERT HICKOX – Regarding reconstructing officer service histories.

Check out your search engine Class of '50 West Point. You may find all the officers in question. I was in Korea 46 to 48 [KMAG] and I did not find the life so good. It was a shit hole. By the time we moved into livable quarters, it was time to rotate back to the States. I won't say I'll never go back there, but if it is at all possible, I'll stay away.

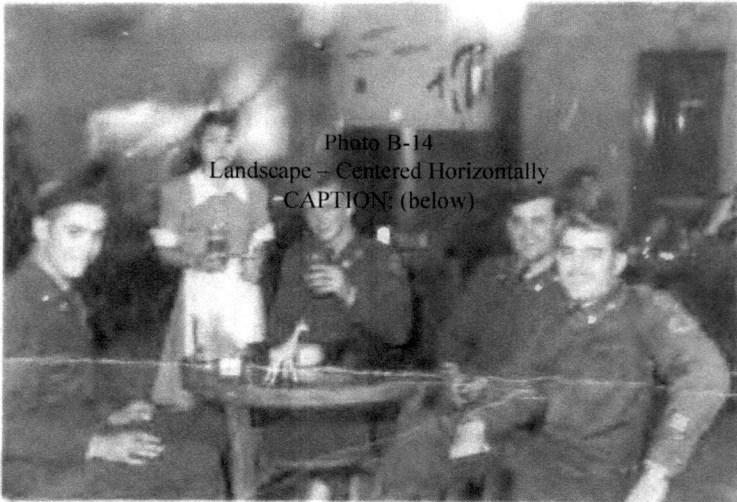

? THISTLE   FRYE   KING

"It was taken in '50 right after Frye and I [Thistle] made staff."

BIO-14.3   10 NOV 2002 – HANDWRITTEN LETTER FROM
             ALFRED THISTLE TO ROBERT HICKOX –
             Regarding Garabed Kenoian, Bob's "little Arab
             buddy".

Here are some pics that the Arab had. I went down to see him
last week. He looked good and had a better memory than when I
saw him in 1950-51. His sister Sally was with him. He wants to live
alone and gets along well. He attends functions at the VFW and
drives around in his own car.

They had to remove the plate he had in his head. It became
infected. ...He doesn't remember much about what happened to
him [in Korea]. Probably the best thing for him.

Hope you can scan these [pics and send them] on to the others. I
would like them back so I can return them to [Garabed]. He was
with the 1st Cav before he came to us.

BIO 14.4   21 NOV 2001 – HANDWRITTEN LETTER FROM
             ALFRED THISTLE TO ROBERT HICKOX -
             Regarding the 65th Engr Cbt Bn Crest.

Another good day and bad day. I got shot down on removing the
stent. Draining too much fluid.

Anyway, I got more info from [Lawrence] Donovan and thought
you could use it in your book. Do you remember what the battalion
motto was back in '49 and '50? I've been trying to find a color pic
so I could look at the pins, but no luck.

This pic [from Donovan] was taken in 1953. No word on if they
were all POWs. Any name sound familiar to you?

...Hope you all didn't eat too much [sic]. Full stomachs can hurt.
A bigger and better day is coming. Megan [Hickox] will like it a lot
better. Just thought maybe this is some help in your quest for
[accurate] history.

Take care, be good. Don't forget the reunion in Reno.

Robert Donald Ivison
Bio-15

Rank – PFC   MOS: Unknown   RA12284786
                              Onondaga, NY

SERVICE: Japan Occupation Army
                              Korean War

HIGHLIGHTS

BIO 15.1   JUN 2020 – INTERVIEW WITH MARY HICKOX

Q: How did Bob describe the wound that led to him
             receiving his second Purple Heart?

MARY: Bob said: "Fighting was bad. Tracers were flying all
             over the goddamn place. We were firing at anything that
             moved. I saw one gook that I was homing in on. Out of
             nowhere, this [other] little gook bastard jumps up, fires,
             and I feel my leg explode. I turned and mowed the little
             bastard down. I yelled for a medic. Everything got quiet.
             I woke up in the hospital thinking this is my ticket home.
             But I couldn't leave the guys. I couldn't leave Bob
             [Ivison] there. I had to go back."

BIO 15.2   11 MAY 2002 – ROBERT HICKOX EMAIL TO
             BILL BOWLING – Regarding the death of Bob
             Ivison.

I was looking through some copies of old newspapers I received
from a friend's sister. [Bob Ivison] was with the 35th and was killed
in May '51. Awarded the DSC [Distinguished Service Cross].

After I was reported missing/KIA, he volunteered for a line company (he had been driving a jeep for the CO) "to get even for me". He had come over to the company (ours) and asked what happened to me. One person said I was missing, another said they saw me shot, and another told him I had been overrun, shot, and bayonetted. This was all in the newspaper article. As I sat there reading it, I felt like I was reading my obituary from fifty years ago.

Weird! Anyway, he went out to get even for me. He singlehandedly wiped out an MG nest and killed a bunch of gooks before they killed him. He's buried not too far from us and I go to the cemetery a couple of times a year. He was only nineteen when he was killed. Dumb kid.

BIO 15.3   KOREAN WAR PROJECT – REMEMBRANCE ENTRY 29617 – ROBERT D IVISON – CONTRIBUTED BY PATRICK SHAUGHNESSY

Remembering PFC Robert Donald Ivison United States Army
E CO 2 BN 35th Infantry Regiment - DSC Citation

The President of the United States takes pride in presenting the Distinguished Service Cross (Posthumously) to Robert Donald Ivison (RA12284786), Private First Class, U.S. Army, for extraordinary heroism in connection with military operations against an armed enemy of the United Nations while serving with Company E, 2d Battalion, 35th Infantry Regiment, 25th Infantry Division.

Private First Class Ivison distinguished himself by extraordinary heroism in action against enemy aggressor forces in the vicinity of Chonjo-ri, Korea, on 20 May 1951. On that date, Private Ivison's company was given the mission of attacking and securing the position of a well-entrenched and fanatically determined enemy force holding Hill 198. Moving in a frontal assault up the hill, the unit was pinned down by intense and accurate enemy small-arms and automatic weapons fire. As the enemy began to roll grenades down among the group, Private Ivison, observing that both the platoon leader and platoon sergeant had been wounded, realized that his comrades must move from their precarious position on the slope or face annihilation. Jumping up from his position, he rushed through the accurate, point-blank enemy fire toward a hostile machine-gun emplacement, shouting words of encouragement to his comrades and urging them forward. With his automatic rifle, he killed the two enemy machine gunners and, although mortally wounded in his charge up the hill, he continued to fire at the now retreating enemy. His actions so inspired his comrades that they charged up the slope, routing the enemy from their position.

Headquarters, Eighth U.S. Army, Korea: General Orders No. 615 (August 5, 1951)

BIO 15.4   EIGHTH UNITED STATES ARMY COMBAT INFORMATION BULLETIN #1 (declassified) – Describing North Korean infantry tactics.

EDITOR NOTES: This excerpt helps a reader envision obstacles faced by Robert Ivison and fellow infantrymen when in combat.

Infantry Tactics – Division tactics include a frontal attack with a strong flanking movement supported by artillery and tanks. The unit attacking frontally is widely dispersed and keeps up heavy fire while flanking elements [maneuver]. Reports indicate that enemy infantry will infiltrate our line disguised as refugees in civilian clothing carrying disassembled firearms and uniforms in bundles. …Infantry moves toward our lines disguised as farmers whose dress is predominantly white. Women and children often accompany these groups. When they reach a point adjacent to and behind friendly lines, they assemble their weapons.

Weapons carried by disguised infiltrating elements are rifles, .30 cal machine guns, mortars, and grenades. Upon a given signal, fire is directed from ridges upon friendly flanks and rear, forcing friendly forces to retire. …The enemy usually had sufficient time to determine very accurately the route of withdrawal [MSR] and placed his automatic weapons and heavy weapons accordingly.

> *Women had machine guns strapped to their backs in a manner that made it look like they were carrying a baby. When they were within killing range of US troops, they dropped to their [hands and] knees and two TEENAGERS dropped with [her] and manned the machine gun [while it was on her back]. Women and children carried grenades and USED THEM.*
> *- public electronic message board*

In an attack, a group of eight or ten enemy will raise their hands as if to surrender. When fire is lifted and friendly personnel move out to accept these prisoners, a company-sized enemy force will launch an attack from concealed positions. While friendly forces concentrate fire on this group, another enemy force is sent around the flanks.

Guerillas – North Korean soldiers are coming through our lines as refugees, securing arms and uniforms behind our lines. Guerilla units are well-trained in demolition work and carry 800 grams (1.75 lbs) of TNT each. They travel on foot and are armed with American BARs, M-1 rifles, water-cooled machine guns, and Japanese rifles.

> *At 0045 hours, Company B, 1st Battalion 35th Infantry Regiment, reported they were under heavy attack and that two tanks attached to them from Company B 89th Medium Tank Battalion had been knocked out by enemy bazooka fire and satchel charges. The enemy held the satchel charges against the tanks and died in the explosion.*
> *- 89th Mdm Tank Battalion History*

Refugees – In one case, a group of approximately 200 refugees consisting of women, children, and old men walked into the battle position from the direction of the enemy. They proceeded through the battle position creating confusion as our forces rounded them up for processing. At this time, the enemy launched a frontal attack, the lead elements mingling with the stragglers of the refugee group. The refugees had no weapons or uniforms, and upon interrogation, revealed that they were directed by the North Koreans to proceed in the direction taken.

One [U.S.] dawn patrol surprised a group of North Korean soldiers eating in a village. This patrol captured two bundles. Each bundle contained a complete change of clothing (farmer white) and a package of money (approximately 5,000 S.K.Won). Military equipment, hand grenades, and small arms were found in the area.

> *In July '50, we got ambushed at night outside Taegu and nearly overrun by civilians. Even women and children would carry burp guns, machine guns, and mortars. It got so bad [that when] we were [being pushed into the sea along] the Pusan Perimeter, we had no choice but to eliminate the [civilian] danger. We received these orders from [General Walton] Walker's HQ.*
>
> *- Robert Hickox*

LESSONS LEARNED
1. Defensive Tactics – Defensive positions MUST have depth. Linear defense so far has proved unsatisfactory. Refugees must be forcibly denied and sent back toward enemy lines. During withdrawal, a move of at least 5000 yards is needed to give sufficient time for reorganization reconnaissance and reoccupation.
2. Security – Infiltration methods used by North Korean troops are effective. Friendly personnel should be well dug in and prepared to fire in ANY direction. The defense plan must be complete and wired in.
3. Planning – All positions must be carefully selected. An example of poor judgment is reflected in the selection of infantry positions at the base of a vertical stone cliff where enemy artillery and mortar fire against the cliff could

reduce the positions. Precautions must be taken to evacuate both personnel and equipment. In one instance, an abandoned U.S. M-24 tank, recovered and used by the enemy, was destroyed in a different sector.

4. Tactical Air Support – Priority of targets in the area, method of control, and directional landmarks MUST be predetermined. Too much time is wasted by requesting aircraft to orbit while details are being calculated. This responsibility belongs to the unit CO and not the TACP.

5. Artillery – A positive system of communication must be established between G3 Air at Division, TACPs, and Division artillery. In many cases, aircraft have failed to locate lucrative targets which could have been marked by artillery fire had such communication and coordination existed. G-3 should evaluate requests for airstrikes prior to submission to JOC. With limited airstrike capability, air effort is wasted or misused on targets such as a "battery of artillery" that turned out to be a mortar position within artillery range or a "concentration of troops" that turned out to be a squad.

6. Commo – To establish better control and communication between ground elements and Liaison and Tactical Air Control Aircraft, the following modifications are authorized for SCR 300 radio networks...

...The above installation increases the range of the SCR 300 from 3 miles to an effective range of 40-60 miles depending on terrain and weather.

DECLASSIFIED BY AUTHORITY OF: Tago 830584
ON: 24 May 1983
BY: Smith (Vetock 2/25/98)

Robert LaForrest Young
Bio-16

Rank - CPL   MOS: 04745   RA 11188480

SERVICE: Japan Occupation Army
                  Korean War

Photo B-16
Portrait – centered
(no caption)

OBITUARY
https://www.bchfh.com/memorials/Young-
Robert/1046228/obituary.php

HIGHLIGHTS

<u>BIO 16.1</u>   9 NOV 2000 – ROB YOUNG EMAIL TO ROBERT
HICKOX – regarding service history.

I sure was there for a while. I was with the 2nd Division, Co K,
38th Infantry Regt. We got there on August 19th, 1950. I caught a

mortar on the 5th of September. My brother was in A Company and he caught one on the 6th. His was a leg wound and they sent him to Japan. Mine was in the side and the neck. They sent me to Japan also, but felt I had not had enough so they sent me back for seconds. The only seconds I liked was chow. I did have a chance to see my brother in Osaka before I went back. They sent him to a stateside hospital and me to the frozen north.

I was in the Kunu-ri roadblock when the Chinks overran us [Memoir Chapter 13 – ed.]. I had a hand grenade take my right knee out from under me. I was lucky the roadblock was broken. I got evacuated to Japan and then to the same hospital as my brother in Massachusetts.

The 2nd was there to hold the line so the 8th Army could get the hell out of there. That was about the 27th and 28th of November, as you know. I feel damn lucky to be alive after that and pleased to get wounded and not taken POW as you were. I am sure my wound was a lot better than what you guys went through. I have talked with a few from my company and others who were POWs and you all should have gotten more than the two Purple Hearts I got.

…do you know about free phone systems on the internet? I could use them to call old buddies. If you do not have one or two of them, you should. I can help with that. Send me your phone number.

BIO 16.2   22 AUG 2002 – ROB YOUNG EMAIL TO ROBERT HICKOX – Regarding PTSD and memory loss resulting from combat.

For some reason, a lot of my memory of the horrors has left me. I must have blocked out a lot of it. When I went to the VA to check on PTSD, I was very concerned about not remembering. As I talked to the shrink, I found some things came back. I still have a hard time [because] I can't remember more. I also felt I did not do my part because the Chinks rubbed me out twice. I really had only about three weeks on the Pusan Perimeter before they got me. After some time in a Japanese hospital, I got back to my company up north.

There I got the second one (million $$$ one). That was only 2+ weeks after getting back. The Chinks and NK had us pretty well enclosed [at Kunu-ri]. We might have had a better chance if the South Koreans had not broken and left our flank open.

...As time goes on and I talk to others, things become clearer. I don't remember ever taking a crap [during combat], which may be why some friends say I am full of shit. I remember taking a leak only once. That was at the time of my first wounding. We had just moved back to our daytime position. We had been in our foxholes all night and were not about to get out to relieve ourselves. When we moved back, I was having a real good draining session when the mortar took me down. Still don't know who put it back. LOL. Hope you enjoy this small part of my war.

KMAG – 17 May 1948

Appendix 3

HOSTILE DEATHS – 65TH ENGR BN – KOREA

1950

Rank	Name	Type	Date	MOS	RA Number	Comp	Branch	Grade	Home County	
CPL	Burkham Rodney F	KIA(MIA)	7/18/1950	03-729	RA18100522	RA	ENG	E4	Grayson	TX
PVT	Kornmiller Donald	SIA	7/19/1950	05-729	RA151984415	RA	ENG	E2	Hocking	OH
PFC	Navarro Julio Q	MIA	7/19/1950	05-729	RA10103243	RA	ENG	E3	Hawaii	HI
PVT	Sparks Clyde A	SIA	7/23/1950	05-729	RA19246943	RA	ENG	E2	Yakima	WA
PVT	Barnett Robert M	KIA	7/25/1950	05-729	RA14279775	RA	ENG	E2	Pinellas	FL
PFC	Griffin Raymond E	SIA	7/25/1950	05-729	RA13257804	RA	ENG	E3	Washing	PA
PVT	Lassiter Howard R	SWA	7/25/1950	05-729	RA14268520	RA	ENG	E2	Thomas	GA
2LT	MacDonald Roderick	SWA	7/25/1950	01-331	O-1686782	NG	ENG	O1	N Haven	CT
CPL	Brenna Odell C	KIA	7/29/1950	05-729	RA17218585	RA	ENG	E4	Marshall	MN
	Brenna – see BIO 3.3									
PVT	Marshall Richard L	KIA(MIA)	7/29/1950	05-729	RA19319540	RA	ENG	E2	Latah	ID
PFC	Bosford Albert C	KIA	8/2/1950	05-729	RA12115924	RA	ENG	E3	Warren	NY
CPL	Brabant John F	KIA(MIA)	8/2/1950	03-729	RA21914105	RA	ENG	E4	St Lawr	NY
PFC	Dowell Charles D	KIA(MIA)	8/2/1950	05-729	RA13280851	RA	ENG	E3	Chester	PA
PVT	Howell Harold	KIA(MIA)	8/2/1950	05-729	RA14354048	RA	INF	E2	Colquitt	GA
PFC	Lujan Herman J	KIA(MIA)	8/2/1950	05-729	RA18253651	RA	ENG	E3	Quay	NM
2LT	MacDonald Roderick	KIA(MIA)	8/2/1950	01-331	O-1686782	NG	ENG	O1	N Haven	CT
CPL	Moody Nathan	SWA	8/2/1950	03-729	RA14270268	RA	ENG	E4	Barnwell	SC
SFC	Peden John W	SWA	8/2/1950	01-729	RA42031096	RA	ENG	E7	Kings	NY
PFC	Rylance Loren	KIA(MIA)	8/2/1950	05-729	RA19329968	RA	ENG	E3	Orange	CA
PVT	Smallwood Howard	KIA(MIA)	8/2/1950	00-035	RA15421790	RA	ENG	E2	Pike	KY
SFC	Smiley James R	KIA(MIA)	8/2/1950	01-729	RA17013120	RA	ENG	E7	Alameda	CA
PVT	Swank Philip O	KIA(MIA)	8/2/1950	05-729	RA17273516	RA	ENG	E2	Sullivan	MO
PVT	Sylvia Gordon E	SWA	8/2/1950	05-729	RA11183560	RA	ENG	E2	Bristol	MA
PVT	West Kenneth R	KIA	8/2/1950	04-745	RA38799392	RA	ENG	E1	Carter	OK
PFC	Whitehead Dana L	KIA(MIA)	8/2/1950	05-729	RA15267457	RA	ENG	E3	Montg	OH
SFC	Fair Curtis A	KIA	8/4/1950 HQ	01-729	RA18050208	RA	ENG	E7	C Costa	CA
PVT	Keith Eul J	KIA	8/4/1950 HQ	05-729	RA18273340	RA	ENG	E2	Oklaho	OK
CPL	Shaw James C	KIA	8/4/1950 HQ	00-776	RA13286436	RA	ENG	E4	Clearfld	PA

BATTLE OF PUSAN PERIMETER - TASK FORCE KEAN KEAN ASSAULTS KPA - MASAN

Rank	First	Last	Status	Date	Code	Service No.	Br.		Grade	County	State
1LT	Sam D	Starobin	SWA	8/7/1950	02-900	O-0050601	---	ENG	O2	Cook	IL
PFC	Edward B	Hoelscher	SWA	8/9/1950	00-776	RA 15415558	RA	ENG	E3	Hamilton	OH
PVT	Thomas	McDowell	SWA	8/9/1950	00-345	RA15294695	RA	ENG	E2	Cayuhoga	OH
PVT	Theodore R	Spears	SWA	8/11/1950	00-014	RA17227777	RA	ENG	E2	Ramsey	MN
SGT	George T	Dowdy	SIA	8/13/1950	03-729	RA3831878	RA	ENG	E5	Kings	CA

TASK FORCE KEAN WITHDRAWS

Rank	First	Last	Status	Date	Code	Service No.	Br.		Grade	County	State
PFC	Glenn I	Beatty	KIA	8/17/1950	05-729	RA15282480	RA	ENG	E3	Stark	OH
PVT	Harry E	Szymanski	SIA	8/17/1950	05-729	RA16318788	RA	ENG	E2	Wayne	MI
CPL	William E	Gibson	SWA	8/19/1950	03-729	RA33435960	RA	ENG	E4	Venango	PA
PVT	Rex A	Shore	SWA	8/19/1950	00-729	RA18281226	RA	ENG	E2	Tensan	LA
SGT	Alfred C	Sliter	KIA	8/19/1950	05-729	RA17243600	RA	ENG	E5	Washing	MO
CPL	Clarence	Wong	SWA	8/19/1950	03-729	RA10103278	RA	MED	E4		HI
PFC	Yukio	Yamamato	SWA	8/19/1950	05-729	RA10103328	RA	ENG	E3		HI
SGT	William L	Pace	KIA	8/22/1950	03-729	RA17101732	RA	ENG	E5	Texas	OK
CPL	Bobby J	Arnette	SWA	8/23/1950	05-729	RA13241526	RA	ENG	E4	Lee	VA

Arnette – see Chapter 8.14

Rank	First	Last	Status	Date	Code	Service No.	Br.		Grade	County	State
CPL	James T	Belcher	SWA	8/23/1950	00-405	RA15416789	RA	MED	E4	Muhlen	KY

Belcher – see BIO 1

Rank	First	Last	Status	Date	Code	Service No.	Br.		Grade	County	State
PFC	William R	Capretto	SWA	8/23/1950	00-729	RA19337727	RA	ENG	E3	LA	CA

Capretto – see Chapter 8.13

Rank	First	Last	Status	Date	Code	Service No.	Br.		Grade	County	State
PFC	Robert F	Scott	KIA	8/23/1950	05-729	RA15420356	RA	ENG	E3	Kenton	KY
SGT	Harold L	Terry	KIA	8/23/1950	03-729	RA17259420	RA	ENG	E5	Jasper	MO

Terry – see Chapter 8.13

Rank	First	Last	Status	Date	Code	Service No.	Br.		Grade	County	State
CPL	William L	Hubbard	SWA	8/24/1950	00-776	RA13263250	RA	ENG	E4	Baltimor	MD
SGT	Earl A	Fair	SWA	8/25/1950	03-729	RA18288515	RA	ENG	E5	Sequoyah	OK
PFC	Guy G	Gallant	SWA	8/25/1950	00-727	RA16267528	RA	ENG	E3	Washten	MI
PFC	Donald	Kornmiller	SWA	8/25/1950	05-729	RA15198415	RA	ENG	E3	Hocking	OH
CPL	Asao	Matsukawa	SWA	8/25/1950	00-078	RA30119256	RA	ENG	E4		HI
PFC	Bud T	Palmatier	KIA	8/26/1950	05-729	RA16253996	RA	ENG	E3	Shiawass	MI

THE GREAT NAKTONG OFFENSIVE – KPA ASSAULTS PUSAN PERIMETER

Rank	Name	Last	Status	Date	Service No.	RA	Branch	Code	County	State
PVT	William G	Brownell	SWA	9/1/1950	RA13264011	RA	INF	E2	Washingt	DC
PVT	Harvey L	Curran	SWA	9/1/1950	RA16301858	RA	ENG	E2	Wabash	IL
PFC	Choy J	Duck	KIA	9/1/1950	RA19295827	RA	ENG	E3	Alameda	CA
SGT	Marion M	Eck	KIA	9/1/1950	RA3642 1301	RA	ENG	E5	Branch	MI
PVT	Ernest J	Freeman	SWA	9/1/1950	RA11167468	RA	ENG	E2	Worcest	MA
SFC	William	McCormick	KIA	9/1/1950	RA15054235	RA	ENG	E7	Scioto	OH
1LT	Lee J	Parisot	SWA	9/1/1950	O-1686801		ENG	O2	Silver Bow	MT
PFC	James A	Arntson	SWA	9/2/1950	RA27359837		ENG	E3	Carlton	MN
PFC	Marvin A	Cook	SWA	9/2/1950	RA16305873	RA	ENG	E3	Mecosta	MI
SGT	Gene W	Fowler	SWA	9/2/1950	RA44170343	RA	ENG	E5	Davidson	TN
PFC	Robert H	Hickox	SWA	9/2/1950	RA12284788	RA	ENG	E3	Onondaga	NY
		Hickox – see BIO 7								
PFC	Ronald C	Karako	LWA	9/2/1950	RA13306754	RA	INF	E3	Norfolk	VA
CPL	Arthur E	Lashua	SWA	9/2/1950	RA16273518	RA	ENG	E4	Marathon	WI
PFC	Roscoe J	Lawrence	SWA	9/2/1950	RA32746564	RA	INF	E3	Warren	NY
PFC	Leon H	Parson	SWA	9/2/1950	RA17273493	RA	ENG	E3	Decatur	IL
PFC	Norman	Powell	SWA	9/2/1950	RA18322116	RA	ENG	E3	San Saba	TX
PFC	Elmer A	Roesler	SWA	9/2/1950	RA19250827	RA	ENG	E3	Missoula	MT
PFC	Aldin B	Saloway	KIA	9/2/1950	RA19308014	RA	ENG	E3	Lake	MT
		Saloway – see BIO 10								
SGT	Daryl E	Hormann	SWA	9/3/1950	RA17258381	RA	ENG	E5	Roberts	SD
		Hormann – see Chapter 9.6								
PFC	Arthur F	West	SWA	9/3/1950	RA25267807	RA	ENG	E3	Madison	TN
SFC	William E	Akers	SWA	9/4/1950	RA0700786		ENG	E7	Warwick	VA
		Akers – see Chapter 8.13								
PFC	Garabed E	Kenoian	SWA	9/4/1950	RA11185039	RA	ENG	E3	Providence	RI
		Kenoian – see Chapter 9.8								
PVT	Oscar M	Morales	KIA	9/4/1950	RA18319694	RA	ENG	E2	Webb	TX
		Morales – see Chapter 9.8								
PFC	John E	Ott	KIA	9/4/1950	RA15280112	RA	ENG	E3	Ross	OH
PFC	Nickolas	Petcosky	KIA	9/4/1950	RA12286423	RA	ENG	E3	Broome	NY

Rank	First	Surname	Status	Date	Code	Number			Grade	County	State
PFC	Robert G	Schoening	SWA	9/4/1950	05-729	RA19353852	RA	ENG	E3	Whatcom	WA
CPL	James G	Seidl	SWA	9/4/1950	00-673	RA16304870	RA	ENG	E4	Taylor	WI
		Seidl – see BIO 7.4									
CPL	Joe W	Shaw	SWA	9/4/1950	03-729	RA17243228	RA	ENG	E4	St louis	MI
PFC	Leonard D	Stamper	SWA	9/4/1950	00-078	RA18332835	RA	ENG	E3	McLennan	TX
		Stamper – see BIO 13									
PFC	Thomas C	Wall	SWA	9/4/1950	00-082	RA16295546	RA	ENG	E3	Wayne	MI
PFC	Billy R	Agee	SWA	9/5/1950	05-729	RA18322938		ENG	E3	Hamilton	TX
PFC	Theodore R	Spears	LWA	9/6/1950	00-014	RA17272777	RA	ENG	E3	Ramsey	MN
PVT	Allen D	Douglas	KIA	9/7/1950	00-729	RA12299389	RA	ENG	E1	Essex	NY
PVT	Orrie	Hilburn	SWA	9/9/1950	05-729	RA34806160	RA	ENG	E2	Monroe	AL
CPL	Edgar	Belhumeur	SWA	9/10/1950	03-729	RA11154607		ENG	E4	Providence	RI
PVT	Warren A	Forrester	SWA	9/10/1950	05-729	RA16267556	RA	ENG	E2	Jackson	MI
SGT	David D	Pecor	KIA	9/10/1950	03-729	RA19329967	RA	ENG	E5	Orange	CA
CPL	David	Branham	SWA	9/12/1950	03-729	RA15421805	RA	ENG	E4	Floyd	KY
PFC	Bonifacio T	Campos	SWA	9/12/1950	05-729	RA10103220	RA	ENG	E3		HI
CPL	James T	Castle	SWA	9/12/1950	05-729	RA15414760	RA	ENG	E4	Montgomery	OH
SFC	Leon W	Oleson	SWA	9/12/1950	00-824	RA37128134	RA	ENG	E7	Jerauld	SD
CPL	James S	Williams	SWA	9/12/1950	03-729	RA13035542	RA	ENG	E4	Wise	VA
PVT	Duane E	Wilson	KIA	9/13/1950	00-817	RA16220146	RA	ENG	E2	Wayne	IL
PVT	Roy	Bailey	SWA	9/13/1950	05-729	RA12286813	RA	ENG	E2	Allegany	NY
PFC	Arthur A	Boland	KIA	9/13/1950	00-835	RA31288847	RA	ENG	E3	Berkshire MA	MA
PFC	Nicholas	Carvalho	SWA	9/13/1950	05-729	RA29045047	RA	ENG	E3		HI
PVT	Charles G	Duhem	SWA	9/13/1950	05-729	RA16290110	RA	ENG	E2	Winnebago	IL
PFC	Jack E	Ginn	SWA	9/13/1950	05-729	RA15420682	RA	ENG	E3	Kenton	KY
PFC	Rueben G	Janke	SWA	9/13/1950	05-729	RA16308107	RA	ENG	E3	Waupaca	WI
SGT	Raymond W	Morgan	SWA	9/13/1950	00-931	RA42226869	RA	ENG	E5	Oneida	NY
PVT	Warner B	Brown	SWA	9/14/1950	05-729	RA16315646	RA	ENG	E2	Genesee	MI
SFC	Leonard A	Cayer	SWA	9/14/1950	03-729	RA19329906	RA	ENG	E7	Los Angeles	CA
PVT	Genaro S	Cota	SWA	9/14/1950	05-729	RA19348591	RA	ENG	E2	Pinal	AZ
CPL	John A	Crosse	SWA	9/14/1950	03-729	RA16255982	RA	ENG	E4	Cook	IL
CPL	Delford M	Dalberg	KIA	9/14/1950	03-729	RA16300769	RA	ENG	E4	Grant	WI
PFC	Michael J	Drahos	KIA	9/14/1950	05-729	RA12314749	RA	ENG	E3	Middlesex	NJ
CPL	Raymond L	Durgin	SWA	9/14/1950	00-014	RA11156445	RA	ENG	E4	Cumberland	ME
SFC	Fred	Easley	SWA	9/14/1950	01-729	RA07002241	RA	ENG	E7	Pike	MS
CPL	Floyd A	Gim	KIA	9/14/1950	03-729	RA18321401	RA	ENG	E4	Smith	TX
CPL	Alexander J	Gress	SWA	9/14/1950	05-729	RA16007287	RA	ENG	E4	Milwaukee	WI

Rank	First	Last	Status	Date	Code	Service Number	Comp	Branch	Grade	County	State
SGT	Robert J	Hossler	KIA	9/14/1950	03-729	RA15271621	RA	ENG	E5	Seneca	OH
SGT	Edward N	Logan	KIA	9/14/1950	00-060	RA37818431	RA	ENG	E5	Douglas	NE
CPL	Daniel C	Martinez	SWA	9/14/1950	03-729	RA10103287	RA	ENG	E4		HI
SGT	Delbert H	Payne	SWA	9/14/1950	03-729	RA18196355	RA	ENG	E5	Lubbock	TX
PFC	Delbert R	Reed	SWA	9/14/1950	05-729	RA1843227	RA	ENG	E3	Payne	OK
SGT	Glendon H	Smith	SWA	9/14/1950	03-729	RA11187625	RA	ENG	E5	York	ME
PVT	Frederick J	Tanner	SWA	9/14/1950	00-657	RA12348199	RA	MED	E2	Onondaga	NY
PFC	Torao	Tokuyama	SWA	9/14/1950	00-062	RA30118885	RA	ENG	E3		HI
PFC	Tamotsu	Toma	SWA	9/14/1950	00-729	RA10013063	RA	ENG	E3		HI
PFC	Akio	Ueda	SWA	9/14/1950	05-729	RA10103236	RA	ENG	E3		HI
CPL	Carl D	Wills	SWA	9/14/1950	00-861	RA18306210	RA	MED	E4	McLennan	TX
1LT	George M	Wright	KIA	9/14/1950	01-331	O-1688695	NG	ENG	O2	Blue Earth	MN
PFC	Joe W	Zeiler	SWA	9/14/1950	05-729	RA17102071	RA	ENG	E3	Denver	CO

BATTLE OF INCHON BEGINS

Rank	First	Last	Status	Date	Code	Service Number	Comp	Branch	Grade	County	State
PVT	William L	Geary	SWA	9/15/1950	05-729	RA13329304	RA	ENG	E2	Alleghany	MD
PFC	Frank J	Mills	SWA	9/15/1950	05-729	RA28778068	RA	ENG	E3	Polk	OR
CPL	Lyle H	Brandt	SWA	9/17/1950	05-729	RA16308102	RA	ENG	E4	Kewaunee	WI
2LT	Robert	O'Connell	SWA		01-331	O-0062327		ENG	O1	Newport	RI
PVT	Robert A	Gerlack	DOW	9/18/1950	04-745	RA16321922	RA	ENG	E2	Milwaukee	WI

PUSAN PERIMETER OFFENSIVE – 25TH INFANTRY DIVISION ASSAULTS CHUNGAM-NI

Rank	First	Last	Status	Date	Code	Service Number	Comp	Branch	Grade	County	State
PVT	Donald K	Bock	SWA	9/20/1950	00-590	RA15293555	RA	ENG	E2	Clinton	OH
PFC	Kenneth W	Dow	SWA	9/20/1950	00-164	RA19318931	RA	INF	E3	Yakima	WA
PFC	Richard G	Parsons	SWA	9/20/1950	00-345	RA15279855	RA	INF	E3	Van Wert	OH
PFC	Vernon C	Reinhardt	KIA	9/20/1950	00-060	RA14230138	RA	ENG	E3	Catawba	NC
SFC	Robert E	Rutledge	SWA	9/20/1950	01-729	RA13167374	RA	ENG	E7	Sullivan	TN
PFC	Dwaine E	Serjeant	SWA	9/20/1950	05-729	RA19361622	RA	ENG	E3	Benton	OR
PFC	Roland V	Stemini	SWA	9/21/1950	05-729	RA13277506	RA	ENG	E3	Baltimore	MD
CPL	Wayne E	Brenizer	SWA	9/21/1950	03-729	RA27045936	RA	ENG	E4	Jackson	MI
CPL	Lee F	Davison	SIA	9/21/1950	04-677	RA19261086	RA	ENG	E4	San Mateo	CA
SGT	Ralph M	Dillow	SIA	9/21/1950	00-405	RA13319632	RA	ENG	E5	Washington	OR

SECOND BATTLE OF SEOUL BEGINS

Rank	First	Last	Status	Date	Code	Service No.		Branch	Grade	County	State
CPL	Ross R	Rickard	KIA	9/25/1950	03-729	RA19290383	RA	ENG	E4	Yolo	CA
PFC	Allen Roland	Goode	MIA	9/26/1950	05-729	RA11159561	RA	ENG	E3	Hancock	ME
SGT	Joseph A	Heiser	SIA	9/26/1950	00-821	RA06824708	RA	ENG	E5	Pierce	WA
PFC	Reuben G	Janke	SWA	9/26/1950	05-729	RA16308107	RA	ENG	E3	Waupaca	WI
PVT	George F	Silva	SWA	9/26/1950	05-729	RA31361780	RA	ENG	E2	Bristol	MA
PFC	Carl L	White	KIA	9/26/1950	05-729	RA18145760	RA	ENG	E3	Craighead	AR
SGT	Claude F	White	SWA	9/26/1950	00-359	RA13265746	RA	ENG	E5	Northampton	PA
PFC	Richard	McIntosh	SWA	9/29/1950	00-931	RA19284233	RA	ENG	E3	Riverside	CA
PVT	James L	Kemp	SIA	9/30/1950	00-137	RA14040255	RA	ENG	E1	Clarke	MS

BATTLE OF KUNU-RI – CHINESE FORCES OVERRUN 65TH ENG COMBAT BATTALION

Rank	First	Last	Status	Date	Code	Service No.		Branch	Grade	County	State
SFC	William E	Akers	CAP	11/27/1950	01-729	RA0700786	RA	ENG	E7	Accomack	WV
		Akers – see Chapter 9.8									
PFC	James A	Arntson	CAP	11/27/1950	05-729	RA27359837	RA	ENG	E3	Aitkin	MN
CPL	Robert Charles	Bockey	MIA	11/27/1950	03-729	RA15410346	RA	ENG	E4	Adams	WV
PFC	Anthony J	Bruneio	CAP	11/27/1950	05-729	RA13264979	RA	INF	E3	Adams	PA
		Bruneio – see Chapter 13.5									
PFC	Bernard	Buli	CAP	11/27/1950	05-729	RA13334990	RA	INF	E3	Adams	PA
		Buli – see BIO 3									
SGT	Lester W	Byers	CAP	11/27/1950	03-729	RA19322171	RA	ENG	E5	Ada	ID
1LT	Hayward	Cameron	CAP	11/27/1950	01-331	O-2204143		ENG	O2	Adams	MS
		Cameron – see Chapter 6.3									
SGT	Calvin M	Cox	POW	11/27/1950	03-729	RA10736287	RA	ENG	E5	Bay	FL
SFC	Charles P	Cuccaro	CAP	11/27/1950	01-729	RA33947883	RA	ENG	E7	Adams	PA
PFC	Francis R	Curtin	CAP	11/27/1950	05-729	RA16144048	RA	ENG	E3	Adams	IL
CPL	Lawrence E	Donovan	CAP	11/27/1950	00-861	RA13309915	RA	MED	E4	Adams	PA
		Donovan – see Chapter 5.6									

Rank	First Name	Last Name	Status	Date	Unit	Service Number		Corps	Grade	County	State
SGT	Brady H	Drake	CAP	11/27/1950	03-729	RA13312718	RA	ENG	E5	Adams	PA
PFC	James D	Ferguson	CAP	11/27/1950	05-729	RA15291641	RA	ENG	E3	Adams	OH
CPL	Delmas F	Floyd	CAP	11/27/1950	03-729	RA18281341	RA	ENG	E4	Acadia	LA
PFC	Robert E	Fogle	CAP	11/27/1950	05-729	RA15279455	RA	ENG	E3	Adams	OH
SFC	David	Frye	KIA	11/27/1950	01-729	RA15114530	RA	ENG	E7	Kanawha	WV
		Frye – see Chapter 16.10									
MSG	Alton Earl	Harper	POW	11/27/1950	01-729	RA14034967	RA	ENG	E8	Edgecombe	NC
		Harper – see Chapter 13.8									
CPL	Harrison O	Harper	SWA	11/27/1950	03-729	RA14283255	RA	ENG	E4	Oconee	SC
		Harper – see BIO 6									
PFC	Samuel Carson	Harris Jr	MIA	11/27/1950	05-729	RA14276188	RA	ENG	E3	Sullivan	TN
CPL	Raymond D	Hess	CAP	11/27/1950	03-729	RA13320414	RA	ENG	E4	Accomack	VA
PFC	Robert H	Hickox	CAP	11/27/1950	01-729	RA12284788	RA	ENG	E3	Onondaga	NY
		Hickox – see BIO 7									
PFC	Kenneth J	Johnson	POW	11/27/1950	05-729	RA12114523	RA	ENG	E3	Broome	NY
		Johnson – see Chapter 7.4									
PFC	Paul Emert	Little	POW	11/27/1950	05-729	RA14297815	RA	ENG	E3	Washington	TN
SGT	Emmette B	Martin	CAP	11/27/1950	00-861	RA15250403	RA	MED	E5	Barbour	WV
PT	John D	Martin	CAP	11/27/1950	05-729	RA19290302	RA	ENG	E2	Alameda	CA
SGT	Clifford L	Neal	CAP	11/27/1950	03-729	RA38517449	RA	ENG	E5	Arkansas	AR
PVT	Louis	Otero	POW	11/27/1950	05-729	RA18255873	RA	ENG	E2	Lincoln	NM
SGT	John M	Patton	CAP	11/27/1950	03-729	RA18285763	RA	ENG	E5	Adain	OH
CPT	Anthony	Pecoraro	CAP	11/27/1950	01-337	O-0059873	RA	ENG	O3	Adams	WA
		Pecoraro – see Chapter 16.10, Bio 11, Bio 12									
PFC	Robert G	Schoening	MIA	11/27/1950	05-729	RA19353852	RA	ENG	E3	Whatcom	WA
CPL	Donald V	Sherrick	CAP	11/27/1950	03-729	RA17256203	RA	ENG	E4	Adair	IA
PFC	Bennie D	Smith	CAP	11/27/1950	00-861	RA14258149	RA	MED	E3	Anderson	TN
PFC	Russell G	Smith	CAP	11/27/1950	00-903	RA17265588	RA	ENG	E3	Buffalo	WI
PFC	Lloyd Dale	Stidman	KIA	11/27/1950	05-729	RA15267441	RA	ENG	E3	Breathitt	KY
PFC	Edward Junior	Stone	POW	11/27/1950	05-729	RA14271565	RA	ENG	E3	Jeff Davis	GA

Rank	First Name	Last Name	Status	Date	Code	Service Number	RA	Branch	Grade	County	State
SFC	Alfred D	Thistle	SWA	11/27/1950	00-572	RA31510248	RA	ENG	E7	Middlesex	MA
		Thistle – see BIO 14									
SGT	Stanley M	Wegrzyn	CAP	11/27/1950	03-729	RA36958829	RA	ENG	E5	Adams	IL
		Wegrzyn – see Chapter 13.8									
PFC	Curtis James	Wells	MIA	11/27/1950	05-729	RA16264063	RA	ENG	E3	Huron	MI
SFC	General John	Wilson	MIA	11/27/1950	01-729	RA45045383	RA	ENG	E7	Claiborne	TN
		Wilson – see Chapter 13.7									
SFC	Osburn	Wilson Jr	SWA	11/27/1950	05-729	RA16265673	RA	ENG	E7	Wayne	MI
SFC	Linden B	Zirkle	CAP	11/27/1950	01-729	RA13317916	RA	ENG	E7	Accomack	VA
SGT	William H	Bowling	SWA	11/28/1950	03-729	RA16275082	RA	ENG	E5	Warren	IL
		Bowling – see BIO 2									
1LT	Norbert O	Schmidt	SWA	11/28/1950	01-331	O-0059123		ENG	O2	Wayne	MI
		Schmidt – see Chapter 13.7									
CPL	Doyle	Decker	SWA	12/1/1950	03-729	RA38783984	RA	ENG	E4	Haskell	OK

1951

Rank	First Name	Last Name	Status	Date	Code	Service Number	RA	Branch	Grade	County	State
SGT	Robert L	De Sota	SWA	1/29/1951	03-729	RA15271527	RA	ENG	E5	Putham	OH
CPL	Moses M	Hayashi	SWA	1/29/1951	04-812	RA30102582	RA	ENG	E4		HI
PFC	Joseph E	Kilby	SWA	1/29/1951	03-729	RA13305847	RA	ENG	E3	Fauquier	VA
SGT	Chester J	Noe	SWA	1/29/1951	03-729	RA37259379	RA	ENG	E5	San Joaquin	CA
SFC	Allan J	Nuzum	SWA	1/29/1951	01-729	RA16277873	RA	ENG	E7	Monona	IA
PFC	Howard J	Waitt	SWA	1/29/1951	00-345	RA06978643	RA	ENG	E3	Camden	NJ
CPL	Samuel E	Whitfield	KIA	1/29/1951	04-081	RA13235578	RA	ENG	E4	Southampton	VA
CPL	Joseph W	Bielawa	SWA	2/3/1951	03-729	RA12115802	RA	ENG	E4	Rensselaer	NY
PVT	Edvins	Plavnieks	SWA	2/3/1951	03-729	RA13350358	RA	ENG	E2	Montgomery	MD
2LT	John H	Cain	SWA	2/6/1951	01-331	O-2021009	RA	ENG	O1	Middlesex	MA
CPL	Gerard J	Gaumond	SWA	2/6/1951	00-861	RA11177739	RA	MED	E4	Hampden	MA
SGT	Roy W	Jackson	SWA	2/16/1951	03-729	RA13165903	RA	ENG	E5	Tazewell	VA
SGT	Charles W	Albright	SWA	3/7/1951	03-729	RA15378273	RA	ENG	E5	Carter	KY
CPL	Francis J	Aldinger	SWA	3/7/1951	03-729	RA13282512	RA	ENG	E4	Philadelphia	PA
PVT	Terrance	Fletcher	KIA	3/7/1951	03-729	RA16304314	RA	ENG	E2	Jo Daviess	IL

Rank	Name	Surname	Status	Date	Code	Service Number	Svc	Branch	Grade	County	State
CPL	Asami	Miyazono	SWA	3/7/1951	03-729	RA30127325	RA	ENG	E4		HI
CPL	Joseph E	Teti	DOW(SWA)	3/7/1951	03-729	RA13276254	RA	ENG	E4	Washington	DC
CPL	Gerald E	Arnold	SWA	3/8/1951	03-729	RA16306795	RA	ENG	E4	Vernon	WI
CPL	Ronald K	Agena	SWA	3/12/1951	03-729	RA10103146	RA	ENG	E4		HI
PFC	Donald W	Bush	SIA	3/17/1951	03-729	RA18147114	RA	ENG	E3	Eddy	NM
SGT	Albert C	Callaway	SIA	3/17/1950	03-729	RA16277282	RA	ENG	E5	Tazewell	IL
PFC	Cristobal	Morales	LIA	3/17/1951	03-729	RA18367012	RA	ENG	E3	Sante Fe	NM
PFC	Thomas L	Brannock	SWA	3/26/1951	00-345	RA15278586	RA	ENG	E3	Cuyahoga	OH
CPL	William L	Rau	DOW(SWA)	3/26/1951	03-729	ER33682149	ER	ENG	E4	Mercer	PA
PFC	Melvin B	Boggs	SWA	3/27/1951	00-345	RA45046018	RA	ENG	E3	Clay	WV
CPL	Diosdado	Popa	SIA	3/27/1951	03-666	RA10103369	RA	ENG	E4		HI
SGT	Ernest R	Bernard	SIA	4/3/1951	03-729	RA13268161	RA	ENG	E5	Washington	PA
CPL	Joseph S	De June	SWA	4/4/1951	03-729	RA13287002	RA	ENG	E4	Somerset	PA
SGT	John J	Riley Jr	SWA	4/28/1951	00-583	RA13262013	RA	ENG	E5	Baltimore	MD
SGT	Cyril I	Halstead	SWA	5/19/1951	03-729	ER35439751	ER	ENG	E5	Boone	WV
CPL	Claude C	Jackson	SWA	5/24/1951	03-729	RA18345717	RA	ENG	E4	Nueces	TX
PFC	Donald R	McElwain	SWA	5/24/1951	03-729	RA19259820	RA	ENG	E3	San Joaquin	CA
SGT	Hurbert W	Beaubien	KIA	5/25/1951	03-666	RA31419737	RA	ENG	E5	Berkshire	MA
PFC	Laverne G	Benson	KIA	5/25/1951	03-729	RA16319896	RA	MD	E3	Fillmore	MN
PVT	Carl F	Junker	KIA	5/25/1951	03-729	RA13363219	RA	ENG	E2	Montgomery	PA
SGT	Donald N	Miller	KIA	5/25/1951	03-729	RA16317386	RA	ENG	E5	Menominee	MI
SGT	George H	Villacres	KIA	5/25/1951	03-729	RA38595066	RA	ENG	E5	Galveston	TX
CPL	Ernest W	Ullrich	SWA	5/31/1951	03-076	RA16298009	RA	ENG	E4	Cook	IL
CPL	Leland K	Wimmer	DOW(SWA)	7/18/1951	03-359	US56059064	US	ENG	E4	Carbon	UT
SFC	Elman	Jackson	KIA	7/28/1951	01-727	RA38341068	RA	ENG	E7	Childress	TX
PFC	Vincent	Longo	KIA	7/28/1951	03-729	RA12318764	RA	ENG	E3	Kings	NY
PFC	Walter J	Mongeon	KIA	7/28/1951	03-729	RA19385761	RA	ENG	E3	Los Angeles	CA
CPL	Clayton H	Thornton	KIA	7/28/1951	03-729	RA17263596	RA	ENG	E4	Lake	MN
CPL	David O	Archuletta	KIA	8/22/1951	03-666	RA17100970	RA	ENG	E4	Las Animas	CO
PFC	Thomas J	Stevens	SWA	8/30/1951	03-729	ER18263000	ER	ENG	E3	Fort Bend	TX
SGT	John B	Wilson	KIA	8/30/1951	03-729	RA19278290	RA	ENG	E5	Klickitat	WA
SGT	Lawrence	Gillespie	KIA	8/31/1951	03-729	US51067278	US	ENG	E5	New York	NY
PFC	Wilbur G	Enright	SWA	9/1/1951	03-729	US55090139	US	ENG	E3	Wabash	IN
PFC	William A	Poulos	SWA	9/1/1951	03-729	US51084965	US	ENG	E3	Kings	NY
PFC	Carson E	Judd	SWA	9/12/1951	03-359	US52078756	US	ENG	E3	Monroe	FL
PVT	James F	Strait	SWA	9/12/1951	03-729	US55132643	US	ENG	E2	Champaing	IL
CPL	Robert A	Whitcomb	SWA	9/12/1951	03-729	RA11202749	RA	ENG	E4	Middlesex	MA
CPL	Jean A	Ballard	SWA	9/21/1951	03-729	RA14358242	RA	ENG	E4	Lee	FL
PFC	Wilmer G	Neely	SWA	9/21/1951	03-729	RA39480206	RA	ENG	E3	King	WA

Rank	First	Last	Status	Date		Service No.	Svc	Br	Grade	County	State
1LT	Edwin S	Townsley	SWA	9/21/1951	01-331	O-0059094		ENG	O2	Queens	NY
PVT	Willie	Lowery	SWA	10/2/1951	03-666	US53079199	US	MED	E2	Guilford	NC
SGT	Dwight L	Whitten	SWA	unknown	03-729	US55080990	US	ENG	E5	Montgomery	IL
CPL	Lester B	Eckert	SWA	11/9/1951	03-729	US52007804	RA	ENG	E4	Hancock	OH
PFC	Thomas	Weiler	SWA	11/9/1951	03-666	RA19384961	RA	MED	E4	San Francisco	CA
PFC	Benedict	Yeskis	SWA	11/9/1951	03-729	US55105103	RA	ENG	E3	Cook	IL
1LT	Robert L	Fies	SWA	unknown	03-729	O-2203579		ENG	O2	Montgomery	OH
CPL	Neil L	McGurran	SWA	unknown	03-729	NG27771842	NG	ENG	E4	Pembina	ND
SGT	Grover W	Coleman	KIA	unknown	02-014	RA35815003	RA	ENG	E5	Lincoln	KY

1952

Rank	First	Last	Status	Date		Service No.	Svc	Br	Grade	County	State
SFC	Walter E	Jackson	SWA	3/18/1952	01-542	US56077034	US	ENG	E7	Gila	AZ
PVT	Salvat	Giovannotto	LWA	4/23/1952	03-729	US51117354	US	ENG	E2	New York	NY
CPL	Orville G	Freund	SWA	5/15/1952	03-729	US55122265	US	ENG	E4	Fond du Lac	WI
CPL	Martin A	Wanhaaho	LWA	5/15/1952	03-359	US55110596	US	ENG	E4	Houghton	MI
CPL	Albert E	Brown	LWA	5/19/1952	04-014	RA12294729	RA	ENG	E4	Litchfield	CT
PFC	Robert F	Klobucher	SWA	6/13/1952	03-729	US11154579	US	ENG	E3	Norfolk	MA
PFC	Grady W	Pittman	LWA	7/24/1952	03-729	RA53083151	RA	ENG	E3	McDowell	NC
PVT	Cartyle A	Riggs	LWA	8/14/1952	03-729	US55203731	US	ENG	E2	Adams	IL
CPL	Monroe	Younce	LWA	8/14/1952	03-729	RA13304741	RA	ENG	E4	Russell	VA
SGT	Delbert L	Nidy	LWA	9/29/1952	03-729	RA15240777	RA	ENG	E5	Kanawha	WV
SGT	Charles	Burroughs	SWA	unknown	01-729	RA53058349	RA	ENG	E5	Tattnall	GA
PVT	Rafae	Cruz-Mercado	SWA	unknown	01-729	RA50105698	RA	ENG	E2		PR
PVT	Clarence E	Wells	SWA	unknown	01-729	US51042170	US	ENG	E2	Merrimack	NH

1953

Rank	First	Last	Status	Date		Service No.	Svc	Br	Grade	County	State
CPL	Thomas E	Reinen Jr	LWA	1/18/1953	01-821	RA21720257	RA	ENG	E4	Bergin	NJ
CPT	John C	O'Connor	DOW	5/30/1953	01-331	O-1111817	NG	ENG	O3	Providence	RI
PFC	Robert L	Van Horn	DOW(SWA)	5/30/1953	01-014	US55273625	US	INF	E3	Arenac	MI
CPL	Harold G	Call	LWA	7/17/1953	01-729	RA17307315	RA	INF	E4	Christian	IL
SGT	Robert E	Seidl	KIA	unknown		US52182052	Z		E5	Berks	PA

Key:

RA – Regular Army
NG – National Guard
ER – Enlisted Reserve
US – Draft

KIA – Killed in Action
SWA/SIA – Seriously Wounded in Action
LWA/LIA – Lightly Wounded in action
DOW – Died of Wounds

MIA – Missing in Action
CAP – Captured
POW – Prisoner of War

NOTES:

1. The list of Hostile Deaths 65th Engr Bn – Korea in possession of Robert Hickox demonstrates an authentic United States Army Unit as fielded during late 1949. As a result of the National Security Act of 1947, the United States Army and United States Marine Corps experienced reorganization. Many duties formerly assigned to the USMC were transferred to the Army. Bob's document lists MOS for all battalion members. The MOS code given does not match the modern U.S. MOS system. Instead, it presents a hybrid value combining the WW2 MOS system with occupational fields later used by the USMC. The 65th list records a five-digit MOS in an inverted order. Textbook order would list MOS in the form: XXX-YY. Bob's list records YY-XXX.

2. An abbreviated MOS list appears below:

YY:	Occupation (USMC)	XXX:	Specialty (US Army)
00	Support	014	Auto Mechanic
01	Admin	035	Carpenter
02	Intelligence	331	not listed
03	Infantry	345	Truck Driver
04	Logistics	405	Clerk/Typist
05	MAGTF Support – Equipment Operator	729	Pioneer (Combat Engineer)
		745	Rifleman
		776	Radio Operator (low speed)
		900	not listed

QUESTION: Why was James Belcher, a typist who was shot seven times and bayonetted twice, in a foxhole with an M-1 Rifle?

ANSWER: The 29th Commandant of the Marine Corps, General Alfred M. Gray Jr., once stated, "Every Marine is, first and foremost, a rifleman. All other conditions are secondary." The 65th Engineer Combat Battalion is a pioneer battalion similar to the pioneer battalions currently fielded by the US Army and USMC. Personnel assigned to the 65th were often committed as infantry instead of being assigned battlefield engineering tasks.

Michael A. Shaughnessy

APPENDIX 4

25TH Infantry Division History

Tropic Lightning – Korea

August – November 1950

Declassified – 19 Dec 2003
Authority – NND785101

NOTE: Information presented in this section is intended to provide students of military science with insight into the daily operation of a Korean War Era Combat Engineer Battalion. Personnel rosters offer opportunity for a reader to reconstruct service history for a relative who served in the Armed Forces of the United States of America.

The History of the 25th Infantry Division in Korea was prepared and submitted monthly by Adjutant Michael A. Shaughnessy. This report often carried the following cover letter.

HEADQUARTERS
65TH ENGINEER COMBAT BATTALION
APO 25

[date]

SUBJECT: Command Report

TO: Commanding General
25th Infantry Division
APO 25

In compliance with letter, your headquarters, file AG 314.7 (D), subject; Command report, dated 12 December 1950, the attached report is submitted.

FOR THE COMMANDING OFFICER:

MICHAEL A. SHAUGHNESSY
Captain   CE   Adjutant

CREDIT: Reports used in this appendix obtained under the Freedom of Information Act by the Shaughnessy Family.

AUGUST

25.A.1   Activities Summary for August 1950

Command – This section summarizes issues affecting force preservation and mission completion. A summary of command topics is presented below.

1. Road Conditions – Movement south of Sanju was hampered by a road network in poor condition. Rain and heavy traffic restricted repair efforts. Traffic Control squads stationed at critical points relieved congestion.

2. Road Reconnaissance – When the Sammangjen bridge began to fail under Division load, the Division Engineer prohibited crossings by heavy vehicles. Location and construction of an acceptable bypass route became a priority.

3. Task Force Kean – Withdrawal of Task Force Kean from Chinju occurred so rapidly some scheduled demolition projects were not completed. The heavy rock base under Korean roads required extra preparation time for emplacement of a sufficient cratering charge.

4. Naktong River Dam – Near the end of August, the battalion was directed to build a dam across the Naktong River and back the water up, causing floods which would make fords impassable to enemy units. The project was cancelled after engineers estimated it would require twenty days to move the required amount of earth.

5. Emergency Road 24th RCT – The Commanding General ordered a four-mile road over rough terrain to be constructed with all speed. This emergency road was completed in three days by concentrated engineering effort.

S1 – Administrative: This section deals with personnel records, pay, and duty assignments. A summary of S1 topics is presented below.

1. Casualty reporting – new policies concerning efficient requisition of replacement personnel, casualty reporting, disposal of personal effects, and awarding of decorations were implemented per GHQ direction. An improvised casualty reporting book was issued to platoon leaders.

2. MOS Changes – During this period, 58 MOS numbers were changed. Of these, 24 involved the new Communication Career Field.

3. Battalion Table of Equipment and Organization (TOE) – General Order 182, HQ Eighth Army, 29 July 1950, authorized full strength for the battalion. See 25.A.4a below. Replacements received totaled eight officers and seventy-two enlisted

men. Losses during the period were ten officers and eighty-seven enlisted. To offset losses, non-essential personnel in HQ & Service Company were transferred to line units.

4. On 25 August, Chaplain J.R. Himes was assigned to the battalion. Catholic and Protestant Services were conducted during the month.

5. The Adjutant arranged for movies to be shown three nights per week. Books and magazines were distributed to all companies. One RU100 radio was placed in service. The Division news bulletin circulated as requested.

S2 – Intelligence: This section deals with locating enemy units, obscuring friendly movement, and understanding enemy communication. A summary of S2 topics is presented below.

1. Maps – A shortage of acceptable maps for Taegu and surrounding areas developed. Maps 1:50,000 scale printed in Korean and lacking proper contour lines were replaced after extensive travel to and from the base map depot in Pusan.

2. Twin Maps – S2 personnel maintained two situation maps. A tactical map generated from G2 reports was used during briefings. An engineering map displaying roads, bridges, streams, projects, and material dumps was posted publicly.

S3 – Operations: This section deals with troop movement, location of equipment and weapons, and modifications to terrain. Maps coordinates are typically involved in such matters. A summary of S3 topics is presented below.

1. Maintenance Zones – The Masan Operations Area was divided into zones of responsibility. Engineering projects in each zone were assigned by company. Road and bridge maintenance projects and heavy equipment assigned to those projects were recorded on a master map on public display.

2. Task Force Kean – During the advance of Task Force Kean, close support of attacking infantry units was a priority engineering mission. After the planned withdrawal, demolition of targets in the former task force zone became priority. Demolition sites were selected by reconnaissance, plotted on a map, and assigned an index number. These numbers were used to distribute workload to each company.

3. Proper Minefield Recording – proper recording of minefield assets was designated mission critical. Training classes provided instruction for engineer and infantry companies regarding proper marking and recording of minefields. Immediate verbal report of all minefields emplaced was followed by detailed sketches and written reports. This data was compiled on a master map maintained by the Assistant Division Engineer. Visual markers, such a s pickets and wire, were emplaced around select minefields.

4. Commitment as Infantry – After receipt of an Operations Order directing commitment of engineer units as infantry, Ground reconnaissance and map assets were provided to affected personnel. Liaison with 35th Infantry Regiment and 89th Medium Tank Battalion solved communication problems between these units.

S4 – Logistics & Supply: This section deals with who requested (and received) specific clothing, equipment, and food. Road and sea routes used to provide these items fall within S4 jurisdiction. A summary of S4 topics is presented below.

1. Division Airstrip – Two railroad cars filled with 200,000 sandbags shipped from Masan arrived at the division airstrip and were used for constructing revetments.

2. Task Force Kean – In preparation for the Task Force Kean offensive, two units of Bailey bridge, each containing 130 feet of double bridge, arrived on 7 August. The M4-A2 floating bridge with transportation arrived later. After the offensive, the Bailey bridge was returned to 8th Army while the M4-A2 bridge platoon deployed in reserve at Chinhae.

3. Inventory – The supply section received 10,000 barbed wire coils, 3,000 concertinas, 20,000 long pickets, 20,000 short pickets, and 500,000 sandbags.

4. Unfilled Requisitions – Engineer resupply was available only in Pusan. If no representative was on hand when shipments arrived, requisitions remained unfilled. Due to this situation, WOJG Hanson averaged three trips to Pusan weekly to secure supplies.

5. Water Supply – Water supply units were attached at the regimental level and functioned satisfactorily.

6. Korean Labor Records – Initially, 100 Korean laborers were hired per day. When need rose to 300 Korean workers per day, Lt Wright devised an index card system to keep track of days worked and compensation issued. Money and rice served as payment.

COMMO

Wire communications encountered no problems. Division Signal personnel established wire communication between all companies and Division HQ. Requisition submitted for one additional wire vehicle was denied due to a battalion vehicle shortage.

Radio communication remained excellent. Radio SCR 193 Masan operated continuously. Stationary battalion SCR 694 operated as expected. When these units were relocated, communication became disrupted and adjustments proved necessary. Company SCR 300 radios operated satisfactorily.

BATTALION MAINTENANCE

A vehicle shortage resulted from combat losses and operational breakdown. Tires and some repair parts were unavailable through normal channels. Permission was granted to strip vehicles damaged beyond repair for parts. The battalion motor officer traveled to Pusan Ordnance depot numerous times searching for spare parts. A new system of period equipment checks was initiated.

EQUIPMENT MAINTENANCE

Enemy destruction of all but one twenty-ton flatbed trailer necessitated moving heavy equipment by rail. Resulting delay increased with distance travelled. Numerous bulldozer breakdowns occurred due to improperly adjusted tracks or operator error. During mid-August, all equipment was pooled and assigned to Main Supply Route (MSR) improvement.

BATTALION SURGEON

Battalion Aid Station HQ Masan established 3 August. Three medics assigned to each company. On 25 August, Lt LE Goodrich assigned as battalion surgeon. First Aid classes initiated on 27 August to train medics. Medical detachment serving 65th Engr Combat Bn, 72nd Engr Combat Company, and 77th Engr Combat Company.

25.A.2   BATTALION JOURNAL – S3 - (Highlights)

Information contained in this section originates in daily reports filed by elements of the 65th Engineer Combat Battalion. Although these elements sometimes operated independently, they were typically attached to the "Wolfhounds" 27th Infantry Regiment (CO Mike Michaelis – see Hickox Memoir 9.4.1. Where possible, daily activity is summarized in a manner that minimizes the use of military jargon. Emphasis is placed on journal entries preceding the 23 August 1950 firefight on Hill #303 mentioned in Hickox Memoir 8.11.

<u>Summary</u>

3 Aug   1st Platoon Company C sent to support 27th Infantry Regiment at 1715 hours (5:15 P.M.).

4 Aug   1-7. Preparation of selected deployment zone. Includes: 1) construction of hasty minefields; 2) sandbag revetments [improvements] at [proposed Leopard] airstrip; 3) road grading; 4) construction of POW enclosures; 5) Password and alternate created; positive identification required; 6) reconnaissance of road networks: a) Munsan-Chirwon-ni-Yongsang-Miryang route; b) Masan-Chung-ni-Chungam-ni route; c) Masan-Chinhae-Chungchon-ni-Sonsan-Sodongni-Pusan route.

5-6 Aug	All. General road improvements and roadblock emplacement. Construction of [Leopard] airstrip on Chungammi road. Division CP [Command Post] road under construction. Equipment on hand: 7 x 2.5-ton dump trucks, 3 x 0.25-ton trucks, 1 x 0.75-ton truck, 1 x Air Compressor, 1 x D-4 Bulldozer, 6 x 1-ton trucks, 1x 20-ton trailer. Equipment on ship or at Pusan: 6 x 2.5-ton dump trucks, 1 x 0.75-ton shop truck, 1 x 2.5-ton cargo truck, 1 x 0.25-ton truck.
7 Aug	1. 77th Engr C Company – 3rd Platoon returns to Company 1600 hours. Casualties: 1 Officer & 7 Enlisted MIA, 3 Enlisted WIA.
	All. Division CO directs all convoys clear [location] G-3 with all personnel in proper uniform. Continue projects.
8-9 Aug	Extensive road improvement. Reconnaissance teams formed.
10 Aug	Continue Current projects. TRAINING: 1st & 2nd Platoon test fired 3.5' rocket launcher [M20 Bazooka]. Bury enemy dead from previous firefight.
11 Aug	Continue projects. One halted due to enemy activity. 77th Engr C Co – 2nd & 3rd Platoons searched for 1 Officer & 6 Enlisted MIA. Found. 1 Officer & 3 Enlisted evacuated to hospital WIA. 1 Enlisted returned. 2 Enlisted KIA.
12 Aug	All. Continue current projects.
	4. List submitted by Company B for flamethrower squad: CPL Rickard, CPL Davis, PVT Dunham, PFC Teti, CPL Castle, PFC Nidy.
	5. List submitted by Company A for flamethrower squad: CPL Morales, PFC McElwain, PFC Nelson, PVT Collins, PVT Forrester, PVT Miller.
	6. List submitted by 77th for flamethrower squad: CPL Brooks, PFC Thomas, PFC Nathan, PVT Holliman, PVT Johnson, PVT Hinys.
13 Aug	All. Continue current projects.
	3. List of men for flamethrower training from C Company: Sgt Zirkle, PFC Byers, PFC Drake, RCT Morales, PVT Leight, PVT Arutson.
14 Aug	Demolition projects begin. Select bridges prepared and select roads cratered. Repaired and resurfaced bridge on Marine landing road one mile West of Chindong-ni.
15 Aug	Leopard airstrip operational. Large-scale relocation of engineering supply. 1 dozer digging in artillery. 1 dozer digging CP shelter. Large-scale construction of concertina.
16 Aug	Destruction of roads near selected demolition targets. Hasty minefields removed and replaced with standard fields. Infantry Battalions instructed in erection of tactical wire. Wire stock brought to dumps in Battalion areas. Destroyed 2 bridges in Chindong-ni. Laid 78 Anti-Tank Mines.

Detailed

17 Aug 1-2. Large-scale transport of supplies and support of 24th RCT [Regimental Combat Team].

3. 72nd Engr C Company – Minefields laid at (1144.5-1346.1) & (1144.7-1345.9). Separate reports submitted. Built access road to new Regimental CP {Command Post] Parking Area. Demolition equipment & mines hauled from 2nd Bn area to new dump 4 miles NE of Chindong-ni. Assisted Battalions in erection of tactical wire. 3rd Platoon: craters blown on MSR [Main Supply Route] in front of MLR [Main Line of Resistance]. 1 dozer digging in tanks on MLR. 1 dozer constructing roads and digging artillery emplacements. D-4 dozer [bulldozer – Caterpillar D4H LGP] used to dig in Regimental CP. CP located at (1149.2-1347.5).

18 Aug 1. Company A 65th – 1st Platoon prepped to drop 1 pier, 2 spans on road bridge (1142-1368); 2 piers, 3 spans on road bridge (1143-1366). 50 yards east of bridge #2 placed road crater (160 lbs explosives, not fused). 2nd Platoon: 1 squad cleared trees from ends of runway on airstrip in 35th RCT zone. 2 squads made pickets for barbed wire, minefield marking triangles, loaded timber on trailers. 3rd Platoon cut pickets and delivered to CSP [Combat Security Police]. Prepped 2 bridges for demolition West of Chindong-ni on MSR. Prepped 1 bridge for demolition on LST road.
2-4. Positioning of Engineer Supplies and large-scale support of 24th RCT at Masan.

19 Aug 1. Company B 65th – 1st Platoon relieved 2nd Platoon at Company A 35th RCT (1700 hours). 2nd Platoon committed [as infantry] with Company H 35th RCT: (1) enlisted man killed, (4) wounded. 1 squad prepped and guarded demolitions for 35th RCT. 3rd Platoon blew road crater (1147.8-1380.0) 12' deep, 30' wide, 40' long. Maintained road within vicinity 2nd Bn, 35th RCT. Erected 1100 yards wire in 2nd Bn area, 35th RCT.
2. 77th Engr C Company – 1st & 2nd Platoons supported 1st & 2nd Battalions, 24th RCT. 3rd Platoon performed road maintenance and attended flame thrower school.
3. 72nd Engr C Company – 1st Platoon laid 18 Anti-personnel M2 Mines for 1st Battalion, assisted 1st Bn in laying wire. Improved access road to bivouac & water point area. 2nd Platoon laid mines in 3rd Bn area (70 AT M6) (18 AP M2A3) 15 trip flares. 3rd Platoon laid mines (4 AP M2) (29 AP M3) 2 trip flares. Dozer used to construct road to ammo dump, improve road to Medical Company. CP located at Chindong-ni.
4. Company A 65th – 1st Platoon prepped demolitions on bridge & trestle (mark #6 on plan). Prepped overhead trestle on mark #5. 3rd Platoon laid 30 AP mines in front of 2nd Bn 5 RCT.

5. Received memo #3, HQ 89 Medium Tank Battalion, re: employment of tanks with infantry.

6. G-3 req recon of overlay area and demolition plan for defense of Masan. [From:] ADE [Asst Division Engineer]

20 Aug

1. 77th Engr C Company – 1st and 2nd Platoons support 1st & 2nd Battalion 24 RCT. 3rd Platoon maintains roads.

2. Company A 65th   1st Platoon prepped the following:

1 double crater	740 lbs explosives
1 crater	704 lbs explosives
1 culvert	264 lbs explosives
1 Railroad Bridge	86 lbs explosives

2nd Platoon prepared the following:

1 crater	360 lbs explosives
1 crater	468 lbs explosives
1 crater	324 lbs explosives
1 crater	332 lbs explosives
1 crater	180 lbs explosives

TOTAL EXPLOSIVES: 3458 lbs.

Above craters prep on MSR [Main Supply Route] to 5 RCT. 3rd Platoon drained rice paddies on supplementary supply route to 24 RCT. Recon instructions from Major Brown for defense of Masan.

3. 72nd Engr C Company – 1st Platoon constructed bridge on lateral road 3 spans each 15' 30-ton capacity (1147.0-1348.8). 2nd Platoon laid 19 Anti-personnel Mines. 3rd Platoon laid 7 AP Mines, constructed access road to alternate artillery position 2 miles East of CP. Conducted concertina school for infantry A & P Platoons. Laid 4100 yards wire.

4. Company B 65th – 1st Platoon guarding bridge demo for 35th RCT. Transported mines & started minefield in front of 29th Infantry. 3rd Platoon laid 1100 yards wire vicinity 2nd Battalion, 35th RCT.

21 Aug

1. Company A 65th uses 3 platoons (less 1 squad) to construct supplementary route for 24 RCT (30% complete). One squad operated sawmills in Masan.

2. Company B 65th – 1st Platoon laying mines, guarding fused demo sites. 2nd Platoon laying mines and prepping demolitions. 3rd Platoon providing technical assistance in laying barbed wire, prepping demo. D-4 [bulldozer] making

turnaround at Leopard airstrip. 864 Anti-Tank Mines and 560 Anti-Personnel Mines laid. Erected 8000 yards double apron fence and 1000 yards four strand fence.

3. 77th Engr C Company supporting 24 RCT.

4. Demolition Plan for defense of Masan submitted by Company A 65th Engr C Bn.

5. 72nd Engr C Company – 1st Platoon laid 177 Anti-Tank Mines (1148.0-1349.7). 2nd Platoon laid 44 Anti-Personnel Mines (1141.0-1439.1). 3rd Platoon laid 36 Anti-Personnel Mines (1148.3-1349.7). Laid 4700 yards wire.

6. Mines laid in area: AP-78; AT-170; wire – 2800 yards; Operation Report and Mine Reports will follow by special messenger – CO 72nd Engr C Company. Location of new minefields:

    1) AP field at (1141.0-1439.1).
    2) AP field at (1148.3-1349.7).
    3) AT field at (1148.0-1349.7).

22 Aug   1. Company A 65th uses 3 platoons (less 1 squad) to construct supplementary route for 24 RCT (75% complete). One squad operated sawmills in Masan.

2. 72nd Engr C Company – 1st Platoon laid 9 Anti-tank Mines. 2nd Platoon repaired road to 2nd Battalion OPLR [Outpost Main Line of Resistance]. Constructed road to new artillery position. Repaired bridge in 2nd Battalion zone. 3rd Platoon removed unexploded thermite bomb from tank. Destroyed 2 enemy mortars & small amount of ammo on Regimental order. Improved fences on existing minefields. Laid 9 mines and 3250 yards wire.

23 Aug Operations Order 231800 received from Lt. Colonel Brookes. (See below)   Firefight – Hickox Memoir 8.11.

Summary

24 Aug – 31 Aug 1950

    These daily reports detail the large-scale relocation of minefields and wire to support new troop positions. Unusual activity is listed below.

25 Aug   3. 72nd Engr C Company - …2nd Platoon recon shoreline for possible landing sites. Destroyed eight small boats.

26 Aug   5. Constructed cattle enclosures vicinity Chirwon-ri: one at Koman-ri, one at Chindong-ri, one at Chung-ni. Each pen to be 2 strand wire fence. Advise location of pens. Completion date 27 Aug 50. Approximate size 200' x 200'. ADE [Asst Division Engineer]

27 Aug   5. Company A 65th – Built 4 cattle pens – (1151.5-1369.9), (1151.1-1363.8), (1143.7-1366.2), (1149.6-1348.3)

25.A.3   OPERATIONS ORDER – GENERAL SITUATION – HQ ENGR "C" BN – (excerpt)

Maps: 1/50,000   Korea   Uiryong   6819 I
                                 Masan   6919 IV

1. General Situation (summary)

Enemy Forces entrenched on high ground North and West of SIN-SAN (1148.9 – 1371.2) constitute a threat from which attacks can be launched with the objective of cutting or harassing MSR to the 24th and 35th RCTS and possible attacks on Masan.

Supporting fires and concentrations, provided by 64th FA Bn, will be arranged by Liaison Officer. Attacking units will be supported by elements of 89th Med Tk Bn. Initial control of 89th Tk Bn to be 65th Engr "C" Bn. As the situation develops, elements of the 89th Tk Bn will be placed with and in support of attacking companies.

2. 65th Engr "C" Bn

a. Attacks on receipt of further orders, under control of CO, 35th RCT. Use of de-trucking point #1 or #2 will depend on objective given. (See Overlay)

b. Initial orders will be transmitted through the 35th RCT. On receipt of orders directing operations, liaison will be established with the CO, 35th RCT. [Details] For details of assembly area, attack positions, LD and direction of attack, see overlay.

3. [Combat Engineers Reorganized as Infantry]

a. Company A will reorganize as infantry immediately, secure basic load of ammunition, be prepared to move to assembly area on two hours notice. Plan to attack following lead Cos at 500 yards to the attack position, thereafter on orders of Bn CO. CO, Company A will execute reconnaissance for successive positions forward.

b. Company B will reorganize as infantry immediately, secure basic load of ammunition, be prepared to move to assembly area on two hours notice. Plan to attack abreast of 77th Engr "C" Company. Co B on the right and 77th Engr "C" Co on the left.

c. 77th Engr "C" Company will reorganize as infantry immediately; secure basic load of ammunition, be prepared to move to assembly area on two hours notice. Plan to attack abreast of Co B. 77th Engr "C" Co on the left and Co B on the right.

x. Engineer Unit Commanders, Commander Company C, and 89th Tk Bn will execute reconnaissance of routes, assembly area, and assault positions.

Pending receipt of further orders, units will continue present missions.

4.   Ammunition Resupply Point – Initial assembly area. Other Supply and Administration – no change. See SOP.

5.   Support
Initial location of CP, Aid Station, axis of Sig Comm (see overlay). For further Sig instructions see annex.

BROOKES
Lt. Colonel, CE

SIGNAL ANNEX TO OPNS O, HQ 65TH ENGR "C" BN
CORRECTED COPY: DESTROY ALL OTHERS

1-3.   Axis of signal communications, Wire Communications protocol, overlay.

4.   Radio Communications
a.   The radio SCR 193 will remain in Division Command Net No 1 unless the controlling headquarters is the 5th RCT, in which case it will close in Command Net No 1 and open in Command Net No 2…
b.   The Battalion Command Net No 1 (SCR 694) will consist of…
c.   The Battalion Command Net No 2 (SCR 300) will consist of…
d.   All companies will establish SCR 536 nets for company control. Call signs for these nets will be letter designation of company followed by designation of platoon. EG: Able [Alpha] One, Baker [Bravo] Two, etc.

5.   Messenger Communication
All organic companies and supporting units will send two (2) messengers each to message center, this headquarters, upon arrival at initial assembly area. Commanding officer, HQ & SV Company will furnish two messengers for the Battalion Commander.

6.   Visual Communications
a.   Communications officer, this headquarters, will issue extracts of SOI for air-ground panel code identification of CPs and front lines.
b.   When possible, rifle smoke grenades will be utilized for target designation for supporting armor and artillery.

MEMOIR

Pyrotechnics:
1. Red star cluster – enemy attacking.
2. Green star parachute – request supporting fire.
3. Red star parachute – increase range.
4. White star parachute – decrease range.
5. Amber star cluster – lift supporting fire.
6. White star cluster – attack.
7. Green star cluster – withdraw.
8. Amber star cluster – enemy tank attack.

25.A.4   PERSONNEL ROSTER
25.A.4a   STRENGTH REPORT

	1 AUG 50	Authorized Strength	Officers – 36
			Warrant Officers – 8
			Enlisted – 762
		Actual Strength	Officers – 34
			Warrant Officers – 3
			Enlisted – 688

25.A.4b   ROSTER OF OFFICERS   1 Aug 1950

HEADQUARTERS

NAME	RANK	SN	BR	MOS	DUTY
Brookes, Wythe P	Lt Col	045447	CE	01-331	Bn CO
Hatch, McGlachlin	Maj	025578	CE	01-331	Bn Executive Officer
Belote, Lem Y	Capt	01101332	CE	00-600	Bn Motor Officer
Gamble, Charles E Jr	Capt	01303135	Inf	00-200	Bn Commo Officer
Yerks, William F	WOJG	W-907071	USA	02-200	Bn Personnel Officer
Strouse, Robert L	1 Lt	01062084	CE	01-331	Liaison

NAME	RANK	SN	BR	MOS	DUTY
Shaughnessy, Michael A	1 Lt	02011055	CE	02-110	Adjutant
Carney, Leroy F	Maj	01114880	CE	07-010	Asst Division Engr
Schmitz, Roy E	Capt	01645977	CE	07-010	Asst Division Engr
North, Robert E	1 Lt	01642430	CE	09-301	S2
Brown, Stephen D	Maj	0359393	Inf	02-162	S3
Pessa, Joseph J	Capt	01101991	CE	04-010	S4
Wymer, Lloyd E Jr	2 Lt	01688724	CE	09-301	Asst S2
Deveaux, Leroy G	1 Lt	01308489	Inf	05-004	Asst S3
Wright, William	1 Lt	01109770	CE	04-010	Asst S4
Hanson, Clifford N	WOJG	W-903-212	USA	04-000	Supply Off Gen S4

HEADQUARTERS AND SERVICE COMPANY

NAME	RANK	SN	BR	MOS	DUTY
Murray, William R	1 Lt	01322165	Inf	02-900	CO HQ & SV Co
Roller, Martin B	1 Lt	01296907	Inf	01-331	Recon Off
Hiatt, Paul E	2 Lt	02016351	Inf	04-113	Mess, Supply, Trans Off
Sandberg, Norman E	2 Lt	02204188	CE	01-342	Pl Ldr, Bridge Pl
Stroup, Donald F	WOJG	RW-904316	USA	04-880	Pl Ldr, Engr Equip Maint

COMPANY A

McAdoo, Richard F	1 Lt	050609	CE	01-331	CO Company A
Duke, John G	2 Lt	02204428	CE	01-331	Pl Ldr
MacDonald, Roderick	2 Lt	01686782	CE	01-331	Pl Ldr
McGovern, Bernard C	2 Lt	0963208	Inf	01-331	Pl Ldr
Powell, Frank	2 Lt	02204333	CE	04-113	Mess, Supply, Trans Off

COMPANY B

Collins, James M	1 Lt	01106066	CE	01-331	CO Company B
Starobin, Sam D	1 Lt	050601	CE	01-331	Pl Ldr
Parisot, Lee J	2 Lt	01688801	CE	01-331	Pl Ldr
Wright, George M	2 Lt	01688695	CE	01-331	Pl Ldr
Crowell, George A	2 Lt	02204414	CE	04-113	Mess, Supply, Trans Off

COMPANY C

NAME	RANK	SN	BR	MOS	DUTY	MEMOIR
Pecoraro, Anthony	1 Lt	059873	CE	01-331	CO Company C	16.10
Cameron, Hayward	2 Lt	02204143	CE	01-331	Pl Ldr	6.3, 7.2, 7.7, 13.7, Bio-2.1
Perry, Milum D Jr	1 Lt	050594	CE	01-331	Pl Ldr	
Sweely, Joe W	1 Lt	01109053	CE	01-331	Pl Ldr	
Gaston, Marvin M	2 Lt	02208465	CE	01-331	Pl Ldr	

MEDICAL DETACHMENT

| Nowlis, Gerald R | Capt | 0961449 | MC | 03-100 | Bn Surgeon |

Key: CE – Combat Engineer

25.A.4d   DAILY UNIT STRENGTH REPORT

Date	Assigned	Authorized	KIA	WIA	MIA	TOTAL	NB	TOTAL	GAINS	POW/KIA	MEMOIR
1 Aug 50	724	738				9		6			
2 Aug 50	724	738				9		6			
3 Aug 50	724	738				9		6			
4 Aug 50	705	738	3	2	13	27		7			
5 Aug 50	705	806				27		7			
6 Aug 50	705	806				27		7			
7 Aug 50	704	806		1		28		7			

Date	Assigned	Authorized	KIA	WIA	MIA	TOTAL	NB	Total	GAINS	POW/KIA	MEMOIR
8 Aug 50	711	806				28			7	7	
9 Aug 50	702	806		2		30	3	10			
10 Aug 50	697	806				30	5	15			
11 Aug 50	40/653	44/762				2/28	4	19			
12 Aug 50	40/653	44/762				2/28	2	21	2		
13 Aug 50	40/653	44/762				2/28	1	22	1		
14 Aug 50	41/650	44/762				2/28	2	24	2		
15 Aug 50	41/650	44/762				2/28	2	24			
16 Aug 50	41/647	44/762				2/28	2	26			
17 Aug 50	645	762				2/28	1/3	1/29	1		
18 Aug 50	40/649	44/762				2/28	0/1	1/30	5		
19 Aug 50	40/643	44/762	1	4		2/33	0/2	1/32	1		
20 Aug 50	40/650	44/762				2/33		1/32	7		
21 Aug 50	40/649	44/762				2/33	0/3	1/35	2		
22 Aug 50	40/660	44/762				2/33	0/5	1/40	3		
23 Aug 50	40/671	44/762				2/33		1/40	2		8.11
24 Aug 50	41/678	44/762	3	2		2/38	0/1	1/41	14		
25 Aug 50	42/703	44/762				2/38	2/1	3/42	29		
26 Aug 50	42/713	44/762	1	4		2/43		3/42	15		
27 Aug 50	42/713	44/762				2/43		3/42			
28 Aug 50	42/715	44/762	1			2/44	0/1	3/43	4		
29 Aug 50	42/720	44/762				2/44		3/43	5		
30 Aug 50	42/720	44/762				2/44	0/1	3/44	1		
31 Aug 50	42/722	44/762				2/44	0/2	3/46	4		

KEY: STRENGTH – Split values represent Officer/Enlisted. EXAMPLE: 44/762 represents an authorized strength of 44 Officers and 762 Enlisted.

NB – Non-Battle Casualties: a person unavailable to his organization due to injury or disease. Includes persons missing for involuntary reasons other than combat.

GAINS – Replacement: A soldier assigned from a depot garrison to fill an existing vacancy in a line unit.

Return to Duty: Non-Battle Casualties who have recuperated or been recovered from involuntary absence.

KIA – Killed in Action   WIA – Wounded in Action   MIA – Missing in Action

25.A.4e   AWARDS

Name	Company	Date	Award	Date of Deed	MEMOIR
Sgt David D. Pecor	A	15 Aug 50	Silver Star	25 July 50	
Pvt Charles G. Duhem	B	28 Aug 50	Bronze Star	11 Aug 50	

NOTE: Sgt Pecor and Pvt Duhem are listed in the August report as above. These men are listed again in the September report [25.B.4e] with award type inverted. Duhem is listed with a Silver Star while Pecor is listed with a Bronze Star. These appear to be new awards earned later and not clerical errors.

SEPTEMBER

25.B.1　Activities Summary for September 1950

Command – This section summarizes issues affecting force preservation and mission completion. A summary of command topics is presented below.

1. Conversion to Infantry – After considering the use of the Engineer Battalion as infantry, an operations order was issued and a counterattack area designated. During the night of 31 August-1 September, the battalion minus one company attached to 27th RCT relocated to the vicinity of Saga. The 77th Engineer C Company joined the battalion.

    a. During the night of 1 September, the 77th Engineer C Company retreated from its position and set up perimeter defense for artillery located in the valley. The 77th was later forced from this position after the CP received fire from small arms, automatic weapons, and mortar. CP vehicles ran a gauntlet of fire through rice paddies and regrouped in the rear.

    b. At the new CP location, the 77th Engineer C Company, the Battalion Bridge Platoon, and the Battalion Assault Platoon provided security.

    c. The three line companies of the battalion performed infantry missions.

    d. Division Engineer support performed road and bridge maintenance, placed wire and minefields.

2. Breakout from Pusan Perimeter – As the Division swept up the west coast of Korea toward Kunsan, engineer platoons were attached to three armored spearheads to clear mines and breach obstacles. A D-4 bulldozer transported on a 6-ton cargo truck proved to be of great value because the combination could keep pace with the column advance. Three armored sweeps covered the area from: 1) Chindong-ni to Sachon to Chinju; 2) Chinju to Hadong to Kunsan; 3) Chinju to Hamyang to Kunsan. Rearguard engineer companies strengthened bridges and improved bypasses.

3. Bridges – Two stream crossings supported these operations. A 500-foot low level timber bridge carried all divisional loads except for tracked vehicles. Tracked vehicles used a 900-foot ford crossing built up with sandbags. The floating bridge normally carried by the battalion was unavailable after transfer to Army control on 14 September.

4. Multiple CP Locations – During the breakout, the Division operated a tactical CP behind forward elements, a Forward CP twenty miles to the rear, and a Rear CP in Masan.

S1 – Administrative: This section deals with personnel records, pay, and duty assignments. A summary of S1 topics is presented below.

1. Military Pay Orders – The volume of soldier's deposits totals $14,345.00 for the month. [Robert Hickox pay: $82.00 per month. See 3.1. -ed.] Difficulty in pay adjustment continues. Movement of troops and breaks in contact with headquarters have been a barrier.

2. Missing Service records – Eighty Service records were forwarded to hospitals upon evacuation of personnel, but recovery of these records upon return to duty has proven difficult.

3. ROK Personnel – On 21 September, 100 ROKs were assigned to the battalion and distributed to each company. [See ROK Lieutenant Lee – 13.31 -ed.]

4. New Officers – Second Lt Robert K O'Connel and Second Lt Robert F Flynn, who graduated from USMA in June 1950, were assigned as platoon leaders. Captain Lem Belote signed a new Category III expiring 30 April 1954. Five officers were relieved from assignment. First Lt Parisot and Second Lt Barr were evacuated due to combat wounds. Major Brown, Lt Roller, and Lt Deveaux were evacuated as Non-Battle Casualties. Nine efficiency reports included semi-annual Captain reports and reports for officers departing the organization. There were 53 promotions and 3 reduction in rank published by this battalion.

S2 – Intelligence: This section deals with locating enemy units, obscuring friendly movement, and understanding enemy communication. A summary of S2 topics is presented below.

1. Maps – Due to a fast-moving situation, maps were requested faster than they could be supplied. The problem was solved with support from the US Air Force who flew maps to the forward areas.

2. POW Interrogation – While in Chinju, S2 personnel interrogated North Korean prisoners to gain information of engineering importance concerning roads to the West and North.

S3 – Operations: This section deals with troop movement, location of equipment and weapons, and modifications to terrain. Maps coordinates are typically involved in such matters. A summary of S3 topics is presented below.

1. Field Fortifications – During the month, the Operations section stressed the importance of field fortifications. The S3 section operated sawmills, a sheet metal shop, made minefield markers, and constructed concertinas. Projects involved the use of 250 refugee laborers.

2. Kunsan Reconnaissance – After the Breakout from Pusan Perimeter, the battalion reached Kunsan and required extensive reconnaissance of roads, railroads, port facilities, field and coast fortification systems, and engineering material locations. These requests were fulfilled.

S4 – Logistics & Supply: This section deals with who requested (and received) specific clothing, equipment, and food. Road and sea routes used to provide these items fall within S4 jurisdiction. A summary of S4 topics is presented below.

1. Bridge Platoon – During September, equipment belonging to the Bridge Platoon received service and additional assets. A 25-foot utility boat, six 18-ton pneumatic floats, three treadway 6-ton cargo trucks, and bridging accessories arrived at the Engineer Depot.

2. Camouflage – A limited amount of camouflage material was received and used at Division Headquarters Masan. Requisition fulfillment ran about 70%.

COMMO

Due to the distance separating companies from battalion, it was impossible to lay wire between them. Limited wire communications existed between some line companies and the unit they supported. The SCR 193 radio remained in the Division net during the month and handled traffic for the battalion. Messages were relayed to line companies who were attached to a regimental SCR 694 radio net. No additional problems were encountered.

MAINTENANCE

During the first part of September, a shortage of tires of all sizes became critical. Tires for 4-ton and 6-ton trucks became available after making a special trip to the Pusan Ordnance Depot. By the end of the month, this shortage ended and most vehicles received new tires.

25.B.2   BATTALION JOURNAL – S3 - (Highlights)

Information contained in this section originates in daily reports filed by elements of the 65th Engineer Combat Battalion. Although these elements sometimes operated independently, they were typically attached to the "Wolfhounds" 27th Infantry Regiment (CO Mike Michaelis – see 9.4.1. Where possible, daily activity is summarized in a manner that minimizes the use of military jargon. Emphasis is placed on journal entries preceding the Battle of Inchon 15-19 Sep 1950, specifically the 2 Sep 1950 firefight where Robert Hickox was wounded 9.4.3.

An Operations Order (unavailable) reorganized most 65th elements as infantry. These elements were attached to other units as shown.

<u>Detailed</u>

1 Sep

1. Company A constructed 175 ft retaining wall on MSR [Main Supply Route] to 24th RCT.
2. Company A 2nd Platoon probed for mines on MSR to 5th RCT until 310900 Aug 50.
3. Company A 3rd Platoon: 1 squad sprinkling ash MSR to 24th RCT. 2 squads repaired retaining walls on MSR to 24th RCT.

4. Company B attached to 35th RCT.
5. Company C attached to 27th RCT.
6. 77th Engr C Company supporting 24th RCT.
7. 72nd Engr C Company supporting 5th RCT.

2-8 Sep

1. Company A attached to 1st Bn 35th RCT.
2. Company B attached to 1st Bn 29th Inf.
3. Company C attached to 27th RCT.
4. 77th Engr C Company attached to 1st Bn 29th Inf.
5. 72nd Engr C Company supporting 5th RCT.

9-10 Sep

1-5. Companies A, B, C attached to 35th RCT and 24th RCT and assuming defensive positions. 72nd Engr C Company attached to 5th RCT. 77th Engr C Company repairing roads along MSR from Chung-ni to Haman to Chindong-ni.
6. 65th Engr C Bn repairing MSR Masan to Chung-ni. Building pit for gravel. Assisting in airstrip extension at Chinhae. Providing security at 8063rd MASH [Mobile Army Surgical Hospital – TV Series: Hawkeye served at 4077th MASH -ed.] Operating security road patrols from 8063rd MASH to road intersection (1151-1366). Assisting in preparation of plan for defense of Chinhae airstrip. Constructing pickets and concertina.

11 Sep

1. 65th Engr C Bn assisting in planning defense of Chinhae airstrip.
2. Aerial recon made of area north of Masan.
3. Recon of road east from Chirwon.

12 Sep
1. Company B on attack with 25th Recon Company in 35th RCT zone.
2. 4th Platoon 77th Engr sweeping for mines over Engineer road. 7 box-type mines recovered.
3. Enemy removed 2 minefields from (1139.4-1362.4) and (1139.6-1362.3). 20 mines total. Relocated 18 mines 400 yards away. Five mines boobytrapped. Destroyed in place.
4. 65th Engr C Bn maintaining MSR from Masan to Chirwon including streets in Masan.

13 Sep
1. Company B swept for mines in 2nd Bn, 35th RCT area. Removed 5 AT M6 mines apparently laid by enemy.
2. Company B: Whole Company attacked enemy infiltrated rear area 35th RCT MLR [Main Line Resistance].
3. H&S Company supervised camouflage of Lightning CP, installed Water Point for 24th RCT at Haman, installed Water Point for 27th RCT, replaced Water Point for 11th Engr C Bn.

14 Sep
1. Company B attacking enemy with Company I 35th RCT and 25th Recon Company vicinity (1144.3-1372.8).
2. 2nd Platoon Company C attached to 27th RCT vicinity (1149.3-1347.5).
3. 77th Engr swept for mines from (1148.2-1365.2) on MSR to Haman. 4th Platoon laying mines and barbed wire for 24th RCT.
4. H&S Company repairing 1-way loop to Lightning CP.
5. Bridge Platoon departs Masan 141342 Sep 50.

BATTLE OF INCHON BEGINS – 15 Sep 1950

15 Sep
1. Headquarters and Service (H&S) Company repairing road to Division artillery CP.
2. Grade for 800 ft extension of Chinhae airstrip completed.
3. H&S Company constructing minefield marking signs.

16 Sep
1. Company B relieved of attachment to 35th RCT and attached to 24th RCT. Moved to vicinity (1132.8-1358.5). Closed new area 160800 Sep 50.
2. H&S Company widening road and assisting in removal of 89th Tank Bn equipment in 35th RCT area.
3. H&S Company making reconnaissance of Division zone roads.

17 Sep	1. Company B w/2nd Platoon attached to Task Force (?) assaulting ridge vicinity (1132.8-1358.5). 2. 77th Engr C Company searching for mines on MSR [Main Supply Route], Masan-Haman and Engineer road.
18 Sep	1. 77th Engr C Company completed tank bypass at Haman. 2. H&S Company completed removal of tanks and tank retrievers from 35th RCT area. 3. 1 D-7 bulldozer recovered by H&S Company. Disabled by enemy in 35th RCT area.

BATTLE OF INCHON ENDS – 19 Sep 1950

Summary

NOTE: Activity during the balance of the month involves consolidation: regrouping units, repairing roads, repositioning minefields and wire to support current troop positions. Unusual activity is listed below.

19 Sep	5. Mine reported in center of road at (1162.4)-1366.0) 2.5-ton truck wrecked at 1500 hours.
21 Sep	5. H&S Company, Assault Platoon relieved as security guard for 8063rd MASH. Digging gun emplacements for 64th & 90th Field Artillery Battalions.
22 Sep	2. Company B supporting 27th RCT repaired 2 craters and constructed 2 bypasses during the night. Cleared 12,000 yards of road. Removed 10 enemy placed M6 Mines. 5. H&S Company, Assault Platoon training 100 ROK troops. 6. 21 assault boats being procured from Pusan.
23 Sep	4. Recon team, HQ, and HQ & Service Company [elements] made ground recon of [river] crossing at (1122.0-1358.5). Steep banks, water 10' deep, road net poor, unable to recon crossing at (1119.6-1359.8) due to enemy occupation. Air recon made of river in Chinju area. 5. Crossing available approximately 2.7 miles south of Chinju.
24 Sep	2. Company C constructing refugee enclosure at Chindong-ni.

4. 65th [elements] performing recon of river crossing (1119.5–1359.7). Crossing fordable, shifting sands, about 40" water (max), road net fair.

25 Sep   1. 1 platoon [from] Company A supporting Task Force Dolvin.

27 Sep   4. Major Joseph J. Pessa assigned as Operations Officer vice Major Leroy F Carney.

30 Sep   1. Company C repaired bridge at Lightning CP Namwon. 1 platoon w/ bulldozer supporting Task Force: 1st Bn, 27th RCT – objective Yosu.

2. HQ, HQ & Service Company closed Namwon 292330 Sep 50.

3. 2 recon teams accompanying Task Force: 1st Bn, 27th RCT to Yosu to obtain data on roads, railroads, and port facilities.

25.B.3   OPERATIONS ORDER – GENERAL SITUATION – HQ ENGR "C" BN – (unavailable)

An Operations Order 301800 dated 30 Aug 1950 reorganized 65th Engineer elements as infantry. These elements were attached to other units as needed. Occasional elements continued to perform Combat Engineer duties.

25.B.4   PERSONNEL ROSTER
25.B.4a   STRENGTH REPORT

1 SEP 50	Authorized Strength	Officers – 36
		Warrant Officers – 8
		Enlisted – 762
	Actual Strength	Officers – 41
		Warrant Officers – 3
		Enlisted – 744

STRENGTH REPORT

30 SEP 50	Authorized Strength	Officers – 36
		Warrant Officers – 8
		Enlisted – 762

Actual Strength

Officers – 38
Warrant Officers – 3
Enlisted – 687

25.B.4b.   ROSTER OF OFFICERS   30 Sep 1950

HEADQUARTERS

NAME	RANK	SN	BR	MOS	DUTY	CHANGE
Brookes, Wythe P	Lt Col	045447 CE		01-331	Bn CO	(relocated 25 Sep 50)
Hatch, McGlachlin	Maj	025578 CE		01-331	Bn XO	(CO 26 Sep 50)
Carney, Leroy F	Maj	01114880	CE	01-331	Bn XO	
Clift, John D	Capt	01115530	CE	00-600	Bn Motor Officer	(replaced by Belote)
Strouse, Robert L	1 Lt	01062084	CE	01-331	Liaison (omitted)	(ret Pl Ldr Co B)
Himes, John R	Capt	0516265	ChC	05-310	Bn Chaplain	
Pessa, Joseph J	Maj	01101991	CE	02-162	S3	(replaced Brown)
Belote, Lem Y	Capt	01101332	CE	04-010	S4	(replaced Pessa)
Starobin, Sam D	1 Lt	050601 CE		05-004	Asst S3	(replaced Deveaux)

NOTE: Officer Roster abbreviated. Changes from 1 Aug 1950 Headquarters Complement listed above. See 25.A.4b for full roster.

HEADQUARTERS AND SERVICE COMPANY

NAME	RANK	SN	BR	MOS	DUTY	CHANGE
Donohoe, Patrick J	1 Lt	059102	CE	01-331	Pl Ldr	
Perry, Milum D	1 Lt	050594	CE	01-331	Recon Officer	(replaced Roller, Martin)

NOTE: Changes from 1 Aug 1950.

COMPANY A

Fullerton, Avery S	1 Lt	059124	CE	01-331	Pl Ldr
Mason, John H	1 Lt	060287	CE	01-331	Pl Ldr

NOTE: Changes from 1 Aug 1950. Fourth Platoon Leader added.

COMPANY B

Frech, David F	1 Lt	059131	CE	01-331	Pl Ldr
O'Connel, Robert K	2 Lt	062327	CE	01-331	Pl Ldr

NOTE: Changes from 1 Aug 1950. Platoon Leader Starobin, Sam D, 1 Lt, promoted to HQ Asst S3. Platoon Leader Parisot, Lee J, 2 Lt, WIA 1 Sep 1950.

COMPANY C

NAME	RANK	SN	BR	MOS	DUTY	MEMOIR
Schmidt, Norbert O	1 Lt	059123	CE	01-331	Pl Ldr	13.7, 13.9, 16.10
Flinn, Robert F	1 Lt	062327	CE	01-331	Pl Ldr	

NOTE: Changes from 1 Aug 1950. Platoon Leader Perry, Milum D Jr, 1 Lt, promoted to HQ Recon Officer. Platoon Leader added.

MEDICAL DETACHMENT

Nowlis, Gerald R	Capt	0961449	MC	03-100	D/S 35th RCT	
Goodrich, Edward O	1 Lt	0979146	MC	03-100	Bn Surgeon	(replaced Nowlis)
Nalbone, Charles J	Capt	0347741	MSC	03-506	Med Asst	

25.B.4d DAILY UNIT STRENGTH REPORT

Date	Assigned	Authorized	KIA	WIA	MIA	TOTAL	NB	TOTAL	GAINS	POW/KIA	MEMOIR
1 Sep 50	43/725	44/762							3		
2 Sep 50	42/724	44/762	0/4	2/8		4/64	1	3/47	12		9.4.3
3 Sep 50	42/724	44/762	0/1	0/7		4/65	3	4/51	15		
4 Sep 50	43/726	44/762	0/1			4/65	3	4/56	7		
5 Sep 50	42/711	44/762	0/4	0/10		4/79	9	5/63	8	4	
6 Sep 50	43/717	44/762	0/1			4/80	2	5/65	10	2/190	
7 Sep 50	43/736	44/762	0/1			4/80	1	5/66	20	3	

Date										
8 Sep 50	42/733	44/762	0/1			4/81	3	6/69	1	2
9 Sep 50	42/733	44/762				4/81	3	6/72	3	
10 Sep 50	42/728	44/762	0/1	0/3		4/85	4	6/76	3	4/5
11 Sep 50	42/728	44/762				4/85	2	6/78	2	
12 Sep 50	42/723	44/762	0/2			4/87	4	6/82	2	12
13 Sep 50	42/717	44/762	0/1	0/8		4/96		6/82	3	
14 Sep 50	41/713	44/762	0/1	0/5		4/102	1/2	7/84	4	

BATTLE OF INCHON BEGINS – 15 Sep 1950

Date										
15 Sep 50	39/693	44/762	1/5	1/13		6/120	5	7/89	3	7/54
16 Sep 50	39/690	44/762	0/2			6/122	3	7/92	2	
17 Sep 50	38/690	44/762	0/1	1/0		7/123	1	7/93	2	
18 Sep 50	39/692	44/762				7/123	1	7/94	3	0/25
19 Sep 50	39/691	44/762				7/123	4	7/98	4	

BATTLE OF INCHON ENDS – 19 Sep 1950

Date										
20 Sep 50	38/684	44/762	0/1	1/6		8/130	5	7/103	5	
21 Sep 50	39/686	44/762				8/130	1	7/104	4	
22 Sep 50	38/684	44/762				8/130	1/5	8/109	3	
23 Sep 50	38/680	44/762	0/1			8/131	5	8/114	4	1
24 Sep 50	38/681	44/762				8/131	3	8/117	3	
25 Sep 50	39/680	44/762				8/131	1	8/118	1	
26 Sep 50	38/679	44/762	0/1			8/132	1/1	8/118	1	
27 Sep 50	38/678	44/762	0/1	0/3		8/135		9/119	3	
28 Sep 50	38/679	44/762		0/1	0/1	8/138		9/119	3	
29 Sep 50	38/679	44/762				8/138		9/119		
30 Sep 50	38/682	44/762				8/138		9/119	3	

25.B.4e   AWARDS

Name		Company	Award	MEMOIR
1.	SGT William C Barker	Med Det	Distinguished Service Cross	
2.	SGT James T Belcher	Med Det	Silver Star	11.7
3.	PVT Charles G Duhem	Co B	Silver Star	
4.	SGT Andrew J Sisk	Co B	Bronze Star	
5.	PVT Rex A Shore	Co B	Bronze Star	
6.	PVT Leroy T Marriot	Co A	Bronze Star	
7.	PFC Dale A Weber	Co A	Bronze Star	
8.	PFC Joseph De June	Co A	Bronze Star	
9.	CPL Clarence Wong	Co B	Bronze Star	
10.	CPL James Ewing	Co A	Bronze Star	
11.	1LT Bernard C McGovern	Co A	Bronze Star	
12.	SFC Marshall G Manson	Co B	Bronze Star	
13.	PFC Bonifacio T Campos	Co B	Bronze Star	
14.	PFC Louis V Hathaway	Co B	Bronze Star	
15.	PFC Francis J Kukahiko	Co B	Bronze Star	
16.	SFC Marvin Kempfer	Co C	Bronze Star	Kempfer – 11.12
17.	2LT Roderick MacDonald	Co A	Bronze Star (Post)	
18.	SFC James R Smiley	Co A	Bronze Star (Post)	
19.	SGT David D Pecor	Co A	Bronze Star (Post) (attached)	
20.	PFC Loreen Rylance	Co A	Bronze Star (Post) (attached)	
21.	SFC William Akers	Co C	Bronze Star (MIA)	

15.15

NOTE: Pvt Duhem and Sgt Pecor listed in August report 25.A.4e.

OCTOBER

25.C.1   Activities Summary for October 1950

Command – This section summarizes issues affecting force preservation and mission completion. A summary of command topics is presented below.

1. Kunsan Repair – After arriving in Kunsan, engineer companies repaired roads and removed obstacles. Bridge repair was abandoned due to lack of materials. Eventually, good bridge timbers were located in fortifications built by the North Koreans. These fortifications were demolished and timber salvaged.

2. Taejon Repair – During the second week of October, bridge repair projects using timber recovered from North Korean rail yards began. A local sawmill was used to produce decking. A bridge over the Kum River received 525 feet of replacement sections. The bridge was completed the night before high water washed out a sandbag causeway and floating bridge currently in use.

3. Pyongtaek Infrastructure – The Main Supply Route from the Kum River to Suwon covered seventy-one miles. Engineer units were placed along this route and activity was coordinated by radio from Pyongtaek. Several bridges were constructed while others were repaired. Bypasses were improved. Traffic congestion diminished. In addition to the MSR, the battalion maintained the road from Chichiwon to Chongju and repaired a bypass constructed from sandbags and earth and corduroy used to bypass a permanent bridge. When the battalion moved from Taejon to Pyongtaek, the IX Corps Engineer Section created plans to rehabilitate the Taejon power and water supply. On 24 October, power became available in Taejon. Two sawmills began producing bridge decking.

S1 – Administrative: This section deals with personnel records, pay, and duty assignments. A summary of S1 topics is presented below.

1. Consolidation – Division Rear CP released control of the Personnel Section which rejoined the battalion at Pyongtaek. Battalion Administration was united for the first time since June 1950.

2. Promotion – A total of 48 promotions were recorded during the month. Approximately eighty WDAGO Form 20 records were reviewed for accuracy and errors were corrected. Twenty-five service records were processed and forwarded to other organizations.

3. Military Pay Orders – Soldiers' deposits totaled $16,165.00 for the month.

4. MISC – A chaplain conducted religious services during the month. Movies were shown on four occasions. Most personnel were offered the opportunity to attend the Bob Hope Show.

S2 – Intelligence: This section deals with locating enemy units, obscuring friendly movement, and understanding enemy communication. A summary of S2 topics is presented below.

1. Masan – While the Battalion CP was located at Masan, S2 personnel performed reconnaissance of the area around Taejon searching for access roads other than the main Supply Route (MSR).

2. Taejon – After moving to Taejon on 5 October, the section discovered that an intended move to Pyongtaek would place the Division too far away for easy map supply. The issue was resolved by placing a map truck directly under control of the Assistant Division Engineer.

S3 – Operations: This section deals with troop movement, location of equipment and weapons, and modifications to terrain. Maps coordinates are typically involved in such matters. A summary of S3 topics is presented below.

1. Kunsan Docks – Repairs to the Kunsan docks were abandoned after Divisional orders moved all units to Taejon.

2. MSR Bridges – Upon arrival at Taejon, repairs to all roads and bridges along the Main Supply Route from Waegwan to Taep'yong-ni began.

3. Training – Effective 16 October, all units received certain types of training during lax periods. The 25th Infantry Division HQ published a training schedule.

4. Electric/Water Supplies – From 6 to 10 October, the Operations Officer made a detailed survey of the electrical distribution system and water supply in Taejon.

S4 – Logistics & Supply: This section deals with who requested (and received) specific clothing, equipment, and food. Road and sea routes used to provide these items fall within S4 jurisdiction. A summary of S4 topics is presented below.

1. Kunsan – The S4 Section moved from Kunsan to Taejon on 5 October. During this time, four convoys travelled to Pusan Engineer Depot to procure engineer supplies needed to cover shortages.

2. Pyongtaek – Battalion Staff conducted inspection of all personal items and TOE equipment and ammunition. Requisitions were issued to cover all shortages. During the third week of October, an extra wool blanket, wool sleeping bags, and one set of wool clothing was issued to each man. On 15 October, cold weather clothing was issued to Korean

troops assigned to the battalion. Nine railcars containing bridge timbers, decking, sandbags, and bridge hardware arrived in Pyongtaek.

3. Rations – Rations and fuel were requisitioned daily and delivered to the companies. Trucks relayed rations from Quartermaster Taejon to Battalion to Company. Fuel was shipped by rail.

COMMO
No record.

MAINTENANCE
No record.

25.C.2   BATTALION JOURNAL – S3 - (Highlights)

Information contained in this section originates in daily reports filed by elements of the 65th Engineer Combat Battalion. Although these elements sometimes operated independently, they were typically attached to the "Wolfhounds" 27th Infantry Regiment (CO Mike Michaelis – see 9.4.1. Where possible, daily activity is summarized in a manner that minimizes the use of military jargon.

Detailed

1 Oct

1-6. Company A located at I-ri (CQ 155780). Company B located at Namwon (CQ 5319). Company C located at Kunsan (BQ 9384). 77th Engr C Company located 3 miles East of Kunsan (BQ 9884) based on verbal order from G-3. 65th Engr C Battalion bridge platoon located at Ponsong (DP 3492) attached to 8th Army.

7. 5 x EM, 1 x 1.75-yard crane, 1 x 1.5 yard crane, 1 x 20 ton trailer, 1 x 6T 6x6 prime mover located at Masan awaiting rail transportation.

Summary

2-8 Oct

Infrastructure Repair – all units repairing roads and bridges within assigned zones. River crossings monitored. Heavy equipment arrival at Taejon: 2 x motorized graders, 5 x D-7 bulldozers, 2 x D-4 bulldozers.

9-31 Oct

Paperwork Typhoon – 128 mandatory reports and referred messages logged in journal. Most are status updates or requests for material and labor. Unusual items are listed below.

10 Oct

1. Captain Bang-G4-Tel: reported fire at [illegible]. H&S sent 25 G.I.s and 25 Koreans to fight fire.
2. Sgt Posey with 20 more G.I.s, H&S Company to relieve first fire-fighting detail. Reports fire under control.
4. Captain Schmitz desires to know how much paint was furnished to the MPs and where the paint came from.

6. Major Danley – Leopard 2 – states that all of Company A has moved and he has no contact with them. Wants to know if this office directed [stole his company]. Matter checked by Lt Starobin. Major Danley found [to be] working with erroneous information – no further action.

19 Oct
6. Continuous rain all day.

20 Oct
1. Major Hatch [report] re: A Company Inspection. Found no shortages that would seriously affect Combat Engineers. Clothing and equipment is generally worn out. Checked bridge across Kum River with Captain Collins. Found two spans weakened by high water. Work on by 74th. Checked crossing between Chochiwon & Chongju where B Company is attempting to repair a 125' gap (28' high) with sandbag and earth fill. Work about 50% complete.

2-3. SUMMARY: weather conditions affecting select roads and bridges. MSR bridge imperiled.

8. Still raining all day.

21 Oct
2. SUMMARY: Water has risen two feet overnight. Cascade of messages generated by this fact.

22 Oct
1. GHQ Letter: Submission of monthly Strength & Status Report suspended for the duration of present emergency.

24 Oct
1. 30 G.I. bodies discovered at CS 7065. Give who discovered bodies, how identified, is there evidence of atrocities, condition of bodies. Requested by S2 24th Inf.

2. Company C discovered bodies. Identified by helmet liners with 24th Division insignia. No indication of atrocities. Bodies decayed to skeletons.

6. ADE [report] re: G-3 wants to know when all-out training is possible.

25 Oct
2. S3 to ADE [report]: present MSR over 60 miles. No all-out training possible until relieved of road responsibility.

26 Oct
4. CO & Staff Meeting – 25 subjects discussed including politeness, safe driving, medals, leave, training, pay, and movie projectors. Highlights listed below.

Command # 5 – Supply discipline must be stressed. Last command inspection satisfactory. New one in 2 or 3 weeks. Overages turned in. Line companies may keep additional support weapons, mortars, and BAR.

S1 # 3 – normal leave cancelled. Emergency leave in effect.

S4 – Mountain sleeping bags issued for wool. Parkas issued for wool. New one in 2 or whatever is left – Hickox Memoir 5.4]

Captain Gamble's To Do List: Submit Unit History (in diary form). Requisition athletic equipment and movie projector. Coordinate with A Company S1 regarding movie selection. With A Company S4 regarding athletic equipment. With B Company S1 regarding baggage claims.

6. ADE [report] re: G-3 plans – units concentrate on order. Prepare for further movement. Provide for field security, conduct intensive training. Tentative assembly area 6 miles from Taejon. Be prepared to move at any time.

28 Oct — Major Carney [report] re: power off at Suwon (1100-1230) 29 Oct 50. Power station at Champyang and Tanganri not synchronized. Shutdown necessary for adjustment.

25.C.3 — OPERATIONS ORDER – GENERAL SITUATION – HQ ENGR "C" BN – (none)

25.C.4 PERSONNEL ROSTER

25.C.4a — STRENGTH REPORT

1 OCT 50	Authorized Strength	Officers – 36
		Warrant Officers – 8
		Enlisted – 762
	Actual Strength	Officers – 38
		Warrant Officers – 3
		Enlisted – 687

STRENGTH REPORT

31 OCT 50	Authorized Strength	Officers – 36
		Warrant Officers – 8
		Enlisted – 762
	Actual Strength	Officers – 36
		Warrant Officers – 2
		Enlisted – 693

25.C.4b — ROSTER OF OFFICERS — 31 Oct 1950

HEADQUARTERS

NAME	RANK	SN	BR	MOS	DUTY	MEMOIR
Hatch, McGlachlin	Maj	025578	CE	01-331	Bn CO (26 Sep 50)	
Carney, Leroy F	Maj	01114880	CE	01-331	Bn XO	

7.5

Clift, John D	Capt	01115530	CE	00-600	Bn Motor Officer
Gamble, Charles E Jr	Capt	01303135	Inf	00-200	Bn Commo Officer
Yerks, William F	WOJG	W-907071	USA	02-200	Bn Personnel Officer
Himes, John R	Capt	0516265	ChC	05-310	Bn Chaplain
Shaughnessy, Michael A	1 Lt	02011055	CE	02-110	Adjutant
Robeysek, James W	Maj	01101188	CE	07-010	Asst Division Engineer
Schmitz, Roy E	Capt	01645977	CE	07-010	Asst Division Engineer
North, Robert E	1 Lt	01642430	CE	09-301	S2
Pessa, Joseph J	Maj	01101991	CE	02-162	S3
Belote, Lem Y	Capt	01101332	CE	04-010	S4
Hanson, Clifford N	WOJG	W-903-212	USA	04-000	Supply Off Gen S4
Wymer, Lloyd E Jr	1 Lt	01688724	CE	09-301	Asst S2
Starobin, Sam D	1 Lt	050601	CE	05-004	Asst S3

HEADQUARTERS AND SERVICE COMPANY

NAME	RANK	SN	BR	MOS	DUTY
Murray, William R	1 Lt	01322165	Inf	02-900	CO HQ & SV Co
Mason, John H	1 Lt	060287	CE	01-342	Pl Ldr, Bridge Pl
Perry, Milum D	1 Lt	050594	CE	01-331	Recon Officer
Wright, William	1 Lt	01109770	CE	04-113	Mess, Supply, Trans Off
Stroup, Donald F	WOJG	RW-904316	USA	04-880	Pl Ldr, Engr Equip Maint

COMPANY A

NAME	RANK	SN	BR	MOS	DUTY
McAdoo, Richard F	1 Lt	050609	CE	01-331	CO Company A
Frech, David F (formerly Co B)	1 Lt	059131	CE	01-331	Pl Ldr
Fullerton, Avery S	1 Lt	059124	CE	01-331	Pl Ldr
McGovern, Bernard C	2 Lt	0963208	Inf	01-331	Pl Ldr
Powell, Frank	2 Lt	02204333	CE	04-113	Mess, Supply, Trans Off

COMPANY B

NAME	RANK	SN	BR	MOS	DUTY	MEMOIR
Collins, James M	1 Lt	01106066	CE	01-331	CO Company B	
Donohoe, Patrick J	1 Lt	059102	CE	01-331	Pl Ldr (formerly H&S Svc Sep 50)	
Strouse, Robert L	1 Lt	01062084	CE	01-331	Pl Ldr (formerly Liaison Aug 50)	
Duke, John G	2 Lt	02204428	CE	01-331	Pl Ldr (formerly CO A)	
Crowell, George A	2 Lt	02204414	CE	04-113	Mess, Supply, Trans Off	

COMPANY C

NAME	RANK	SN	BR	MOS	DUTY	MEMOIR
Pecoraro, Anthony	1 Lt	059873	CE	01-331	CO Company C	16.10
Cameron, Hayward	2 Lt	02204143	CE	01-331	Pl Ldr	6.3,7.2, 7.7, 13.7, Bio-2.1
Schmidt, Norbert O	1 Lt	059123	CE	01-331	Pl Ldr	13.7, 13.9, 16.10
Gaston, Marvin M	2 Lt	02208465	CE	01-331	Pl Ldr	
Sweely, Joe W	1 Lt	01109053	CE	01-331	Pl Ldr	
Flinn, Robert F	1 Lt	062327	CE	01-331	Pl Ldr	

MEDICAL DETACHMENT

	RANK	SN	BR	MOS	DUTY
Goodrich, Edward O	1 Lt	0979146	MC	03-100	Bn Surgeon
Nalbone, Charles J	Capt	0347741	MSC	03-506	Med Asst

25.C.4c NON-BATTLE CASUALTIES

NOTE: The following list omits unnecessary medical information. All casualties occurred in Korea.

Name		Company	Date	Diagnosis
	Hickox Memoir			
PVT	Kemp, James L	H&S	1 Oct	sprained knee
SGT	Bruner, Louis J	H&S	1 Oct	fractured wrist

Rank	Name	Company	Date	Injury	MEMOIR
PFC	Everly, Lewis A	H&S	2 Oct	foot injury	
1 Lt	Sandberg, Norman E	H&S	3 Oct	blood poisoning	
SFC	Lennon, Edward J	H&S	12 Oct	blood poisoning	
CPL	Darche, Francis J	H&S	21 Oct	cut upper lip	
PVT	Jenkins, Foster M	A	9 Oct	gunshot wound, left leg	
SFC	Jernigan, Curtis J	A	14 Oct	fractured hip & knee	
PFC	Jackson, Claude C	A	14 Oct	strained ligament	
PVT	Fox, Henry G	A	30 Oct	internal hemorrhage	
SFC	Oberg, Grantley K	B	3 Oct	bruised knee	
MSGT	Francard, Leroy J	C	3 Oct 50	splinter, left hand	7.1, 7.2, 8.6, Bio-2.1, Bio-4
CPL	Davison, Lee F	C	8 Oct	sprained back	
PFC	Stone, Edward	C	11 Oct	fractured right hand	
SGT	Byers, Lester W	C	20 Oct	fractured left thumb	
PFC	McEwen, Irwin H	C	20 Oct	anxiety reaction	
PFC	White, Virgil C	C	21 Oct	sprained hip	
PFC	Leight, Charles W Jr	C	24 Oct	injured right foot	
CPL	Heldman, Cletus B	C	27 Oct	sprained ankle	

25.C.4d   DAILY UNIT STRENGTH REPORT

NOTE: One combat casualty was suffered during October 1950. On 7 October, an officer is listed WIA. Cumulative combat casualties 1 October listed 8/138 end 31 October listed 9/138. Non-battle casualties increased from 1 October listed 9/120 to end 31 October 10/156. See Non-Battle Casualty List above.

25.C.4e   AWARDS

Name	Company	Award	MEMOIR
none			

NOVEMBER

The 25th Infantry Division Record for November 1950 demonstrates noticeable difference from reports submitted during previous months. Detailed presentation of standard material is lacking. The War Diary is not attached. Explanation of listed entries in the Operations Section is accomplished by referring to other military forms and reports. A possible cause for this sudden change is suggested in the following email.

25.D.0 10 FEB 2001 – PATRICK SHAUGNESSY EMAIL TO ROBERT HICKOX – Regarding Patrick's search of the National Archives.

I haven't forgotten about trying to obtain copies of the other War Diaries if they still exist in the National Archives. If they do exist, they may not have much information in them. Notice that my Dad [Adjutant Michael A. Shaughnessy] was putting together the August Diary in early November 1950. And with the retreat in November 1950, documents may have been lost and completing paperwork may have been a low priority.

25.D.1   Activities Summary for November 1950

Command – This section summarizes issues affecting force preservation and mission completion. A summary of command topics is presented below.

1. Truck Company – Orders received on 1 November required all units to move north with the Division. The Battalion formed a truck company of thirty-five (35) 2.5-ton trucks with a wrecker, maintenance vehicles, and convoy control vehicles. Trucks reported to ASCOM City 2 November to haul supplies for the 3rd Logistical Command. Vehicles and personnel remained on this assignment during the move [of the parent unit] to Kaesong. This necessitated the use of rail transportation and shuttling of units. While the Division was located in the Kaesong area, trucks of the Battalion were used on supply runs to Pyongyang and to assist in the shuttle movement of the Division to Kunu-ri.

2. Power and Water Supply – A survey of the Kaesong power and water supply was submitted to Division and Corps. Limited power and water supplies were made available prior to departure from Kaesong.

3. UN Offensive – Shortly after the arrival of the Division in Kunu-ri, the United Nations major offensive began with a drive to the Yalu River. Companies A and B and the 77th Engr C Company were attached to the Regiments. Company C was attached to the armored spearhead called task Force Dolvin and later called Task Force Wilson. While in a defensive

position, this task force was hit at night by an overwhelming force of Chinese Communists. Positions were overrun or surrounded and severe losses were incurred by several units composing the Task Force. When the task force withdrew, Company C had two officers (the Company Commander and one Platoon Leader), thirty-four (34) Enlisted Men, and ten (10) KATUSA personnel missing in action. One man later returned to the unit. The ground on which this action took place was never retaken so the Battalion was unable to determine whether the personnel missing in action had been killed or captured. Air reports indicated a group of military personnel had been surrounded in that general area and some had been captured, but unit identification was impossible. The personnel who did return had been separated early in the engagement and had worked their way to the rear. They were unable to give any information on the other persons listed as missing in action. A general withdrawal began along the United Nations lines and the units of the Battalion were located in the Ch'anangch'on area by the end of the month. Division changed from IX Corps to I Corps during the withdrawal and contact was established with the Engineer Section of I Corps. Several items of Engineer equipment had to be destroyed by units of the Battalion during the withdrawal due to breakdowns and lack of parts and facilities. All equipment that could be moved was recovered.

S1 – Administrative: This section deals with personnel records, pay, and duty assignments. A summary of S1 topics is presented below.

1. Military Pay Orders – General policy Review. Seventy (70) Enlisted Men were promoted during the month. Continued review of service records and WDAGO Form 20 records. Approximately fifty (50) forms remade. Soldiers deposits for the month totaled $13,250.00.

2. Personnel Section – Plans initiated to consolidate the Personnel Section under Division Rear CP control. During the latter part of the month, the Personnel Section and Administrative Section were separated by two hundred (200) miles, causing a loss in coordination. Casualty reporting was lax due to battle circumstances and distance involved. Flow of reports and correspondence were delayed by as much as ten (10) days. Replacements arriving at this unit were without service records or pay records.

3. Troop Strength – At the end of the month, a shortage of sixty-one (61) Enlisted Men and six (6) Warrant Officers existed within the Battalion. Only four (4) replacements were received during the month.

4. Religious Services – As the situation would permit, religious services were conducted by the Battalion Chaplain.

5. Movies – On eight (8) occasions, movies were shown for men of the Battalion.

S2 – Intelligence: This section deals with locating enemy units, obscuring friendly movement, and understanding enemy communication. A summary of S2 topics is presented below.

1. Maps – Maps issued to all units in Kaesong on 4 November. Map overlays obtained from EUSAK Engineer Section. Information on these overlays incomplete.

2. Turkish Brigade – The Turkish Brigade came under control of the Division. Turkish Brigade supplied with Kaesong maps.

3. Yongbon Reconnaissance – Arrival in Yongbon on 22 November necessitated reconnaissance of all roads in the area. Further information gathered by interviewing prisoners of war.

4. Kunu-ri – On 28 November, the S-2 Section moved to the vicinity of Kunu-ri. On 30 November, the section, less the assistant S-2, moved to Oun-ni. The assistant S-2 went along the Changchon-gang to locate a route over which to lead the artillery from their location north of Kunu-ri.

S3 – Operations: This section deals with troop movement, location of equipment and weapons, and modifications to terrain. Maps coordinates are typically involved in such matters. A summary of S3 topics is presented below.

1. Truck Company – Orders received by phone from G-4 to organize a provisional truck company of three (3) platoons of eighteen (18) trucks each. Trucks dispatched to Inchon on 2 November and attached to the 55th T Truck Battalion. Lt. Sam Starobin, assistant S-3, placed in command of this provisional truck company.

2. Tosong-ni – Orders received from Division HQ on 5 November to move units to the vicinity of Tosong-ni. Company A attached to 35th RCT. Company B attached to 27th RCT. Due to a shortage of trucks provided to the provisional truck company, this movement made partly by rail. Trains arrived in Munsan-ni on 8 November.

3. Kaesong – Reconnaissance and repair started upon arrival at Kaesong. On 17 November, the 25th Division issued Operations Instruction #16. This document ordered units to move to the vicinity of Sunchon in North Korea. Companies A, C, and H & S moved together while Company B remained attached to 27th RCT. All units arrived in Kunu-ri instead of Sunchon on 22 November. Reconnaissance and work assignments delegated to companies. Company A responsible for construction of a one thousand (1000) foot airstrip.

4. UN Withdrawal – By the end of November, withdrawal to Pyongyang had been completed. All railroads and virtually every bridge on the main roads had been demolished. During the withdrawal from Kunu-ri, the S-3 Section had to abandon a one-ton trailer loaded with TOE equipment. Equipment lost included Survey Equipment Set #6, Drafting Set #3, and other items of lesser value but important to the operation of the section.

S4 – Logistics & Supply: This section deals with who requested (and received) specific clothing, equipment, and food. Road and sea routes used to provide these items fall within S4 jurisdiction. A summary of S4 topics is presented below.

1. Winter Clothing – The S-4 Section located in Pyongtaek on 1 November. Parkas, pile caps, and wool gloves issued to all members of the provisional truck company.

2. Turkish Brigade – Turkish Brigade inspected for equipment shortages. Requisitions submitted to cover these shortages.

3. Back Orders – Issue of backordered winter clothing completed by the Division Quartermaster on 15 November. These included the issue of shoe packs and ski socks. [Not all back ordered winter clothing reached C Company attached to Task Force Dolvin. Robert Hickox had a sweater while other men had nothing. See Hickox Memoir 5.44. -ed.]

25.D.2   BATTALION JOURNAL – S3 - (Highlights)

Information contained in this section originates in daily reports filed by elements of the 65th Engineer Combat Battalion. The November Monthly Report demonstrates a drastic format change. Records of daily activity, transparent in previous monthly reports, have become an impenetrable maze of military jargon and administrative form numbers. Section activity is vaguely stated. Details are implied by references such as "Unit Report 32", which is not supplied. Value for the civilian reader is minimal. Highlights are presented below.

EXAMPLE – NEW FORMAT

1 Nov
1. Prov 35 trks, rpt Ascom City 021200 Nov to haul supplies for EUSAK.
2. Prov 6 x 2.5-ton trks w/drvs for sev days DS. Rpt BN CP 020830 Nov 50.
3. Prov 11 x 2.5-ton trks w/drvs for sev days DS. Ready to roll 020830 Nov 50.
4. Prov 9 x 2.5-ton trks, 1 jeep for serv mission. Req officer for convoy commander.
5. Prov 9 x 2.5-ton trks w/drvs for sev days [illegible] Rpt Bn 020830 Nov 50.
6. Unit Report No 31.

S-1   Located within the battalion at Pyongtaek, Korea, handling personnel problems arising.

S-2   Picked up maps in Seoul to augment our depleted supply.

S-3   Received orders from G-4 to organize a truck company of three platoons of eight trucks each. Lt Starobin, assistant S-3, was placed in charge.

S-4   The section is located in Pyongtaek. Four trucks of the section were released to form a provisional truck company. Issued parkas, pile caps and gloves to those drivers selected. Received seven carloads of Class IV supplies.

Date	Section	Entry
2 Nov	S-2	Battalion mail truck fired on by automatic weapon vicinity of (CR 431 579) at 1920 [hrs]. Reported to G-2.
4 Nov	S-1	Published the daily bulletin and handled personnel and administrative duties for the battalion.
6 Nov	S-3	Units of the battalion enroute to the new area. Due to the number of trucks furnished for the provisional truck company, part of the movement is being made by rail.
9 Nov	1.	Company C repairing two bridges north of Kaesong.
10 Nov	2.	AP minefield located by Lt Schmitz (BT8209). Also, MG position (enemy) (BT8108). Reported Unit Report 40.
	S-4	Water point #4 opened at (BT7803). The assistant S-4 spent the day at Ascom City drawing engineer supplies.
12 Nov	S-4	1056 x A & B Rations received and issued to companies. No PX rations.
13 Nov	3.	Company B completed the airstrip.
	S-2	Interrogated one POW brought in by Company C. No information of value was received from him, so he was sent to the POW enclosure.
14 Nov	2.	Company A completed ammo salvage job at junction of Yesong river and Hwanghae-do.
	S-4	The S-4 checked status of the supply of engineer equipment at the Turkish Brigade. 661 x B rations drawn and issued. No PX rations received.
15 Nov	1.	Memo to all staff sections – narrative history 1-12 Nov past due.
16 Nov	S-4	Issued winter clothing to companies. 666 B rations drawn and issued. Also, 50-in-1 PX rations drawn and issued. Shoepacks and ski socks received from quartermaster.
17 Nov	S-4	Shoepacks and ski socks issued to companies. The assistant S-4 and the supply SGT departed with three trucks for Ascom City for supplies. Received 472 B rations and 472 PX rations for issue to H&S and Company C.
18 Nov	1.	Class on cold weather clothing to be held HQ Company 25 Division Mess Hall 1030 hrs. Section chiefs to attend.
19 Nov	2.	20/11/50 EUSAK Tank notes.
21 Nov	S-1	Prepared for movement north. Started packing all equipment.
	S-2	Made preparations for move north to new area. Issued maps to units.
	S-3	Preparations were made for expected move.
	S-4	Drew Turkey for 656 men for the 23rd. No PX rations were received. Drew 50 C-4 rations for one platoon of Company A. Loaded supplies on trucks preparing to move. Issued engineering supplies to Turkish Brigade.
22 Nov	1-4.	Multiple units depart Kaesong and arrive (YE4403)
		All sections – confirmed arrival vicinity Yongbon.

23 Nov

4. Company C departs (YE4403) to join Task Force Dolvin 1100 hrs.

24 Nov

S-3   Received data on roads and bridges in the area and allocated work. Priority on bulldozers given to artillery units.

25 Nov

1. Reported AP mines at (YE396243) & AT mines at (YE390193) quantity unknown.

2. General Kean to Sgt Till: Corps Commander landed on airstrip this AM – very rough. Contact Major Bloom and ascertain if he is satisfied with strip. If not, put blade to work. Satisfied.

3. 77th Engnr maintains road from Kuryong (YE475133) to Ipsok (YE495184). Road from Ipsok east to (YE397146) is dirt one way.

4. Company A constructed bypass from (YE391135) to (YE397146). Repaired bridge at (YE376109). CP location at (YE392135).

S-2   Interrogated prisoners for information of engineering value. Prepared overlays of enemy minefields, listing type and pattern. Supplied to Division.

26 Nov

1. Supplied 6 GI guards for the railhead at Sidong-ni from H&S Company.

S-2   Prepared Division overlays of roads in the area. Received from company B a new type of enemy hand grenade which was sent on to I Corps.

27 Nov

1. 1100 hrs   HQ I Corps: Opns O # 44 HQ I Corps dated 21 Nov 50

2. 1110 hrs   19 E Gp: SO # 75 HQ 19 E Gp dated 28 Oct 50

3. 1115 hrs   Weekly Activities Report Company C dated 20 Nov 50

4. 1120 hrs   ETIB #6 dated 18 Nov 50

5. 1700 hrs   90th FA Bn requires dozer to dig gun emplacements.

6. 1730 hrs   S-3 dispatched dozer to 90th FA Bn.

7. Company A attached to 27th RCT effective 262200 Nov 50

8. Company C – tentative 50 MIA. [Enemy] occupied positions (YE4222-YE4223). Lost 1 jeep, bedding, and hvy weapons.

9. S-2 reported new roads in immediate vicinity and northern area good for military use. Recon working on access roads to defense lines.

10. Telephone: received call 0500 hrs – sent H&S detail to fix bridge.

28 Nov

S-4   Received 216 B rations for issue to H&S Company. Received 70 C rations and issued to the Recon section and water points.

MEMOIR

25.D.3　　OPERATIONS ORDER – GENERAL SITUATION – (unavailable)

25.D.4 PERSONNEL ROSTER

25.D.4a　　STRENGTH REPORT 1 NOV 50

Authorized Strength　Officers – 36　Warrant Officers – 8　Enlisted – 762

Actual Strength　Officers – 36　Warrant Officers – 2　Enlisted – 694

STRENGTH REPORT 30 NOV 50

Authorized Strength　Officers – 36　Warrant Officers – 8　Enlisted – 762

Actual Strength　Officers – 36　Warrant Officers – 2　Enlisted – 701

25.D.4b ROSTER OF OFFICERS　　30 Nov 1950

HEADQUARTERS

NAME	RANK	SN	BR	MOS	DUTY
Hatch, McGlachlin	Lt Col	025578 CE		01-331	Bn CO
Carney, Leroy F	Maj	01114880	CE	01-331	Bn XO
Clift, John D	Capt	01115530	CE	00-600	Bn Motor Officer
Perry, Milum D Jr	1 Lt	050594	CE	00-600	Bn Motor Officer
Stroup, Donald F	CWO	RW-904316	USA	04-880	Asst Bn Motor Officer
Roller, Martin B	1 Lt	01296907	Inf	00-200	Bn Commo Officer
Yerks, William F	WOJG	W-907071	USA	02-200	Bn Personnel Officer

7.5

NAME	RANK	SN	BR	MOS	DUTY
Zlogar, William A	Capt	0969693	ChC	05-310	Bn Chaplain
Robeysek, James W	Maj	01101188	CE	07-010	Asst Division Engineer
Shaughnessy, Michael A	1 Lt	02011055	CE	02-110	S1
Starobin, Sam D	1 Lt	050601	CE	09-301	S2
Pessa, Joseph J	Maj	01101991	CE	02-162	S3
Belote, Lem Y	Capt	01101332	CE	04-010	S4
Wymer, Lloyd E Jr	1 Lt	01688724	CE	09-301	Asst S2
Wells, Paul D	1 Lt	01824543	CE	05-004	Asst S3
Hanson, Clifford N	WOJG	W-903-212	USA	04-000	Asst S4

HEADQUARTERS AND SERVICE COMPANY

NAME	RANK	SN	BR	MOS	DUTY
Murray, William R	1 Lt	01322165	Inf	02-900	CO HQ & SV Co
Mason, John H	1 Lt	060287	CE	01-342	Pl Ldr, Bridge Pl
Wright, William	1 Lt	01109770	CE	04-113	Mess, Supply, Trans Off
Cain, John H	2 Lt	02021009	CE	04-880	Equipment & Maint Officer

COMPANY A

McAdoo, Richard F	1 Lt	050609	CE	01-331	CO Company A
Frech, David F	1 Lt	059131	CE	01-331	Pl Ldr
Fullerton, Avery S	1 Lt	059124	CE	01-331	Pl Ldr
McGovern, Bernard C	2 Lt	0963208	Inf	01-331	Pl Ldr

COMPANY B

Collins, James M	1 Lt	01106066	CE	01-331	CO Company B
Donohoe, Patrick J	1 Lt	059102	CE	01-331	Pl Ldr
Strouse, Robert L	1 Lt	01062084	CE	01-331	Pl Ldr
Duke, John G	2 Lt	02204428	CE	01-331	Pl Ldr
Barr, Thomas J	1 Lt	02014764	CE	01-331	Pl Ldr

| Crowell, George A | 2 Lt | 02204414 | CE | 04-113 | | Mess, Supply, Trans Off |

COMPANY C

NAME	RANK	SN	BR	MOS	DUTY	MEMOIR
Pecoraro, Anthony	1 Lt	059873	CE	01-331	POW	16.10
Cameron, Hayward	2 Lt	02204143	CE	01-331	POW	6.3, 7.2, 7.7, 13.7, Bio-2.1
Schmidt, Norbert O	1 Lt	059123	CE	01-331	WIA	13.7, 13.9, 16.10
Sweely, Joe W	1 Lt	01109053	CE	01-331	Pl Ldr	
Flinn, Robert F	1 Lt	062327	CE	01-331	Pl Ldr	
Letellier, Carroll N	1 Lt	060118	CE	01-331	Pl Ldr	

MEDICAL DETACHMENT

	RANK	SN	BR	MOS	DUTY	
Goodrich, Edward O	1 Lt	0979146	MC	03-100	Bn Surgeon	
Nalbone, Charles J	Capt	0347741	MSC	03-506	Med Asst	

25.D.4c NON-BATTLE CASUALTIES

NOTE: The following list omits unnecessary medical information. All casualties occurred in Korea.

	Name	Company	Date	Diagnosis	Hickox Memoir
CPL	Carlisle, Kenneth F	H&S	7 Nov	leg burns	
PFC	McKim, Elvin B	H&S	10 Nov	Infected feet	
SGT	Alamo, Victor M	H&S	16 Nov	compression of brachial plexus	
PFC	Marrical, Charles R	H&S	23 Nov	rupture	
Capt	Gamble, Charles E Jr	H&S	24 Nov	persistent vomiting	Appendix IV, 25.C.2–26 Oct
PFC	Chang, Earl L	A	17 Nov	liver trouble	
CPL	Teti, Joseph	B	14 Nov	burns, right hand and face	
1 Lt	Gaston, Marvin C	C	9 Nov	bone disease	
SGT	Gower, Samuel R	C	10 Nov	heart trouble	

25.D.4d.   Daily Unit Strength Report

Date	Assigned	Authorized	KIA	WIA	MIA	TOTAL	NB	TOTAL	GAINS	POW/KIA
1 Nov	37/677	44/762				9/138		10/156		
2 Nov-26 Nov	37/677	44/762				9/138	26	12/182	33	4
27 Nov	36/675	44/762		1/3		10/141		12/182	3	

MEMOIR 13.31

C Company (attached to Task Force Dolvin)

Date	Assigned	Authorized	KIA	WIA	MIA	TOTAL	NB	TOTAL	GAINS	POW/KIA
28 Nov (reported)	unknown	circa 120	0/1	0/5	2/34	2/40				0/175
28 Nov (final)			0/1	1/6	2/34	3/41				

NOTE: Listed figure for enemy KIA (175) records the battalion total. Separate figures for Task Force Dolvin and battalion proper are unavailable.

Date	Assigned	Authorized	KIA	WIA	MIA	TOTAL	NB	TOTAL	GAINS	POW/KIA
29 Nov	34/635	44/762				12/181		12/184	1	
30 Nov	34/635	44/762			0/1	12/181		12/184	1	

25.D.4e Awards

	Name	Company	Award	MEMOIR
1.	SGT Louis A. Naylor	A	Bronze Star	
2.	SFC Jack M. Wiggins	A	Bronze Star	
3.	CAP Richard F. McAdoo	A	Silver Star	
4.	1 Lt Avery S. Fullerton	A	Bronze Star	
5.	CPL Claude F. White	A	Bronze Star	
6.	1 Lt John G. Duke	A	Bronze Star	
7.	SFC Norman R. Mason	A	Bronze Star	16.10
8.	Anthony Pecoraro	C	Silver Star	
9.	PFC Roland Sternini	C	Silver Star	
10.	SGT Joseph G. Cody	H&S	Bronze Star	
11.	PFC Roland Sternini	C	Bronze Star	

12.	1 Lt	Hayward Cameron	C	Bronze Star	6.3, 7.2, 7.7, 13.7, Bio-2.1
13.	SGT	Hubert W. Beaubien	Med	Bronze Star	
14.	CPL	George Heffner	A	Bronze Star	
15.	CPL	Herbert Wagner	A	Bronze Star	
16.	PFC	Kinlaw H. Richardson	A	Bronze Star	

25.D.4f COMBAT CASUALTY LIST 27 NOV 1950 – C COMPANY – 65TH ENGINEER COMBAT BATTALION
TASK FORCE DOLVIN

Name			RA	Type	Company	Hickox Memoir
1.	SFC	Frye, David	RA15114530	KIA	C	16.10
2.	1 Lt	Schmidt, Norbert, O	O-59123???	WIA	C	13.7, 13.9, 16.10
3.	PFC	Smith, Russell G	RA17265588	WIA	C	
4.	SFC	Wilson, Osborn	RA16265673	WIA	C	
5.	SFC	Thistle, Alfred D	RA31510248	WIA	C	Bio-12
6.	SGT	Bowling, William H	RA16275082	WIA	C	Bio-2
7.	CPL	Decker, Doyle	RA38783984	WIA	C	
8.	CPL	Harper, Harrison O	RA14283255	WIA	C	Bio-5
9.	CPL	Sherrick, Donald V	RA17256203	MIA	C	
10.	CPL	Hess, Raymond D	RA13320414	MIA	C	
11.	CPL	Floyd, Delmas F	RA18281341	MIA	C	
12.	CPL	Bockey, Robert C	RA15410346	MIA	C	
13.	SGT	Wegrzyn, Stanley M	RA36958829	MIA	C	13.8, 16.10
14.	SGT	Patton, John M	RA18285763	MIA	C	
15.	SGT	Neel, Clifford L	RA38517449	MIA	C	
16.	SGT	Drake, Brady H	RA13312718	MIA	C	
17.	SGT	Cox, Calvin M	RA10736287	MIA	C	
18.	SGT	Byers, Lester W	RA19322171	MIA	C	
19.	SFC	Zirkle, Linden B	RA13317916	MIA	C	

No.	Rank	Name	Service No.			
20.	SFC	Wilson, General John	RA45045383	MIA	C	13.8
21.	SFC	Akers, William E	RA 7007826	MIA	C	15.15
22.	MSGT	Harper, Alton E	RA14034967	MIA	C	16.10
23.	PFC	Johnson, Kenneth J	RA12114523	MIA	C	7.41
24.	PVT	Otero, Louis	RA18255873	MIA	C	
25.	PVT	Martin, John D	RA19290302	MIA	C	
26.	PFC	Wells, Curtis J	RA16264063	MIA	C	
27.	PFC	Stone Edward J	RA14271656	MIA	C	
28.	PFC	Stidham, Lloyd D	RA15267441	MIA	C	
29.	PFC	Schoening, Robert G	RA19353852	MIA	C	
30.	PFC	Little, Paul E	RA14297815	MIA	C	
31.	PFC	Hickox, Robert H	RA12284788	MIA	C	Bio-6
32.	PFC	Harris, Sam C Jr	RA14276188	MIA	C	
33.	PFC	Fogle, Robert E	RA15279455	MIA	C	
34.	PFC	Ferguson, James D	RA15191641	MIA	C	
35.	PFC	Curtin, Francis E	RA16144048	MIA	C	
36.	PFC	Buli, Bernard	RA13334990	MIA	C	Bio-3
37.	PFC	Bruneio, Anthony J	RA13264979	MIA	C	13.32
38.	PFC	Arnison, James A	RA27359837	MIA	C	
39.	SFC	Cuccaro, Charles P	RA33947883	MIA	C	
40.	PFC	Smith, Bennie D	RA14258149	MIA	C (attached)	
41.	SGT	Martin, Emmette B	RA15290403	MIA	C (attached)	
42.	CPL	Donovan, Lawrence E	RA13309915	MIA	C (attached)	5.42
43.	1 Lt	Cameron, Hayward	O-2204143	MIA	C	6.3, 7.2, 7.7, 13.7, Bio-2.1
44.	Capt	Pecoraro, Anthony	O-59673	MIA	C	16.10

TOTAL CASUALTIES – TASK FORCE DOLVIN

NOTE: Casualty type in this report (25th Infantry Division Monthly) varies from the report presented in Appendix III. Individuals listed MIA in this report may have returned to unit at a later date or been located and converted to WIA.

APPENDIX 5
TASK FORCE DOLVIN

On 22 November 1950, Operations Order #15, Headquarters 25th Infantry Division, were received at Headquarters 89tth Medium tank Battalion, forming another in a series of Armored Spearheaded task forces. In the past, this type of task force proved beneficial to the UN efforts by driving a highly mobile striking force into the heart of the enemy.

Task Force Dolvin was formed because the Division zone was too wide for a two regimental front yet the Division Commander desired to keep one regiment in reserve. In order to narrow the zone of the 24th Infantry Regiment and because the right boundary of the 35th Infantry Regiment was an unfordable river, Task Force Dolvin was put in the center.

The Task organization of Task Force Dolvin was as follows:
  HQ 89th Medium Tank Battalion (-)
  B Company 89th Medium Tank Battalion
    Attached: 8213th Ranger Company
  E Company 7th Infantry Regiment
    Attached: Assault Gun Platoon
    89th Mdm Tank Bn
  25th Reconnaissance Company
  Reconnaissance Platoon, 89th Medium Tank Battalion
  77th FA Battalion, G/S; Priority of fires to
    TASK FORCE DOLVIN.
  C Company 65th Engineer Combat Battalion

At 0830 hours 22 November, the advance CP departed from vicinity 404080 (sheet 6333 III) moving to YONG PO DONG (395132) (sheet 6333 I) arriving about 1030 hours.

The zone which Task Force Dolvin moved in had previously been held by the 2nd Battalion, 7th Cavalry regiment, 1st Cavalry Division. At 1145 hours, the major elements of 2nd Battalion 7th Cavalry Regiment [completed occupation] by 1600 hours. The units of the Task Force spent the day enclosing their assigned areas, marrying up, resupplying, and preparing defenses for the night.

Brigadier General VERNARD WILSON, Assistant Division Commander, 25th Infantry Division, arrived at Task Force Dolvin CP about 1630 hours and informed Lt Col DOLVIN that the task force was being reinforced by another Rifle Company from the 35th Infantry Regiment. Plans for the employment of this additional strength were included in Operations Order #6 which was issued to the Unit Commanders at 1100 hours 23 November 1950.

Patrols from the 8213th Ranger Company were sent out 5000 yards to the front of Task Force Dolvin's positions to observe any enemy activity. Patrol #1 left about 0900 returning about 1400. Patrol #2 left the CP area at 1400 returning about 1730. Neither patrol made any contact or observed any enemy activity.

In addition to the normal pre-mission activities of resupplying and marrying up of the teams, a Thanksgiving dinner, with all the trimmings, was enjoyed by all units.

The Task Force Liaison Officer arrived at the CP about 1900 with the message that "H" hour had been announced as 1000 hours 24 November 1950.

The night of 23-24 November was quiet in the Task Force sector and passed without incident.

All units crossed the LD [Line of Departure] Vicinity 399153 at 1000 hours on the 24th (see Opn O #6, HQ 89th M Tk Bn, attached overlay and map). At 1000 hours, two American POWs reported into the Task Force CP stating that they had been brought within 3 miles of our lines and told by the Chinese Communists to proceed down the road and they would make contact with the Americans. They also reported the location of 28 more American POWs at 416201 who were unable to walk due to wounds. The POWs were members of the 8th Cavalry Regiment. In compliance with a division directive, attack plans were not altered as a result of this information. The POWs were contacted at 1329 hours and the Battalion Aid Section, with additional ambulances from 25th Infantry Division medics, evacuated them to the rear.

Objective one (1) and two (2) were secured by Company B 35th Infantry Regiment. Company B 89th Medium Tank Battalion seized and secured objective 3. Company E 27th Infantry Regiment seized and secured objective 4 at 1400. The forward CP moved from vicinity YONG PO DONG (395131) to (418211) arriving at 1630. The Reconnaissance Platoon 89th Medium Tank Battalion screened between the left flank of Task Force DOLVIN and the right flank of the 35th Infantry Regiment and maintained contact between the leading elements of these two forces during the advance.

The forward elements of the Task Force received small arms and automatic weapons fire from the high ground to the right of the road vicinity 434213 which was in the vicinity of objective 5. Company E 27th Infantry Regiment moved up, secured objective 5, supported by the Assault Gun Platoon and assisted by elements of B Company 89th Medium Tank Battalion from the draw vicinity 420216. After Company E 27th Infantry Regiment secured objective 5, Company B reinforced [and] moved to objective 6 and consolidated the position for the night. Company B had their tanks in the general vicinity of 425223 covering to the E, W, [S], and N.

Company B 35th Infantry Regiment consolidated and secured objective 3 for the night, while the Reconnaissance Platoon 89th Medium Tank Battalion maintained contact with elements of the 35th Infantry Regiment at contact point "H" (373178) and also maintained an outpost in vicinity hill 205 (397196). The 25th reconnaissance Company continued to screen the right flank, its CP located vicinity (417215).

The night of 24-25 November passed without incident.

The attack continued on the morning of the 25th with Company B 35th Infantry Regiment moving to objective 7, at 0830 hours. This objective was secured without resistance. About 1000 hours, however, rather heavy opposition was encountered along the high ground vicinity 450230. While Company B 35th Infantry Regiment was securing objective 7, Company E 27th Infantry Regiment sent a patrol to objective 10 and found it unoccupied. The remainder of the Company was ordered by Lt Col DOLVIN to occupy objective 10. During the consolidation of objective 10, Company B 89th Medium Tank Battalion reinforced, moved to objective 8.

By 1840 hours, the defensive positions for Task Force DOLVIN were reported to G-3 25th Infantry Division, as follows: Company E 27th to occupy objective 10 extending from about 450243 to 453247 with one platoon. Another platoon was occupying the point at 458255, the CP plus one platoon and the Assault Gun Platoon was located vicinity 456247. The Ranger Company occupied objective 8 with Company B tanks deployed from a point about 455241 to about 460238 blocking the road to the northeast and assisting and blocking the draw between objective 8 and 10. The Reconnaissance Platoon of the 89th Medium Tank Battalion had set up a road block vicinity 454235. The tactical CP of Task Force DOLVIN was located 446231, and the advance CP at 416210. Company B 35th Infantry Regiment reinforced, was to occupy north prong of objective 7 and tie in with Company C 65th Engr C Battalion deployed along the river from about 446237 to about 443230. One platoon of the 25th Reconnaissance Company was deployed on objective 6and the remainder of the Company was screening between contact points "F" (440230) and "G" (395219).

A message was received from G-3 at 2115 hours that the 2nd Battalion of the 27th Infantry Regiment was to move into an area south of Task Force DOLVIN forward CP. The center of the 2nd Battalion area to be in the vicinity of 415204. Guides would be furnished by Task Force DOLVIN to meet the convoy at IPSOK (408184). The personnel would dismount 300-400 yards north of IPSOK and travel the rest of the way on foot. Further instructions from the Commanding General were that this Battalion would only be committed upon receipt of orders from him. At the same time, G-3 was informed that the situation of our forward elements was very fluid. The enemy was attempting to get between objective 8 and objective 10. The Task Force CP was receiving a heavy concentration of mortar, small arms, and automatic weapon fire, but felt that with the aid of the 8th FA Battalion, we would be able to handle the situation.

At 2215 hours, Company B of the 35th Infantry Regiment reinforced, reported they were unable to take the ridge line beyond objective 7 due to very heavy resistance. Lt Col DOLVIN ordered the Company Commander to withdraw his troops and form a line generally from about 449231 to about 454233. It was felt by the Task Force Commander that the trail between the river and objective 10 might have become a possible threat, at which he ordered reserves to tie in with the Engineers along the river.

The forward platoon, located at approximately 458255, reported they were receiving a very heavy attack. This attack was proceeded by the enemy sending one or two individuals near the positions who could speak very fluent English. These individuals asked how many men were in the position. The infantry, deceived by the voice, readily gave the number in the position. Shortly thereafter, the position was overrun by a large enemy force and the remainder of the platoon forced to withdraw to a point 453247 tying in with the other platoon located there. The reserve platoon, which was located at 457247, was committed and it joined in a defensive position with the other platoon on objective 10. The Assault Gun Platoon and the Company CP withdrew from the former reserve platoon position. The Assault Gun Platoon went into position to cover objective 10 from the south and also cover the river to the NW and W. The Company CP moved to the location of Task Force DOLVIN Tactical CP.

The attack on objective 10 was contained at about 2250 hours and at about 2300 hours another large-scale attack was made on objective 8. The attack was finally contained about 2330 hours. However, the commanding officer felt that another attack was being prepared because of the sounding of whistles and catcalls to the front of his forward positions. At about 2350 hours, a message was received from the Company Commander of Company "B" 89th Medium Tank Battalion that the enemy was close enough to his tanks to throw hand grenades. Objective 8 about 2358 received another attack estimated to be battalion sized. The Company Commander felt that he had sufficient force to withstand the assault.

G-3 was informed of the situation at 0031 hours and also informed that the 2nd Battalion 27th Infantry Regiment had closed in their prescribed area at 0015.

The attack on objective 8 was contained around 0045 hours. At 0250 hours, G-3 reported the 77th Field Artillery Battalion had one battery overrun by an enemy force and one gun captured.

Lt Col DOLVIN reported at 0205 that his forces on objective 8 had been forced to withdraw and that he was going to stabilize the line across the southern end of objective 10 and the northern tip of objective 7. The remainder of the night was spent stabilizing the defensive positions and preparing to retake the high ground on objective 8. Artillery fire in large concentrations was continuously placed on objective 8, northeastern tip of objective 10 and the high ground to the northeast of objective 8.

The enemy continued to be very active to the front and at several times the enemy soldiers charged directly down the road toward two of the tanks of Company "B" in an attempt to throw hand grenades into the tanks. Their mission was not completed due to the accurate firing of the coaxial machine guns. With the coming of dawn, the enemy attack gradually ceased. About 0745, Lt Col DOLVIN reported to G-3 that he was going to have air attacks on the high ground vicinity objective 8, and then launch a counterattack to regain objective 8. G-3 informed Lt Col DOLVIN to hold up on the attack until General KEAN gave his approval.

Company "E" 27th Infantry Regiment continued to hold objective 10, in conjunction with the air, heavy artillery, and tank fire which was placed on objective 8 in an effort to discourage any counterattack the enemy may have been planning at that time. The forward observer on objective 10 reported a large number of enemy killed in an effort to withdraw from the rear slope of objective 8.

Lt DICKSON, the liaison pilot, reported about 0900 that approximately one battalion of enemy was digging in on the forward slope of objective 9 (480250) and that it appeared to himthat the enemy was building a roadblock at 478254. Artillery was called for and adjusted by Lt DICKSON with very good results.

At approximately 0945 hours, the Commanding General of the 25th Infantry Division told Lt Col DOLVIN to get word to Lt Col

MILLER, C.O. 1st Battalion, 24th Infantry Regiment to move his Company "B" between Companies "A" and "C", so that a secure line would be formed from the 25th Reconnaissance Company on the left to Lt Col Miller's Company "A". He also told Lt Col DOLVIN that he would not resume the attack but to await further instructions. However, he was authorized to adjust his lines in order to put his troops in more suitable defensive positions.

A message was received from G-3 that General WILSON was enroute to Task Force DOLVIN's CP and upon the arrival of General WILSON he would assume operational control of Task Force DOLVIN and the 1st Battalion of the 24th Infantry Regiment. Thus Task Force WILSON was formed.

The Ranger Company, having suffered heavy losses on objective 8, was to be withdrawn and returned to Division CP. The 77th Field Artillery Battalion continued to support Task Force WILSON. The 2nd Battalion 27th Infantry Regiment (-) remained in Division Reserve. General WILSON had more detailed instructions and also a new boundary overlay.

General WILSON arrived and assumed command of the Task Force at 1220 hours and immediately appointed Major MORAND his S-3; Major GOOLSBY assumed the duties of S-3, 89th Medium Tank Battalion. General WILSON issued instructions for the forward elements of Task Force DOLVIN to withdraw from objective 8 and 10 and form new defensive positions in the vicinity of objective 7 and objective 6, also tying in with the 2nd Battalion of the 27th Infantry Regiment in the general vicinity of objective 3. This was accomplished by filtering the units from their forward positions thus preventing any mass movement of troops at any one time. For disposition of the troops on the night of the 26th and 27th November, see map. The TAC CP 455243 moved to the advance CP location 418211 closing at 2005 hours.

Company "B" 89th Medium Tank Battalion closed in its new area at 2035 hours and was disposed as follows: 1st Platoon attached Company "B" 35th Infantry regiment (-), 1st Platoon in Task Force Reserve vicinity 423208; Company "B" 35th Infantry Regiment closed in new area at 2040 hours vicinity 445227 and made physical contact with Company "C" 24th Infantry Regiment. However,

Companies "A" and "B" of the 24th were never contacted in this position.

The S-3 of the 89th Medium Tank Battalion reported to G-3 25th Infantry Division at 2155 hours that the position was quiet and the new positions had been consolidated. He further reported that the C.O. felt the enemy was massing for an attack. Company "E", withdrawing from objective 10, reported hearing whistles and other noises to their direct front. By the time of the withdrawal, no contact was made.

At about 2330 hours 26 November, Battery "C" of the 8th Field Artillery Battalion was attacked by a strong enemy force from the north and within the next thirty minutes all three of the batteries had been attacked.

At the 2400 hourly report, the Platoon Leader of the Reconnaissance Platoon 89th Medium Tank Battalion reported by radio that an enemy patrol was in his area, about 400 yards to his left front, and that he expected contact within 15 minutes. The patrol was estimated by him to consist of between 40 and 60 men.

At 0016 hours 27 November, the Platoon Leader Reconnaissance Platoon 89th Medium Tank Battalion, notified the S-3 that he was receiving enemy fire and was attempting to penetrate his position. Shortly thereafter, the Reconnaissance Platoon was engaging the enemy in a heavy firefight. At 0035 hours, Captain NEAL, Company Commander, Company "B" 89th Medium Tank Battalion, was ordered to send a section of tanks to the draw vicinity 416207. At 0045 hours, Company "B", 1st Battalion 35th Infantry regiment, reported they were under heavy attack and that two of the tanks attached to them from Company "B" 89th Medium Tank Battalion had been knocked out by enemy bazooka fire and satchel charges. The enemy held the charges against the tanks and destroyed themselves in the explosion.

The attack on the Task Force CP continued and at 0130 hours the reserve Infantry Company, Company "E" 27th Infantry Regiment, plus the Assault Gun Platoon, 89th Medium Tank Battalion, was ordered to high ground west of the Task Force CP to reinforce the Reconnaissance Platoon 89th Medium Tank Battalion. The Assault gun Platoon with part of the infantry company mounted moved into position from 414212 to 414214. This force moved to the right flank of the Reconnaissance Platoon 89th Medium tank battalion taking the enemy fire and holding the position until the remainder of the Infantry Company arrived and consolidated the ridge.

The intensity of the attack increased at 0200 hours. At 0250 hours, the 8th Field Artillery Battalion reported the road to the rear, vicinity 414196, had been cut and an enemy roadblock established. The action in the CP area lessened until 0330 hours at which time another attack was launched against the Task Force CP with renewed intensity. 25th Reconnaissance Company had withdrawn to a line from 418213 to 419215 forming a defense to the west and northwest. Company "B" 89th Medium Tank Battalion sent a section of tanks to 418213 to protect the left flank of the 25th Reconnaissance Company and also deliver heavy fire upon the enemy which was attempting to infiltrate down the draw. Another section of tanks was sent up the road to 420207 to form a roadblock and to cover the high ground and nose (see map) which had been formerly occupied by Company "F" 27th Infantry Regiment. Company "F" (-) one platoon had been relieved from that position by Brigadier General WILSON and placed in line with personnel from Headquarters 89th Medium Tank Battalion from 417208 to 417207. The attack at 0330 lasted for approximately 30 minutes at which time the pressure seemed to decrease against Company "C" 65th Engineer (C) Battalion which reported at about 0400 hours receiving a strong attack on their position NW, E and SE estimated to be in battalion strength. The Company was forced to withdraw from their position with extremely heavy casualties.

There was a period of about an hour in which the whole front was comparatively quiet except for sporadic small arms firing.

At 0530 hours, the third attack was launched against the Task Force CP. This was preceded by the blowing of bugles, whistles, and general catcalling along the entire front. Enemy mortar and artillery fire was placed on front line positions and around the CP area. The mortar fire was very accurate causing considerable vehicular damage and personnel casualties. This attack, an all-out effort on the enemy's part to overrun the Task Force CP, lasted until

0645 hours. It became necessary to employ every available man, except for one switchboard operator, on the line in defense of the Task Force CP.

It was imperative that the position occupied by the Task Force CP be held at all cost due to the fact that part of the defense perimeter was the high ground overlooking the road used as the MSR. If this position had been abandoned to the enemy, with his superior numbers, could have established a roadblock of sufficient strength to definitely decrease the fighting efficiency of the Task Force. The high ground directly west of the CP area overlooked the entire Task Force position and could have effectively been used by the enemy to direct mortars and small arms fire onto the position. If such a roadblock had been set up, it would have taken a large portion of the Task Force to neutralize it and the enemy could have concentrated his efforts on the forward position. Such maneuver might have created havoc within the Task Force[*]. At the same time, the number of casualties in the Task Force was increasing to the extent that normal channels could not take care of their evacuation and the Task Force Commander had no idea of leaving them to the mercy of the enemy.

For these reasons, an all-out successful effort was made to hold the area.

By 0715 the attack had been stopped and the Infantry Reconnaissance Platoon and the tanks consolidated the high ground to the west of the CP to defend against any further attack. At this time, Task Force WILSON received orders to withdraw to a rear position. The reserve battalion was order to attack forward to extricate Company "G" 27th Infantry Regiment and then to attack to the rear to clear the enemy roadblock which was preventing withdrawal of the task force.

- With the road already cut to the rear, the Task Force Commander felt he did not have sufficient forces to eliminate a possible second roadblock and engage the enemy to the front.

Below are links for units mentioned in this appendix. The Korean War project contains resources useful for descendants of Korean War veterans who wish to reconstruct family history.

Korean War Project
https://www.koreanwar.org/

KMAG – Korean Military Advisory Group
https://www.koreanwar.org/html/units/kmag.htm

25th Infantry Division
https://www.koreanwar.org/html/units/25thunk.htm
https://www.25thida.org/

B Company 89th Mdm Tank Battalion
Assault Gun Platoon 89th Mdm Tank Battalion
Reconnaissance Platoon 89th Mdm Tank Battalion
https://www.koreanwar.org/html/units/89tnk.htm

8213th Ranger Company
https://www.koreanwar.org/html/units/8ircoa.htm

E Company 7th Infantry
https://www.koreanwar.org/html/units/7idunk.htm

25th Reconnaissance Company
https://www.koreanwar.org/html/units/25recon.htm

77th Field Artillery Battalion
https://www.koreanwar.org/html/units/77fab.htm

C Company 65th Engineer Battalion
https://www.koreanwar.org/html/units/65en.htm

Notes

Editing a memoir set seventy years in the past is difficult. Primary sources are hard to locate. Eyewitnesses are deceased, addresses of record are vacant or host new occupants, and phone numbers are disconnected. Newspaper articles found in scrapbooks have been trimmed for looks and lack information identifying the original publication. Archived photographs were copied and shared among Korean War survivors without indicating the original copyright holder. War stories were passed along an email chain with no link to the originator. Decades later, after all memoir contributors have died, an outsider discovers a mysterious pile of tribal legends that must be declared public domain and accessed under the doctrine of fair use.

After examining more than five thousand documents and photographs preserved by the Hickox estate for use in this memoir, it became clear that Bob's archive resulted from group participation. Numerous emails from Bob's war buddies record greetings and political comments mixed with updates on personal efforts to obtain information needed for the memoir. Mary Hickox confirmed that Bob's friends expected to be rewarded for their efforts by inclusion in his memoir. A family member of one veteran described the group relationship as a "boy's club" to which each member devoted a great deal of time.

Twenty years later, as an outsider, I inherited the dormant Hickox memoir project. Editing Bob's memoir using his archive required me to favor documents that demonstrate implied reprint consent. Documents lacking this consent were used to confirm facts recorded elsewhere but are not reproduced here. More than one archive contributor is not recognized in this memoir because the information donated appears intended as reference material only.

Regarding contributors who gave implied reprint consent, ethics and courtesy require an editor to contact descendants of these veterans to discuss the inclusion of desired material after it is reviewed and approved by family consent. Unfortunately, it is difficult to locate survivors who have control over the estates of Korean War veterans. Addresses change and phone numbers become disconnected. Email vanishes into dormant social media accounts or is swept into spam folders. Public database searches sometimes suggest an estate has no surviving members. Occasionally, an individual refuses to reply to legitimate contact efforts. In these cases, the doctrine of fair use permits one to include correspondence that cannot be vetted by the surviving family.

Families of Korean War veterans who supported publication of the Hickox memoir are acknowledged in the opening pages of this book. Veterans whose contribution has been included based on the doctrine of fair use are discussed below. Each case mentioned involves implied consent recorded in one or more archive documents or involves fair use.

***

Tribal legend is often unfair. Several Korean War veterans created an extensive paper trail, while others were recorded by a single reference. Some have no descendants who can tell their stories. Bernard Buli appears in one public-domain photograph. Lawrence E. Donovan has no surviving relatives. He contributed to the Hickox archive using Alfred Thistle as a messenger. Lawrence Donovan's contribution appears per the fair use doctrine.

Harrison Harper, a man of few words, is attested in the equivalent of two postcards. None of Harper's telephone conversations were recorded, nor were his reunion activities. Attempts to locate his descendants failed. Including Harrison

Harper in the Hickox memoir requires claiming fair use of his postcard messages.

Garabed Kenoian, Bob's "little Arab buddy" who suffered a serious head wound on September 4, 1950, loaned Bob a stack of photographs for inclusion in the memoir. These photos were delivered by Alfred Thistle [BIO-14.3], who served as a messenger. Since no eyewitnesses of this exchange survive, it is impossible to identify Garabed Kenoian's contribution to tribal legend.

Robert McKinney preferred conversation over email. His communications are brief and discuss current events. McKinney traveled often to visit his war buddies. According to Mary Hickox, Bob and Mack met regularly and took off in a vehicle to "paint the town red". See Memoir 1.4 – Bob Hickox Day. McKinney's account of his Korean War experience, published in Greybeards Jan/Feb 2001 Issue, is one of two documents containing details of his three-year deployment in Korea. McKinney's extended family lives in Hurricane Alley along the East Coast. A public database search indicates that some of his relatives have been off grid for more than five years. Attempts to contact the Mckinney estate failed.

Aldin Saloway was killed in Korea. Documents in the Hickox archive were generated by veterans who attended the KWVA 50th Reunion. This limits Aldin's contribution to summaries of battlefield activity. Aldin Saloway's biography is based on comments made by Robert Hickox and material provided by Patrick Shaughnessy. Additional material is drawn from public record.

Harold Soyars has no surviving relatives. His contribution appears per the fair use doctrine.

Robert Ivison appears in a public-domain photograph.

Leroy Francard is preserved in the tribal archive as a villain mentioned in passing. A veteran of World War 2, Francard had military experience before Korea and outranked most soldiers mentioned in the Hickox memoir. As a set-piece villain, his contribution is presented in a prejudiced fashion. I have added data drawn from public record to portray Francard as a rounded individual whose story remains untold.

Some contributors openly consented to inclusion in the Hickox memoir. Leonard Stamper submitted a summary of his military experience to Robert Hickox. This document contains dates of service and injury, names of foxhole buddies, and Stumpy's foxhole nickname *Spider*.

Robert Young enjoyed colorful conversations with Robert Hickox. Young submitted a summary of his military experience that reads like a job resume, complete with a headshot. There is no doubt that Robert LaForrest Young, 2nd Division, Co K, 38th Infantry Regt, who arrived in Korea on August 19th, 1950, and was wounded by a mortar on September 5th, desired inclusion in the Hickox memoir. In recognition of his implied request, Robert LaForrest Young, an instructor who taught a class about the M2 Flamethrower and cannibalized eight units to create two working models, all stenciled with 503 PIR, a regiment that parachuted onto Corregidor five years earlier, has been included in the Hickox memoir.

Other Korean War veterans created an extensive paper trail that did not guarantee immortality. James Belcher, a medic who was shot seven times and bayonetted twice in combat, contributed over five hundred documents to the Hickox archive. Few of these documents discuss Korean War military events. Most Belcher communications discuss current events, family celebrations, pets, weather, and performance automobiles. Belcher comments on military matters only when directly questioned. Jim and his family were displaced by several California wildfires, one of which they could see from their living room window. Some of Jim's children live in Hurricane Alley along the East Coast. Attempts to contact the Belcher estate failed. Addresses of record are vacant, telephone numbers are disconnected, and email accounts are deleted. Jim Belcher's rare comments regarding his Korean War experience are included per the fair use doctrine and only when they contribute to an ongoing discussion involving multiple individuals.

The dead speak. When one is privileged to hear their voices, one is obligated to quote them accurately. Several passages in this memoir contain racist language and battlefield jargon commonly used during the Korean War. Attitudes demonstrated by people in Bob's memoir were produced by the pressures experienced during youth and combat. Initially, I considered deleting all racist language from the account. After giving the matter thought, I decided not to diminish the power of the narrative by surrendering to cancel culture.

The Hickox memoir records a powerful story, a tale of heroes fighting impossible odds. It is the last eyewitness account of a lost age, an age none of us should forget.

Robert Hickox (right rear), others unidentified.

Outlaw Hat

"I think that picture was taken in a beer hall in Osaka. Or maybe the USO in Osaka. You like that 40-mission *crush* in my hat? I received quite a bit of flack over that. Every officer in my camp chewed me out at one time or another. I never got hassle from the MPs. Of course, I never went where there were MPs if I could avoid it. Ha!"

- Robert Hickox

Photo Credits

Index

www.ingramcontent.com/pod-product-compliance
Lightning Source LLC
Chambersburg PA
CBHW071832270326
41929CB00013B/1965